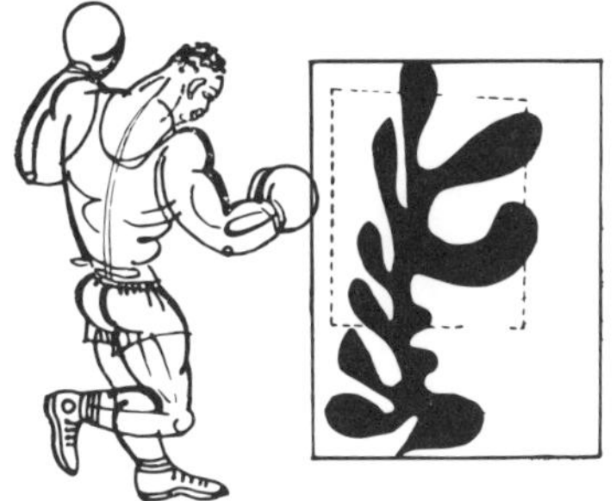

MODERNISM/ MURDERISM

The Modern Art Debate in Kumar

Jyoti Bhatt, Pherozeshah Rustomji Mehta, and the readers of Kumar

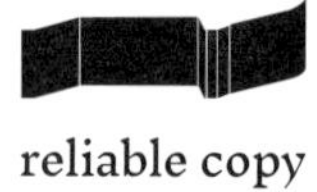

Modernism/Murderism: The Modern Art Debate in Kumar
By Jyoti Bhatt, Pherozeshah Rustomji Mehta, and the readers
of Kumar

Translated by Vasvi Oza

Reliable Copy #7
First Edition – 2000

Editors: Nihaal Faizal and Sarasija Subramanian
Researchers: Sarasija Subramanian and Vasvi Oza
Translation Assistants: Dhaivat Shah and Kadamboor Neeraj
Research Assistants: Kadamboor Neeraj and Stuti Bhavsar
Copy Editor: Stuti Bhavsar
Publication Design: Roshan Shakeel

Unless otherwise credited, all images reproduced in this book
were digitised from copies of back issues of Kumar from
the private collections of Anil Relia, Archer Art Gallery,
Ahmedabad.

Modernism/Murderism: The Modern Art Debate in Kumar
has been made possible through the generous support of Ark
Foundation.

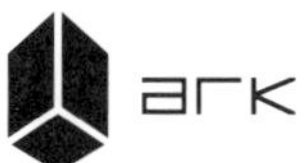

Research towards this publication was supported by Ark
Foundation. Research on Kumar and this debate prior to this
publication was supported by Akar Prakar Contemporary and
Lath Sarvodaya Trust's ArtVarta Research Grant.

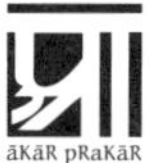
ākāR pRakāR

Printed by Sudarsan Graphics, Chennai

ISBN: 978-81-953472-1-6

Reliable Copy and Vasvi Oza would like to thank Bhairavi Modi, Chinar Shah, Chithra KS, Indrapramit Roy, Noopur Desai, Pankti Desai, Samia Vasa, Santosh Dash, and Shukla Sawant for their comments and suggestions towards this publication; the team at *Kumar* comprising of Late Dhiru Parikh, Jyotiben Modi, Mohammad Rangwala, and the current editor Praful Raval for allowing us access to their archives, their assistance during our research, and for their kind permissions towards this research and publishing project; Anil Relia for making back issues of *Kumar* available to us; Manish Naik and Shabbir Hakim for their assistance in the digitisation process; Tanushree Devaraj for her help in the vectorisation of the illustrations reproduced in this book; and Aaiushi Beniwal, Kavya Oza, Yatri Oza, and the team at Ark Foundation (Nupur Dalmia, Rachita Gupta, and Shilpa Rangnekar) for all their on-ground support in Vadodara.

CONTENTS

EDITORS' NOTE

Modernism/Murderism: The Modern Art Debate in Kumar brings together, for the first time in English, a forgotten debate on Modern Art that took place in the pages of the Gujarati-language periodical *Kumar* in the years between 1959 and 1964.

This debate featured on one side Pherozeshah Rustomji Mehta, a writer and art connoisseur from Karachi, and on the other Jyoti Bhatt, a young artist and recent graduate from the Faculty of Fine Arts, The Maharaja Sayajirao University of Baroda, who had just joined as a teacher there. While Mehta, for his part in the debate, chose to defend what he believed were the timeless and traditional values of art—educated as he was by his numerous visits to museums of Europe in the early 1900s—Bhatt proposed that Modern Art was no stranger to these values, that in fact it had much in common with them, and was extending not just those, but also various other visual traditions forward.

This debate took place across six articles published in *Kumar* and fires were further fuelled by the numerous readers who chose to respond to these articles under the 'Readers Write' column (*Vaachako Lakhe Chhe*) of the periodical. Interestingly, the debate was itself instigated when Jyoti Bhatt, as a regular reader of *Kumar*, chose to respond to Mehta through the 'Readers Write' column. Bachubhai Ravat (the then-editor of *Kumar*) featured this text as a full-length article.

This lively debate, that also offers us a vantage point from which to view the entry of Modernism and its affiliated discourses into the art practices of the region, was brought to our attention by the artist and researcher (and in her new role, translator) Vasvi Oza, who has over the last several years been meticulously studying regional print cultures of Gujarat, with a special focus on Gujarati periodicals. A project by Asia Art Archive in India titled 'Bibliography of Modern and Contemporary Art Writing of South Asia' (2011) first put her in contact with *Kumar*, and the Ila Dalmia Research Grant from FICA (2016), enabled her to continue her study into two periodicals—*Kumar*, founded by Ravishankar Raval and Bachubhai Ravat in 1924, and *Vrishchik*, founded by Gulammohammed Sheikh and Bhupen Khakhar in 1969. A recent grant from Akar Prakar Contemporary under their ArtVarta programme allowed for a more focused entry into this present debate.

A generous grant from Ark Foundation led towards the consolidation of this research into a book and allowed us to enter the picture as editors and publishers, complicating—as usual—all operational processes. As always with our Reliable Copy publications, the editorial process was not as straightforward as this final book might sometimes appear to suggest. Alongside Vasvi, we took on the role of researchers, recruited friends to join us in our efforts at translation, and began tracing the beginnings and ends of this debate. We got in touch with Mehta's grandson Jamsheed Mehta, visited the *Kumar* office in Ahmedabad, digitised old copies of the periodical from the collector and gallerist Anil Relia's archive, and extensively interviewed Jyoti Bhatt (the contents of which promise to be a future publication) who also quickly stepped in to help proof our translations. We are grateful to Kadamboor Neeraj and Dhaivat Shah who joined us in these efforts as both translators and researchers. Thanks are also due to Roshan Shakeel who patiently and thoughtfully designed not just this book, but also the varying levels of information contained within it.

Edited, designed, and organised as this modest volume, the debate now stands as a record of a specific moment of history. The relevance of this moment can be seen not just in what happened to art in Vadodara and Ahmedabad, but also in the practices that the currents of this debate touched, even if indirectly, through its influence on a generation of readers and thinkers who went on to shape art in the wider region. In bringing this debate to light, we hope that we have contributed our small efforts at making accessible histories and regional discourses that continue to slip through the cracks, assumed as they are to be relevant only to very few readers. We believe this to be otherwise, and offer this publication as a first in a line of many such iterations to come.

NOTE ON TRANSLATION

In a conversation with Jyoti Bhatt regarding the herculean task of translating any text, he told us a story of the release of the film *Moulin Rouge* (1952) in Ahmedabad and Vadodara, where the theatres took upon themselves the task of translating its title. As the title's Latin script clearly meant that the words must be English, 'Rouge' was misunderstood as 'Rogue' and hence translated to *'Badmaash'*. 'Moulin', for which a parallel could not be drawn, was given the status of a proper noun—either a place or a person. As a result, two translations of the title were circulated on posters to promote the film: *Moulin no Badmaash* (Rogue of Moulin) in Ahmedabad and *Badmaash Moulin* (Moulin the Rogue) in Vadodara. As in most conversations with him, the anecdote paved the way for a larger vision—in this case, his reasoning that translation is the closest form of reading, a process in which the reader/translator cannot take a single word, phrase, or punctuation for granted. And of course, a clear warning of what ensues if one were to get it wrong.

Working on the translation of the texts that follow has been just that—a close and extremely conscious reading that went through several steps, drafts, people, and languages, before bridging the gap between the original Gujarati writing from over 60 years ago and our English version presented here. This process of translation has been a collaborative one and has involved numerous back and forths with editors, friends, teachers, mentors, and—as luck would have it—even one of the original authors of the debate, across multiple drafts.

In its own way, the subject of these translations is already a Modern Art discourse very much marked by acts of transformation, reading, and even misreading. Popular discourse around Modern Art in the 1950s and 1960s was largely disseminated in English and came to South Asia in the form of academic books, exhibition catalogues, newspaper reports, and articles in periodicals—examples of which are referenced within the debate published in this book. As a result, the articles contend with this past writing, while unveiling new and quirky vernacular-modern vocabulary that transcends the canon of English writing on Modern Art. It is clear in the texts that both Pherozeshah Rustomji Mehta and Jyoti Bhatt are conscious of the heavy reliance on English when it comes to art history and criticism, and so they frequently bring in English words (such as composition, design, and symmetry) within their Gujarati writing.

While Mehta's reliance on English and Occidental terminology is evident in his texts, this could have either been the result of dissatisfaction with the lack of vocabulary in Gujarati for what he would like to put forth, or an awareness that such terms in English were used widely enough in common parlance at that time, for the reader to understand their meanings effortlessly. While he does not shy away from using provocative Gujarati pronouns for the state of modernist art practices, such as *'atishayta'* (extravagance) and *'arajakta'* (anarchy), he also coins his own hybrid terminology—*'a-kala'* (non-art), *'adrishyanism'* (invisible-ism), *'murderism'*, and *'kachumbarism'*—to substantiate his points through tongue-in-cheek humour. Such neologisms—which often bring together more than one language—have been retained either within the main text or as elaborations in footnotes.

Along with English, both Mehta and Bhatt have also used specific references from Sanskrit literature to prove their points, as well as highly colloquial idioms from both Hindi and Gujarati languages. Such non-uniformity of the original text has brought about an interesting and challenging texture to the process of translation and we have tried to retain this as far as possible.

Further, the time period in which these articles were written comes into question repeatedly, particularly in the terms used to reference or describe Modern Art. For example, *'adhunik'* and *'adhyatan'* (modern) are used interchangeably with *'navi'* (new) and *'samprat'* (current or contemporary), which have been retained in the translation as three different words in parenthesis, owing to their historical specificities, even though the author might have meant them as descriptors for the same moment. Another example is the word *'shaili'* (style), that has been used previously in Gujarati scholarship to categorise various historical miniature schools such as Kangra *shaili* or Pahadi *shaili*. Mehta has extended the use of this term to include *'navi shaili'* (new style) or even *'shaili ghelchha'* (stylo-mania) to describe modernist art practices in the West, or *'samanya shaili'* (common style) and *'vyaktigat shaili'* (individual style) to talk about the art practices that were then emerging in the country.

Another word that features heavily in this debate is *'vikrut'* (distorted)—a term used by Mehta to denote the ultimate characteristic of abstract works of art. The word has been associated with visceral expressions, often related to the distortion of bodies, while in its dictionary definition *'vikrut'* is also defined as 'that which goes against the laws of nature'. In Mehta's writing, the reader is offered a similar interpretation of *'vikruti'*—a suggestion that such distortions that characterise Modern Art in the West were seeping into Indian art practices and would devour its beauty and aesthetics. Bhatt picks up this word in particular, and through his responses to these provocations, explains how *'vikrutikaran'* (distortion) in art has always been an integral part of image-making. In fact, he goes a step further and demonstrates how even in literature, similes and metaphors can be considered as examples of distortion in language, using this as a way to redefine distortion and make an attempt to rid it of its negative connotations.

Such terms, along with many others that add to the art historical vocabulary of regional writing, as well as a few that the act of translation could not do justice to (ones that were untranslatable in their history, meaning, or emphasis), have been inserted in ⟨ ⟩ in Gujarati script beside their English translations. Names of colours in Gujarati have also been retained with care, as it was pointed out to us by Bhatt that unlike in English, colours in Indian languages (barring a few primary ones) are always named through descriptors—ash-like (*rakhodiyo*), rose-like (*gulabi*), sky-like (*aasmani*), for example. The hope is that when a reader familiar with Gujarati reads words with such weighted cultural specificity, they will have access to the linguistic reach of the original text, as well as an additional layer of meaning otherwise lost in translation.

One word in particular which we felt would be important to clarify is *'Habsi'*, used initially by Bhatt as a translation for 'Negro', with reference to Henri Matisse's painting 'Negro Boxer'. A word derived from the Arabic *'Habashi'*, translating to 'Abyssinian', *'Habsi'* was used in the Indian subcontinent to initially refer to Abyssinian slaves often employed during the Mughal rule. This term gradually became one that was generalised, to refer to all Black people. The word *'Habsi'* is used by Bhatt both as a part of the title of the painting, as well as to refer to the African-American community. While we have retained 'negro' in the title, we have translated *'Habsi'* to 'Black' when he refers to an individual.

Owing to the fact that the book not only brings together the writings of Mehta and Bhatt—who in themselves both use language and structure in their own ways, with little similarity to each other—but also of the editor of *Kumar*, as well as nineteen readers who contributed, in their own ways, to this debate, one of the biggest challenges was of keeping the individual voices intact. Towards this, we have tried to maintain the character of the original writing as far as possible. For example, the translations of Mehta's writing retain his unexpectedly long and winding sentences, which make one feel out of breath by the time they reach a full stop—a structural technique that doubly emphasises his frustration with Modern Art. Bhatt's writing, on the other hand, is often repetitive both in structure and argument, but this makes his explanations seem like that of a teacher talking to novice students—constantly cajoling them to pay close attention to, and truthfully answer his seemingly rhetorical questions—with the hope that at least one of his many examples will pique their interest and lead to clarity of thought.

Bhatt's clear, pedagogic, and humble writing leans on humour to gently counter Mehta's, or draw the reader into the narrative through rhetoric, while Mehta's witty use of alliteration, casual sarcasm, and humour are very purposefully used to do one of three things—prove his point, garner reader support, or express exasperation. The last of these becomes his way of connecting with the reader's own exasperation with Modern Art, so much so that he often assumes the viewers' position of a 'lay-spectator', to point out the audacity of the modern artist who claims (amongst many other things) that "understanding our new style is beyond *you*".

Besides the sentence structure and writing style, the language used by the different writers also varies. Mehta—a Parsi-Gujarati writer of repute, based in Karachi—oscillates between highly academic terminology (both Occidental and Sanskrit) and colloquial proverbs, while Bhatt—a recent graduate and teacher in his twenties—uses phrases and examples that are culturally specific to Gujarat (particularly Saurashtra, where he is from), with a heavy reliance on Hindu mythology and Indian aesthetics.

Additionally, the readers' responses bring in a wide range of examples and citations— cinema, literature, *shayari*, poetry, Sanskrit Upanishads, amongst many others. In some responses, the reader talks not only of the Modern Art debate, but also of other published content. As these comments shed light on the layered contexts of both the content published in *Kumar* as well the readers' engagement, these have been retained as is.

As cultural and historical specificities became a point of careful consideration, this is most evident in aphorisms and proverbs used by the authors. These play an important role in not only Mehta and Bhatt's articles, but also in the readers' responses. The translation of such aphorisms has been done in one of two ways to assure clarity of meaning. The first—suggested by Bhatt as essential for retaining clarity of thought—is the replacement of the proverb in the main text with an appropriate English proverb, while footnoting the original Gujarati one with elaborations. The second is a transliteration and subsequent elaboration of meaning, where a parallel failed to do justice.

The footnote functions as a key tool within our translation, assuring that while history is not erased from the main text, elaborations are provided to further make the context accessible. Even so, footnotes in this book are used judiciously, only when elaboration is essential to understanding the point being made by the writer. In addition, some footnotes also clarify certain errors and misunderstandings that were part of the original text. Such clarifications are also provided through insertions of words, dates, and phrases by the editors of this book into the main text using ⟨ ⟩, to ensure continuity of thought.

Alongside their writing, the use of quotations and visuals play an essential role in the articles, and in turn in our process of translation. Mehta's writing reflects a sense of betrayal and disappointment on behalf of the public towards the modern artist, while Bhatt's writing suggests possible ways of both understanding and appreciating such art works. In order to substantiate his criticism, Mehta uses popular public opinions (as hearsay), quotes from art scholars from around the world, newspaper reports, his own 'grammar' for effective image-making, or even the refrain, "isn't it obvious, what more can one say?" In contrast to Mehta's ways of substantiating an argument, Bhatt circles back repeatedly to his own hand-drawn illustrations which break down visual vocabulary to its barest bones. Almost never creating a 'new' image, he instead focuses on the dissection of existing patterns, paintings, or parts of paintings. Owing to this, the images in the book feature in two ways. On one hand, we have reproductions of artworks, which have been gleaned out of scans from original issues of *Kumar*. The second are hand-drawn illustrations by Bhatt published within his articles, which have been digitally re-traced and vectorised for clarity of reproduction.

There are some cases in the book where the title of the painting seems to be inaccurate with regards to the sources today, possibly because of the sources through which the images were obtained then. These discrepancies have been left as is, as often the title mentioned is integral to the point being made by the author.

Such discrepancies and slippages in both image and text mark the complexity of such an undertaking, and as our act of translation was always one of conversation and collaboration, we conclude this note by thanking the many people who have worked with us towards this process. Along with the translation team, thanks are owed to Jyoti Bhatt who provided many ingenious solutions and insights into the process, as well as Dr. Parul Dave Mukherji and Dr. Rita Sodha for their generous guidance. We also thank Urvish Kothari for pointing out crucial connections between Gujarati literary history and parts of this translation, and Mayank and Sadhana Oza for their help in contextualising the Gujarati proverbs.

THE MODERN ART DEBATE IN KUMAR

78
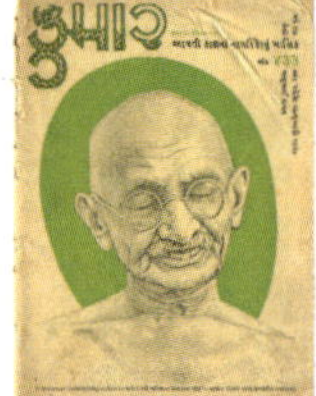
KUMAR #433 · JANUARY 1960

An Article Further Explaining Distortion in Art
Jyoti Bhatt

86
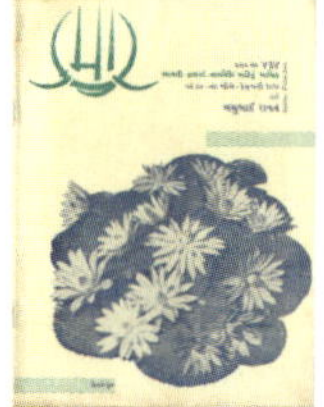
KUMAR #434 · FEBRUARY 1960

Explaining the Reasons for Distortion in Art
Jyoti Bhatt

102
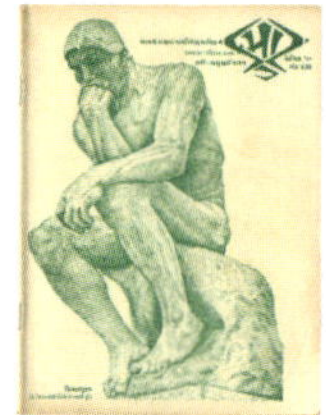
KUMAR #436 · APRIL 1960

Readers Write
Kiranchandra Somnath Joshi

104
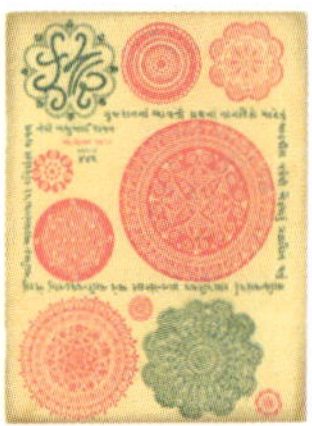
KUMAR #442 · OCTOBER 1960

Readers Write
Dinkar Vaidya 'Min Piyasi'

106
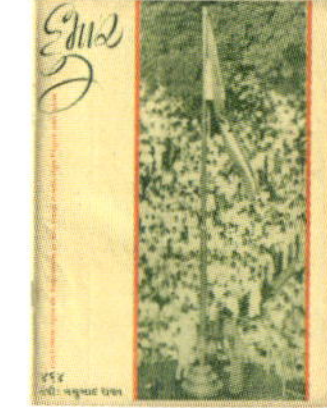
KUMAR #464 · AUGUST 1962

Readers Write
Jayantilal Mehta, Harikrishna R. Pathak

116
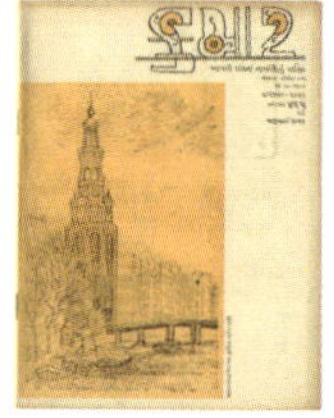
KUMAR #465 · SEPTEMBER 1962

Readers Write
N.G. Bhanwadia

118
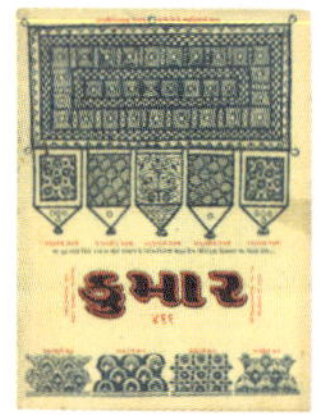
KUMAR #466 · OCTOBER 1962

Readers Write
Suresh Desai

120
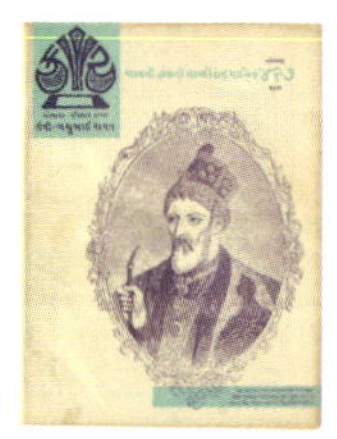
KUMAR #467 · NOVEMBER 1962

Readers Write
N.G. Bhanwadia, Himmatbhai Mehta

124
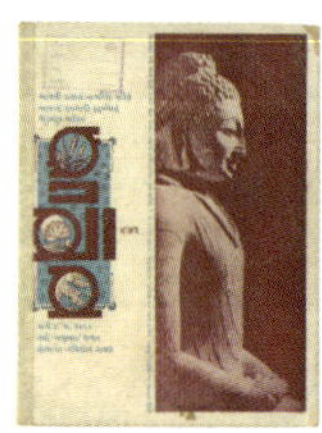
KUMAR #471 · MARCH 1963

Readers Write
Harikrishna R. Pathak

128 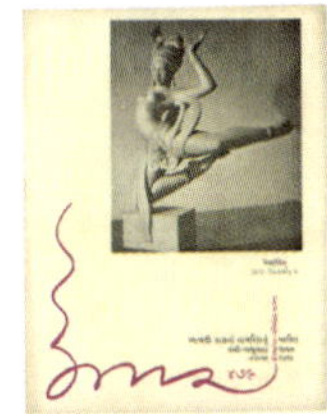

KUMAR #479 · NOVEMBER 1963

Readers Write
Chandrashekhar

130 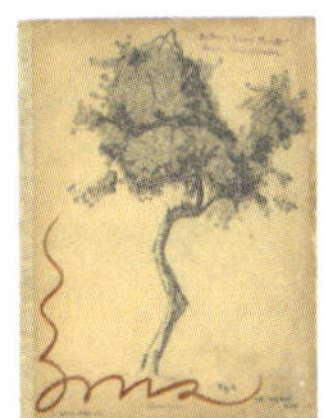

KUMAR #480 · DECEMBER 1963

Readers Write
Pherozeshah Rustomji Mehta

132

KUMAR #492 · DECEMBER 1964

Readers Write
Pherozeshah Rustomji Mehta

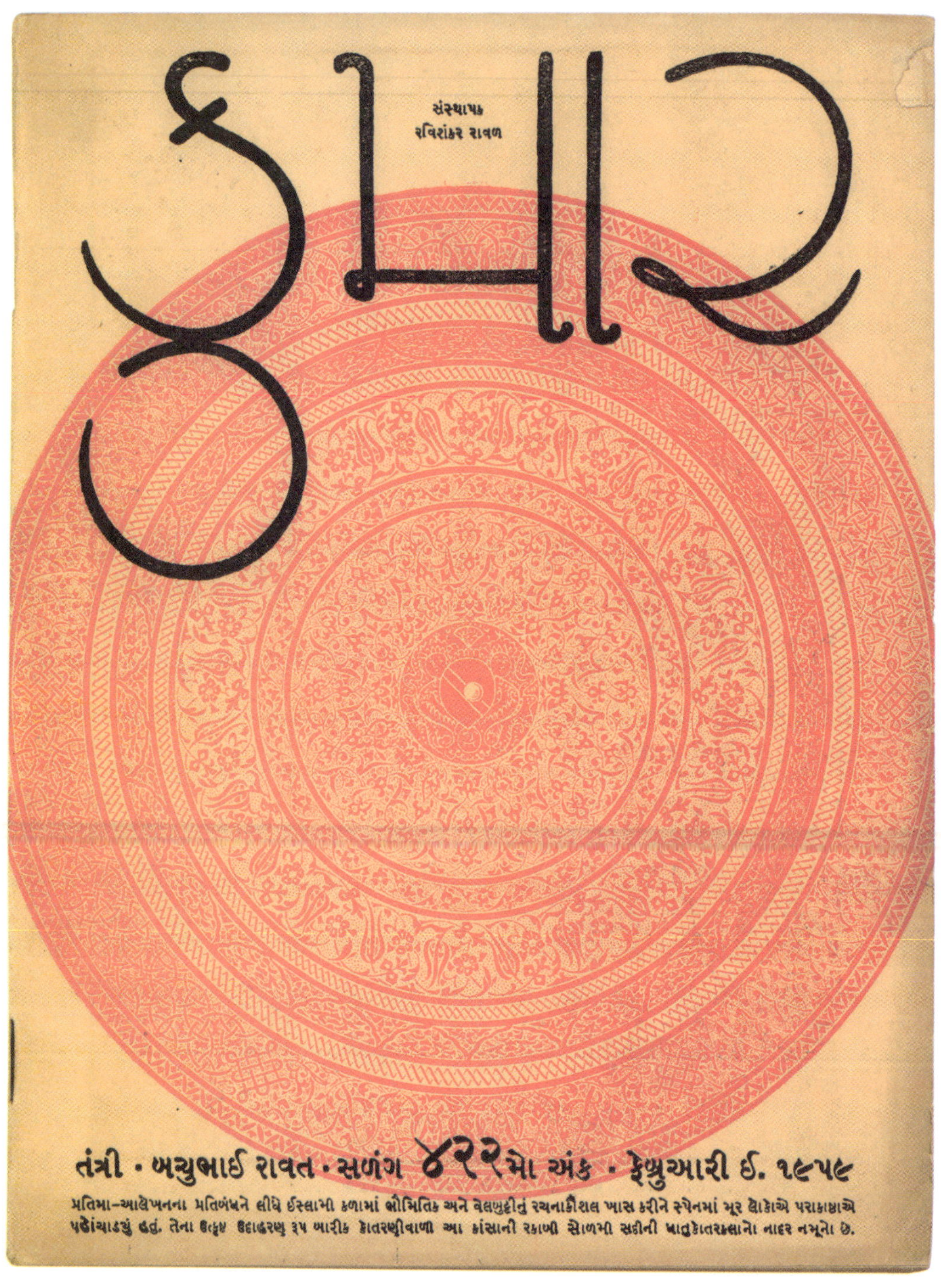

KUMAR #422 · FEBRUARY 1959

Readers Write

I really liked the December ⟨1958⟩ issue of Kumar—owing to the reflective and beautiful articles, and abundance of images. In that, particularly the various sketches rendered by Shri Dinesh Shah of Vinoba Ji are truly admirable. I hope that Kumar continues to benefit from him.

The section 'I am Adventurous' was not to be found. Gujaratis do have some adventurous tendencies, do they not? Or is it that this section did not receive the response it deserved?

Some time ago, there was a discussion amongst us friends. Based on that, ⟨I am⟩ tempted to give a humble suggestion to Kumar. In English and American magazines, we frequently see advertisements regarding coaching institutions that can prove very helpful for painters or artists. Since such organisations run on a commercial basis, the fees of the whole course is not one which is affordable to a middle-class family. That is why it becomes difficult for them to develop painting, music, etc. as a hobby. If some established and professional artists and practitioners of art (such as R.M.R ⟨Ravishankar Mahashankar Raval⟩, Rasiklal Parikh, Shanti Shah), with the help of their pen and brush, start a series of articles such as 'How to Draw and Paint' or 'It is Easy to Draw', it will be extremely compelling and inspirational. While I myself do not have much of an understanding of this subject, I do have a profuse interest in art and artists.

—Jyotish Jani (Goregaon)

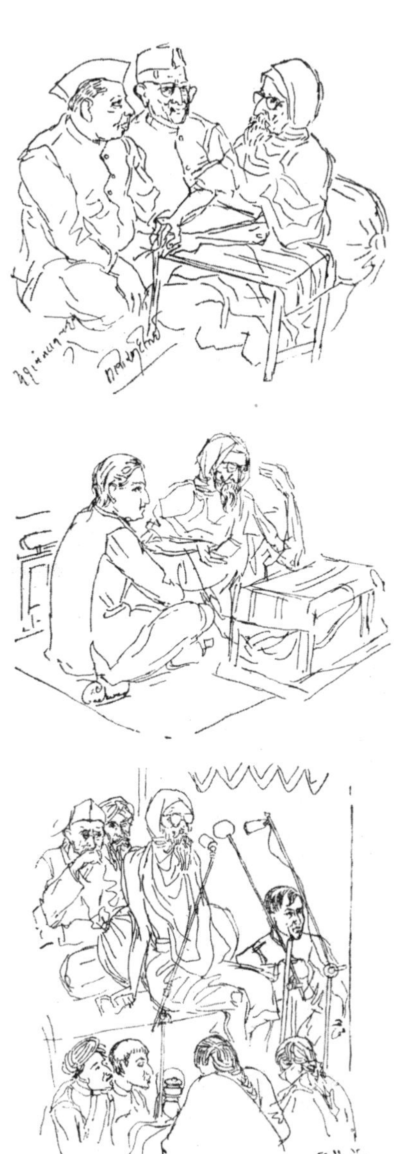

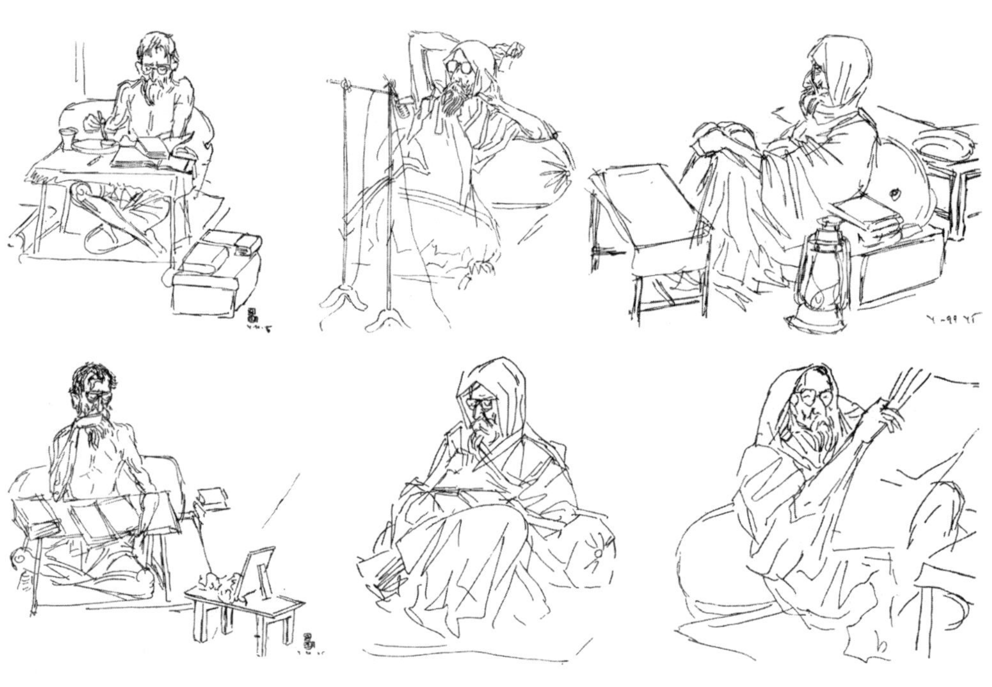

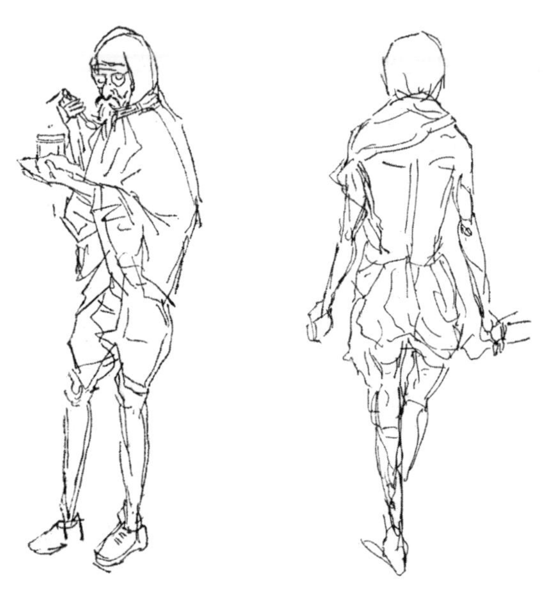

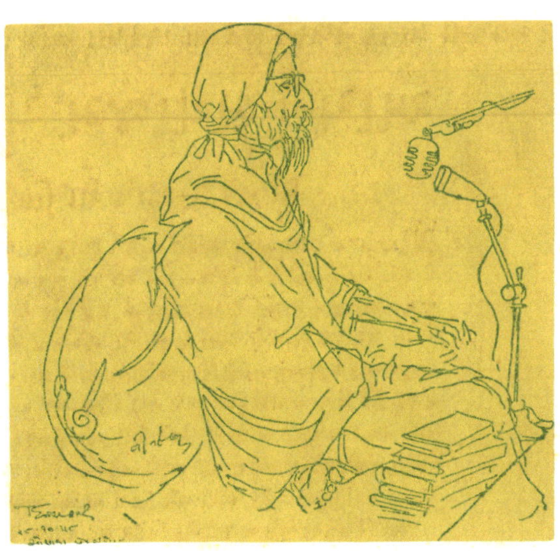

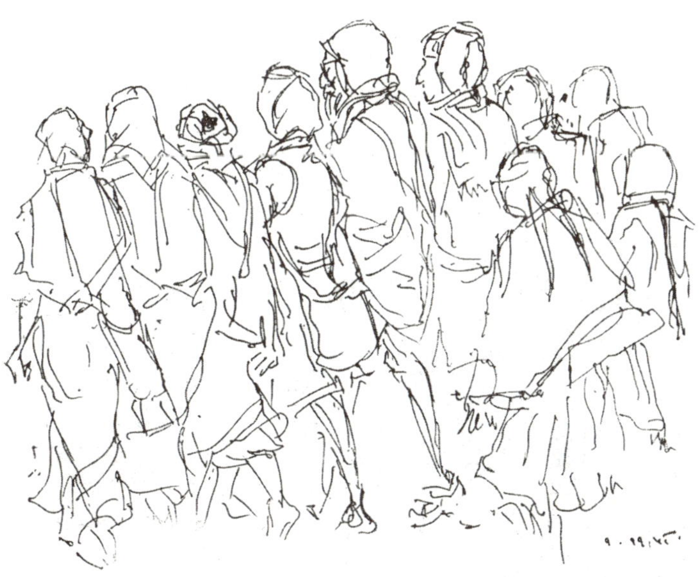

Dinesh Shah's drawings representing what everyday life was like
during Vinoba Bhave's Bhoodan-Gramdan Yatra in Gujarat,
including sketches of various events that Vinoba Ji was involved in.

⟨Published in Kumar #420 · December 1958⟩

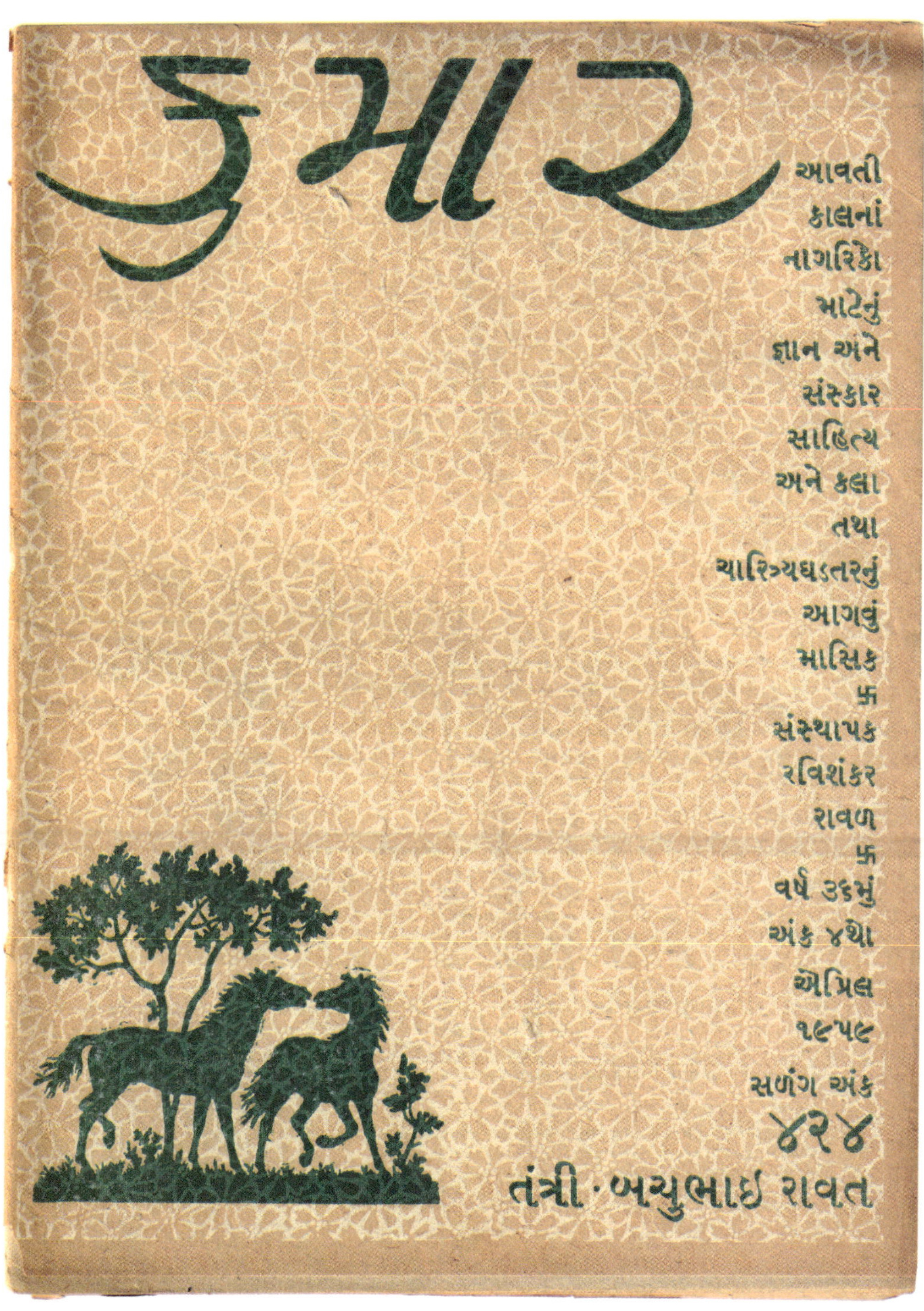

KUMAR #424 · APRIL 1959

Readers Write

Further to what was suggested by Shri Jyotish Jani in February, paintings of the various modern styles cannot be understood by a layperson like myself; which is why many people brush it off by assuming such paintings to be mere blotches of colour or purposeless lines. Can you not give a few examples of paintings of this style in each issue, explaining its constitutive principles and characteristics? For instance, Devnath Mukherjee's painting 'Phool-patro' in the February ⟨1959⟩ issue, might be an excellent work of art, however, like me, a lot of people would not have been able to fully appreciate its essence due to our lack of understanding.

—*Jayendrasinh Jadhav (Junagadh)*

In the March ⟨1959⟩ issue, ⟨we⟩ saw examples of Shri Raghav Ramji Kaneria's modernist style of sculpture.

Nearly ninety percent of people do not have the vision to understand this 'Modern Art'. Often this matter has been discussed amongst us friends, but we couldn't understand if this can truly be called art or not. Is it necessary to pay attention to proportions, outlines, etc. in such paintings? How are these works judged and what are their measures of value? Many such questions arise and the mind remains restless. Therefore, it is a request that you publish articles, paintings, and sculptures shedding light on this Modern Art in Kumar, so that many like us can get a new perspective.

—*Ramnik Bhatt (Rajkot)*

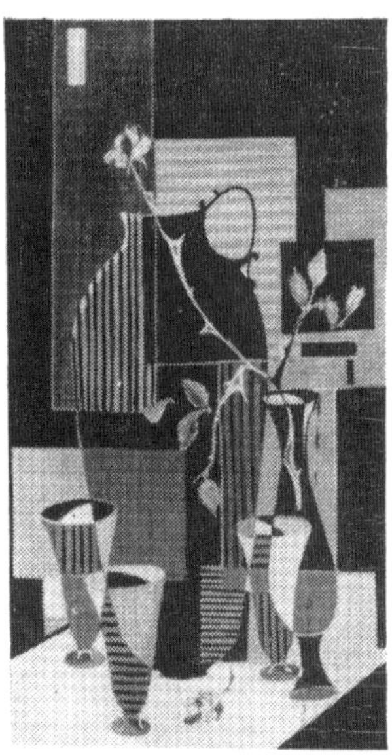

'Phool-patro' ⟨Flower Vase⟩ · Artist: Devnath Mukherjee · This painting has been purchased for an American gallery.

⟨Published in Kumar #422 · February 1959⟩

[*We have been receiving many such vehement opinions against 'Modern Art'. A veteran has already sent us a descriptive article (including the opinions of world-renowned thinkers) which we are going to publish, and along with this we invite opinions of others who appreciate Modern Art. In the meanwhile, we have been making efforts as per the information available to us (for example, about Vitthal and Prabha Badgelvar's artworks) and will continue to do so. Yet, our invitation still stands for unique and unfailingly perceptive writings.]*

⟨*—Editor*⟩

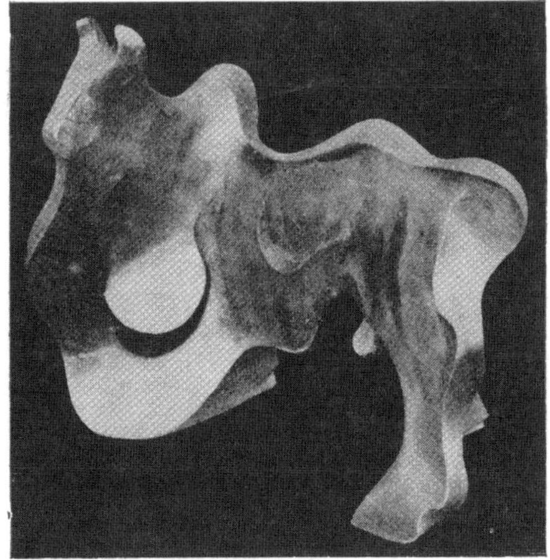

I

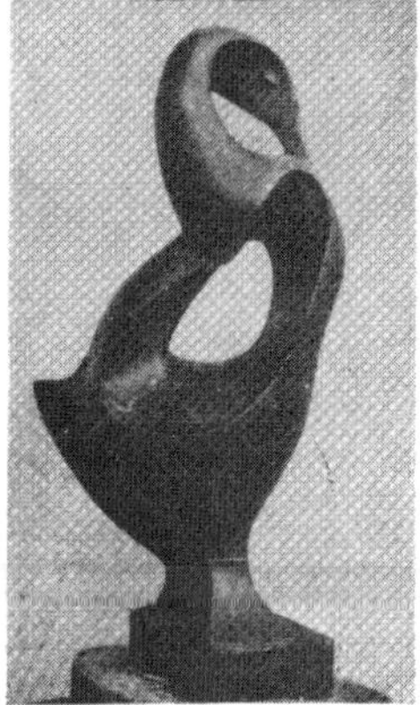

II

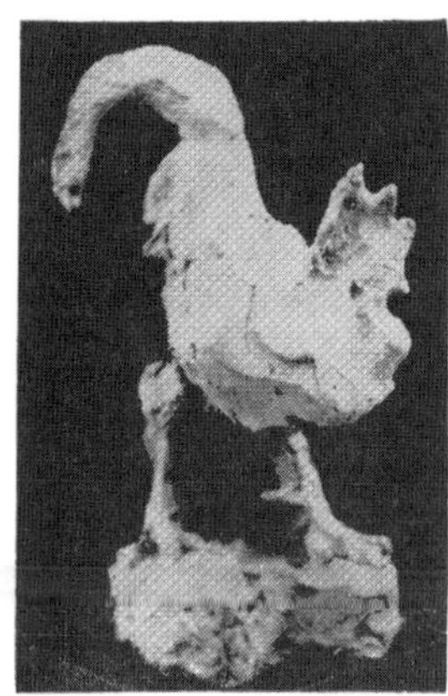

III

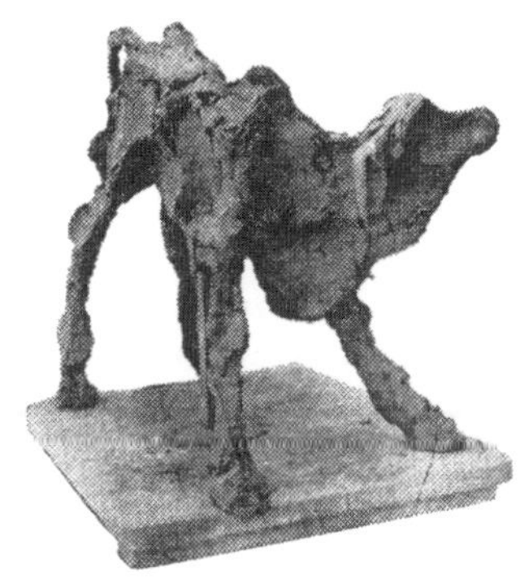

IV

I. 'Nandi' ⟨Bull⟩ · In this year's National Art Exhibition, within the category of modern style in sculpture, a prize of Rs. 1000 was won solely by this sculpture, which was deemed worthy. Artist: Raghav Ramji Kaneria

II. 'Batak' ⟨Duck⟩ · In this year's Art Exhibition for the Mumbai region, a prize of Rs. 500 was won by this second sculpture of Kaneria.

III. 'Kukdo' ⟨Rooster⟩ · A sculpture made in cement.

IV. 'Vaachardu' ⟨Calf⟩ · A sketch made in clay.

Birds, animals, other creatures, and their various manifestations are Kaneria's favourite subjects.

⟨Published in Kumar #423 · March 1959⟩

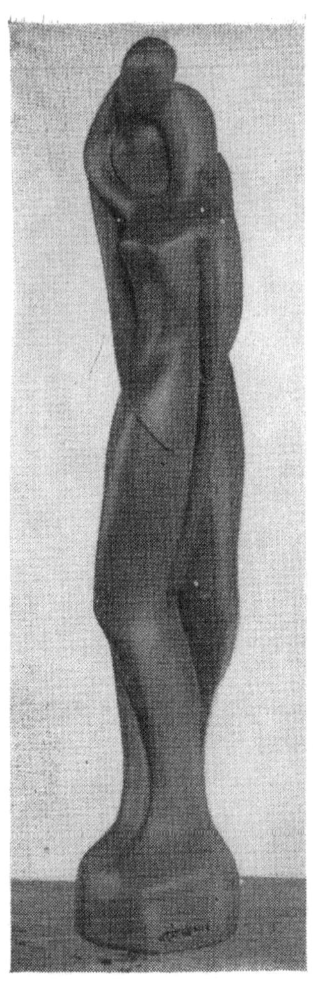

I

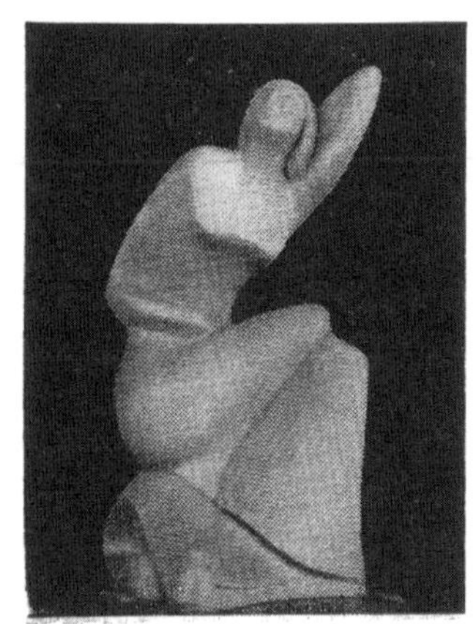

II

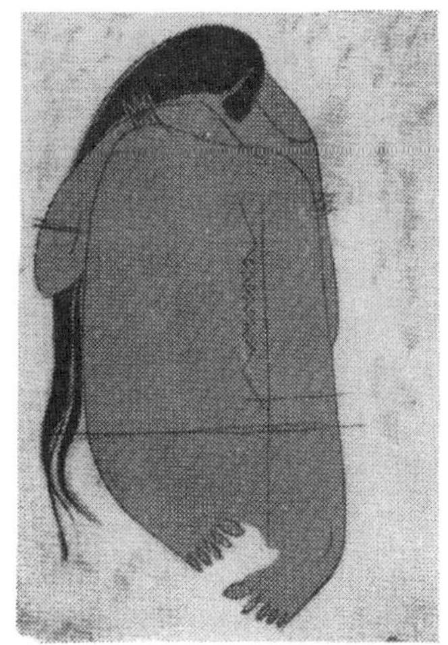

III

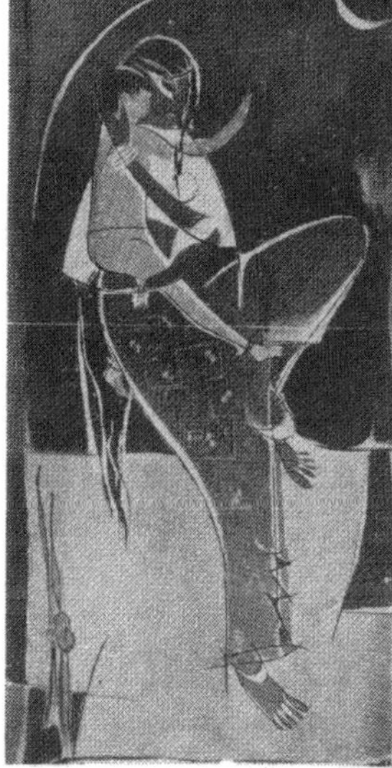

IV

I.   'Jeevansathi' ⟨Life Partner⟩ · A sculpture by Vitthal Badgelvar
II. 'Swapnasheel' ⟨Dream-like⟩ · A sculpture by Vitthal Badgelvar
III. 'Bhagnash' ⟨Broken⟩ · A painting by Prabha Badgelvar
IV. 'Chandamama' ⟨Moon⟩ · A painting by Prabha Badgelvar

⟨Published in Kumar #412 · April 1958⟩

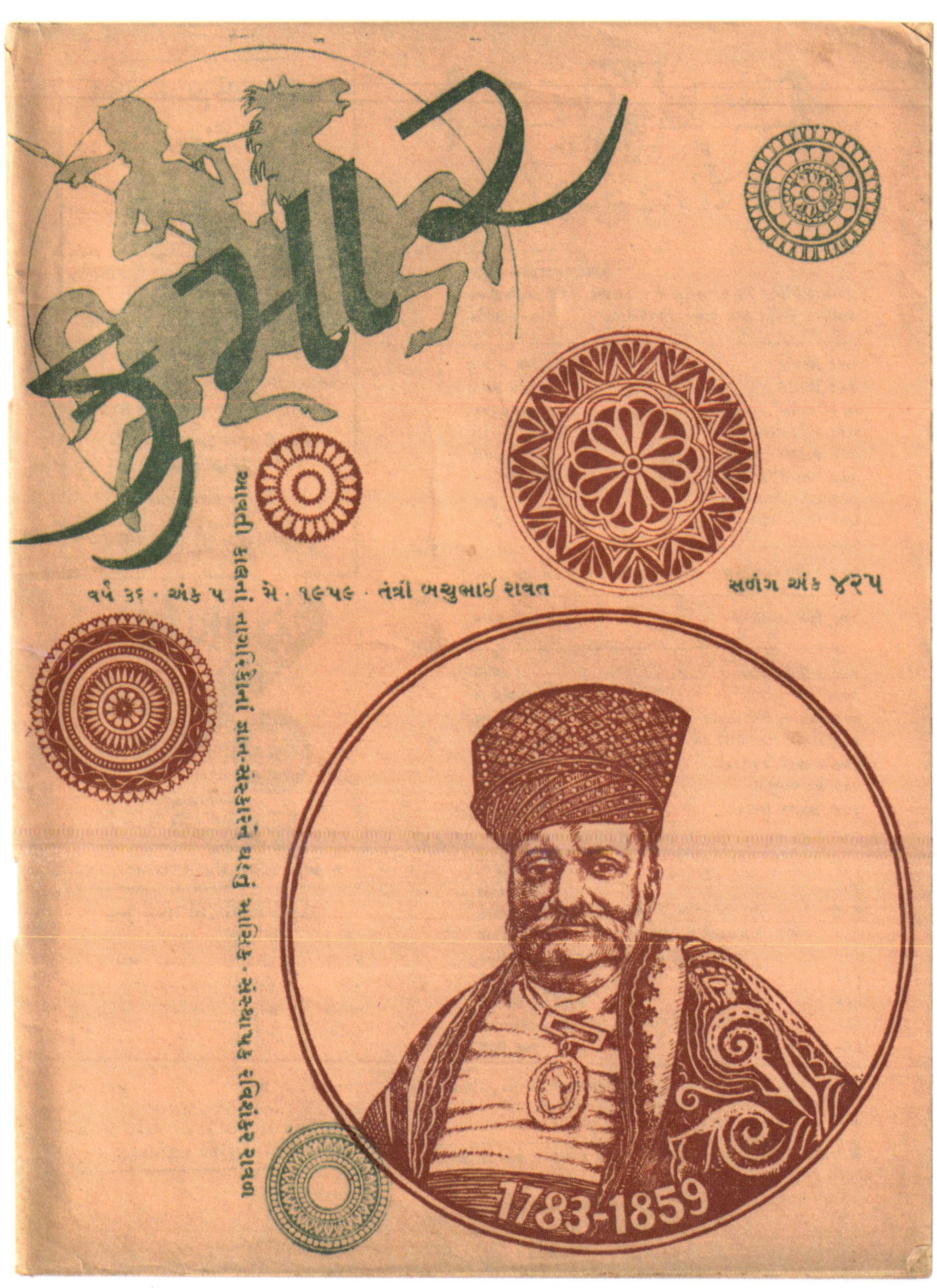

KUMAR #425 · MAY 1959

Readers Write

In the 'Readers Write' from the April ⟨1959⟩ issue ⟨we⟩ read a response about 'modern sculpture'. It is still understandable that in modern sculpture, gracefulness of line is rendered without a face or a clear figure; not just that, but along with proving the point that curves in nature are attractive, it also makes us aware of both movement and rhythm. However, in 'modern painting' only the artists themselves can understand the purpose behind these lines and colours—lines and colours just like a child's naive scribbles! The viewers get nothing out of it.

I had asked a known emerging artist of today, and he had responded that all that 'Modern Art' is doing is surely destroying art.

Moreover, in poetry too, if the phrase *'Vakyam rasatmak kavyam'*[1] is true, then can flavourless phrases that have no core emotion ⟨મુદ્દલ રસ⟩, without the effect of auspiciousness or lucidity, be called poetry? There is nothing to say about the personality of the creators of such poems; however, isn't there a need to think about the evaluation of just their creation and its various kinds? Accepted that novelty is needed, uniqueness is needed; but why should it necessarily be flavourless, repulsive, and disgusting? However in Sanskrit, *'bibhatsa'* is also a Rasa, and so it can be included in poetry! *'Bibhatsa'* means repulsive—not vulgar. But as repulsive as covered with urine-blood, etc... Can someone shed light on this? What do you think?

Hakim Agha Jaan had told the poet Ghalib:
> *Agar apna kaha tum, aap hi samjhe to kya samjhe,*
> *Maza kahneka jab hay, ek kahe, aur dusra samjhe.*
> ⟨What is understood at all, if only you understand what you have said,
> The joy of speech is then, when one says, and the other understands.⟩

Shouldn't the public gain something from art and poetry?

—*Dinkar Vaidya 'Min Piyasi' (Bhadreshi)*

---

1 — Cited from the scholar Vishwanath's Sahityadarpana, a treatise on poetics and aesthetics believed to have been written before 1384 AD, this phrase translates to: "Only those sentences that are delightfully flavourful can be called poetry."

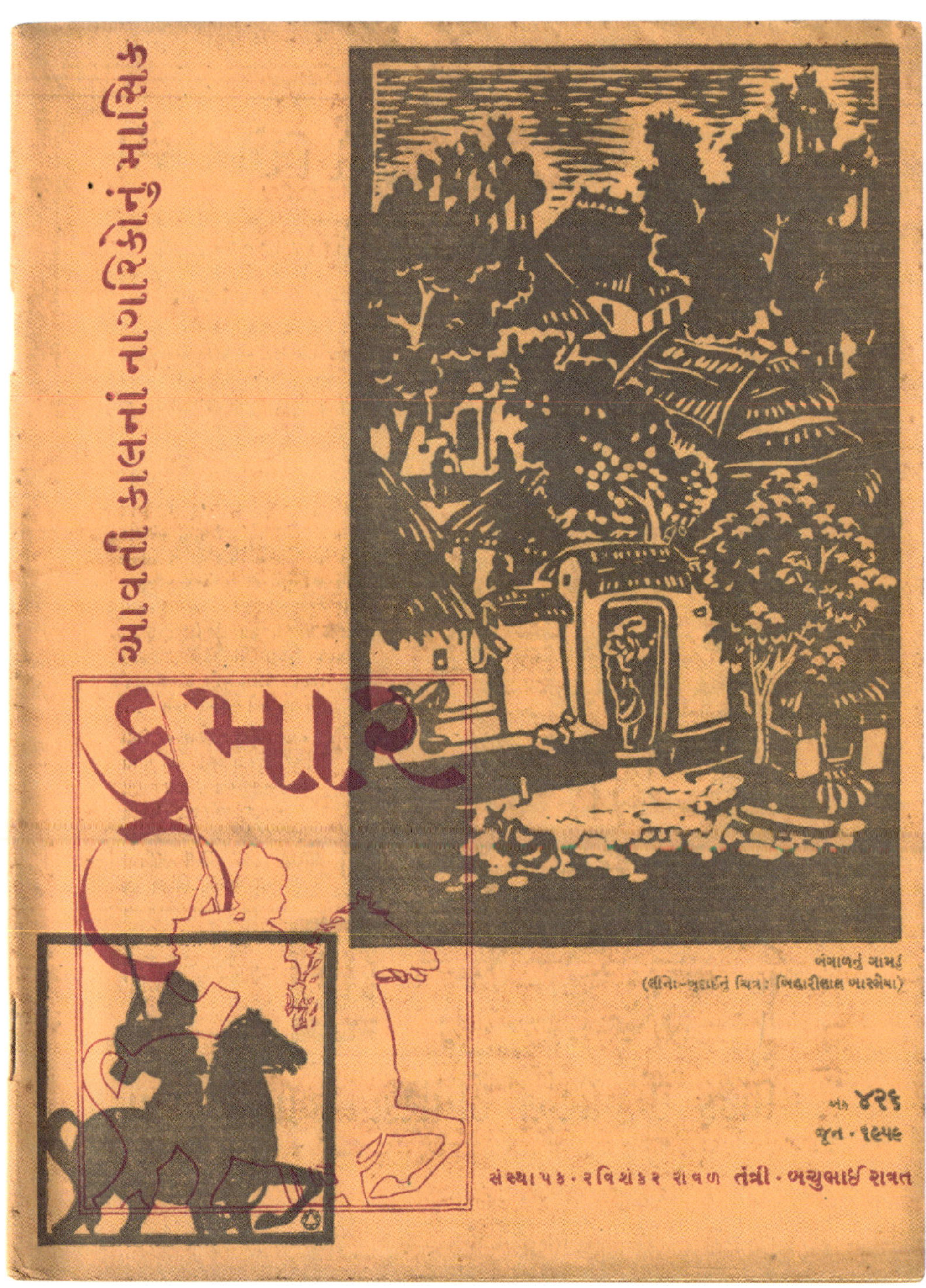

બંગાળનું ગામડું
(લીનો–કટનું ચિત્ર: બિહારીલાલ બારેઇયા)

અંક ૪૨૬
જૂન · ૧૯૫૯

સંસ્થાપક · રવિશંકર રાવળ   તંત્રી · બચુભાઈ રાવત

આવતી કાલના નાગરિકોનું માસિક

KUMAR #426 · JUNE 1959

'MODERN ART'
A DEBATE ON CURRENT PAINTING STYLES

Pherozeshah Rustomji Mehta

The author of this article has been researching art for many years, and has written on and off in periodicals about this subject. Today, even at the age of 80, he has picked up his pen and made the effort to write on this controversial subject, and this shows his acute urge to explain to the public the prestige and discursivity of art; and since his objection of the new art practises is inspired by goodwill for the public rather than for art or the artist, it is worth respecting, in spite of anyone feeling adversely about his thoughts and opinions. As far as possible, Kumar has been appreciative of new art, and considering this fact, perceptive counter responses with similar examples are welcome.

—Editor

It is possible to write a whole book about the day-by-day increase in current painting styles of non-art ⟨અ-કળા⟩, extravagance, and anarchy; however, for now, I have decided to present only a concise criticism which is relevant to this subject.

MODERNISM! MODERNISM!!

Of late, 'modernism'—a word all of three syllables[2]—is rolling off everyone's tongue with regards to any and all art. For quite some time now, in the name of 'originality',

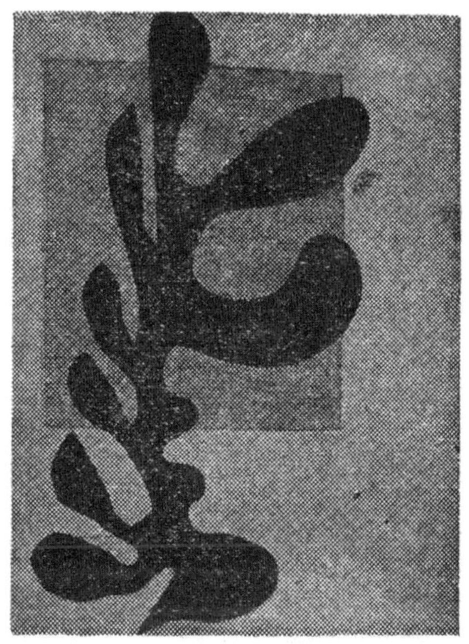

'Negro Boxer' · Artist: Henri Matisse

'newness', and 'uniqueness', an extreme sense of bizarreness and anarchy has entered the field of painting, just as it has in literature and poetry, architecture and sculpture, and objects and decoration; these make us painfully yearn for the subject-specific aesthetics of tastefully created artworks by the great masters of centuries past.

---

2 — In the Gujarati text, Mehta has used the word 'સાડાપાંચિયો' (*saadapanchiyo*, meaning '5 and ½') to describe the number of alphabets in the Gujarati transliteration of the word 'modernism'—મોડર્નિઝમ. In the Gujarati script, the sound of the alphabet 'r' is considered half.

STYLO-MANIA

As we recall the history of painting from the East and the West, we can clearly see that at the turn of every era, in response to the prevalent artistic trends, there came about a kind of 'modernism'—novelty and innovation. So then why is today's modernism so odd? The reason is that today's modernism has caught a peculiar disease. The name of this disease is 'Stylo-Mania' ⟨શૈલી-ઘેલછા⟩. From the fertile soils of France, after the *ripened* 'Cubism' emerged, the West saw an overflow of multiple newer 'isms', such as Futurism, Dadaism, Surrealism, Abstractionism, Constructivism, Neoplasticism, etc., of which there seems to be no end in sight.*

[* All of these combine to approximately thirty odd names, of which some are: Impressionism, Post-Impressionism, Neo-Impressionism, Expressionism, Cubism, Dadaism, Futurism, Symbolism, Cloisonnism, Abstractism-Abstractionism-Concrete Art, Constructivism-Suprematism, Elementarism, Jugendstil (Modern), Synthetism, Plasticism, Neo-Plasticism, Surrealism, Superyurenism[3], Orphism, Pointillism-Divisionism, Purism, Rayonism, Eclecticism, Intimism, etc.]

As and when a new unique 'ism' emerges, with it its 'new style' is bound to appear. However, such is the misfortune of art: these new styles did not stay within their limits, instead they transformed into a state of frenzy.

Any good painting thrives on the character of its style. Style devoid of character ends up nowhere. A good style always in itself should either be of acceptable taste or be long lasting; filled with aesthetic value and usually agreeable; but when one sees the lines of the new painting styles of today, we are reminded of the proverb *'oonth na adhare ang vaanka'*[4] ⟨which indicates that one may endlessly find fault with others, with complete disregard for one's own⟩; and the hodge-podge, blotchy application of colour presents a distorted ⟨વિકૃત⟩ image in our eyes, like that of a four-legged, manged, diseased stray dog wandering through the narrow lanes of a village! Seeing this cartwheeling nature of today's modernism, one wonders if it is 'modernism' or 'murderism'?!

STYLE, WHAT'S THAT?

On 25th August, 1753, the French scholar ⟨G.L. Leclerc, Comte de⟩ Buffon is quoted to have said a memorable phrase at the French Academy: "Style is the man himself." Expanding on this definition of style, Buffon clarified that, "style is nothing but the rhythm and order that the writer or artist places in their own work while creating it." So, in the process of creating an object, just as subjective internal rhythm and order arise within the creator, so do styles. However, Buffon also stated that, "but, any style must be instinctive and simple".

Be it writing or painting, there are two categories of styles: (1) common style ⟨સામાન્ય શૈલી⟩ (2) individual style ⟨વ્યક્તિગત શૈલી⟩. When the artist expresses in the popular style ⟨પ્રચલિત શૈલી⟩ of their time without any noteworthy contribution, that style is known as the 'common style'; however, when the artist blends their own new expression

---

3 — The list of 'isms' has been transliterated from Gujarati script, and 'Superyurenism' in specific is not a movement according to current sources. Even so, it has been retained as per the original.

4 — The Gujarati proverb *'oonth na adhare ang vaanka'* used here is derived from a famous poem by Dalpatram, a 19th century Gujarati poet and social reformer from Ahmedabad. The poem is about a camel who is finding faults in every other animal and bird's body, to which the fox responds by saying, "we may have one or two crooked body parts, but you have no limbs that are not crooked!" This proverb is popularly used in Gujarati vocabulary to describe someone who always finds faults in others and is unwilling to look at their own.

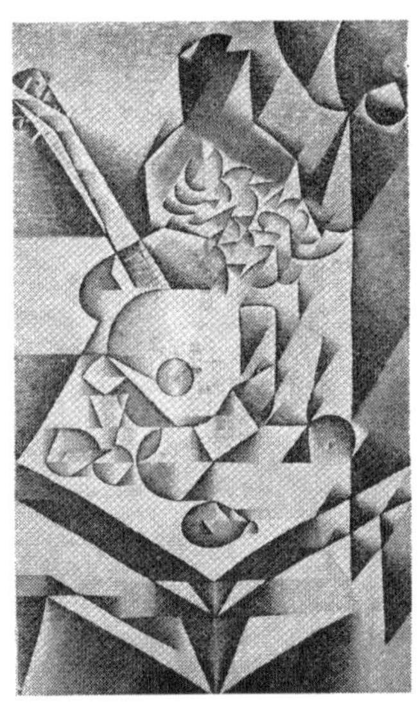

I

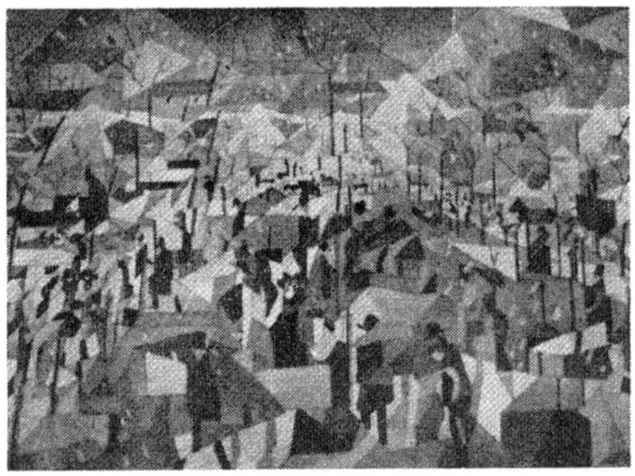

II

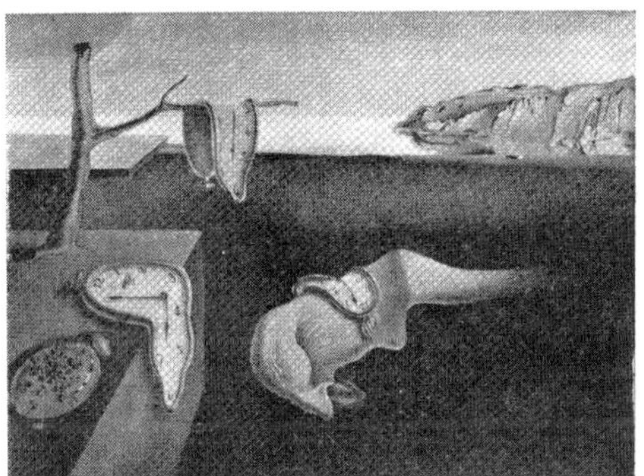

IV

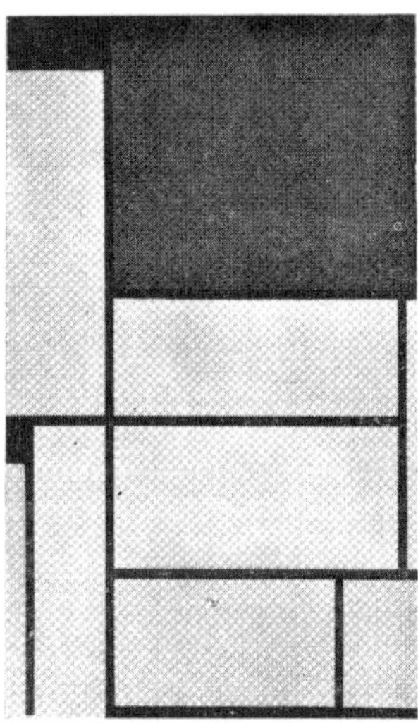

III

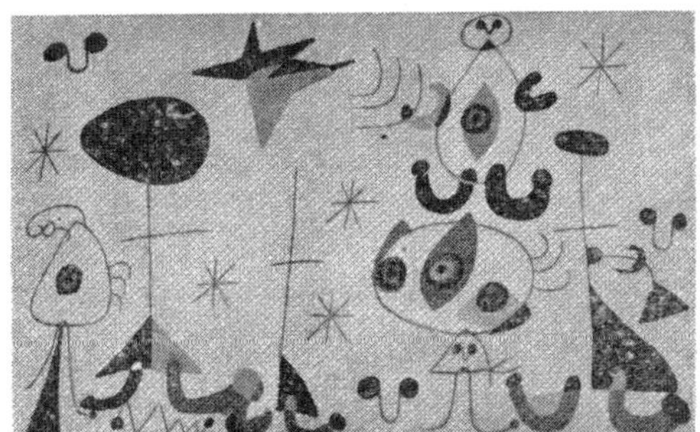

V

Five Styles of Modern Art:

I.   Cubism: 'Still Life with Flowers', 1912 ·
     Artist: ⟨Juan⟩ Gris
II. Futurist Art: 'Le Boulevard', 1911 ·
     Artist: Gino Severini
III. Neo-Plasticism: 'Tableau', 1921 ·
     Artist: ⟨Piet⟩ Mondrian
IV. Surrealist Art: 'The Persistence of
     Memory', 1931 · Artist: Salvador Dalí
V.   Abstract Art: 'Snob Party at the
     Princess's', 1944 · Artist: ⟨Joan⟩ Miró

and spirit with the present styles, then their style is lifted to the status of being personal, i.e. individualistic. Depending on the individualistic style of the artist being well or poorly expressed, or of strong or weak spirit, the work will result in either more (*or less*) elegance and beauty, or ugliness, or distortion. Moreover, when this individual style rears its contradictory head and becomes excessive, then it starts becoming crazy, absurd, ambiguous, impure, and shocking, and even obscure and immensely unpleasant. These days, the 'new styles' or so-called 'individualistic' styles are more or less like this, presenting to us an undesired kind of 'modernism' within art.

WINDING, WANDERING, STIFLING WIT

One expects that this 'new' example of 'new' art of a 'new' style in current times would result in the flourishing of the modern artists' artistic knowledge, arising from the development of the 'scientific age'; but using this knowledge they have hardly provided any poetic, divine, scenic, interesting, or even attractive elements to be remembered for posterity. Although these loud-mouthed modernists boastfully claim that their artworks are 'scientific', owing to their pretentious efforts of bringing only 'novelty' to the table, their scientific intellect or knowledge about art seems to be forgotten, stuck, wandering, and suffocating in some dark narrow alley of 'newness', as if struggling on a paper or canvas.

"UNDERSTANDING OUR NEW STYLE IS BEYOND YOU"

The creators of 'new painting styles' repeatedly tell us, "you ordinary lay-spectators will never be able to comprehend our new painting styles. You want purity of form in the painting, and exciting gracefully curved contours; but you need to understand that the distortion of forms also holds a place in painting. Moreover, this distortion is not futile. But, since you only like those paintings in which the formation of meaning and its mysteries are revealed clearly and swiftly, you should know that we aren't imitators of an 'antiquated' style of the past. You must understand that shapes in nature and shapes in art can be different. Decoding the meaning of our new artworks of the new age is not an easy task. In order to understand our paintings, you should have an expert like us who knows 'new art' and can explain it to you", etc. etc.

It is unanimously accepted that there will also be distortion of forms in paintings, but this distortion should not be such that it presents an altogether different (inverted) shape in comparison to the intended form! For instance, when an artist says, "look, that's a running dog", and instead of a dog one sees a bent and broken, four-cornered elliptical metal machine scurrying away— then that absurdity and 'distortion' is in fact 'non-art', which makes a mockery of art. Of what use is this distortion of forms that is not harmonious with the theme of the painting? There is no room for a 'distortion' that is so unhinged and frivolous that it flouts all 'limits' and 'restraints' (which are no doubt essential) in painting or art.

Now there is no dearth of these trashy ⟨વિક્ષત⟩ artworks of the new 'isms' or 'new styles'. As an example, look at the 'abstract' style painting 'Temptation of Saint Anthony' shown here. Here, in the name of distortion of form, one sees an absolute disaster. This is an ideal example of 'abstractionism'! Even if we let our eyes sink entirely into the painting, we are unable to discern, or even imagine, where St. Anthony is hiding or the objects that 'tempt' him. All over the painting, from top to bottom, here and there, one only sees a worn-out pile of long and wide planks or a heap of iron beams, which is an absolutely incomprehensible absurdity!! It will not be wrong to call this kind of an 'abstractionism'

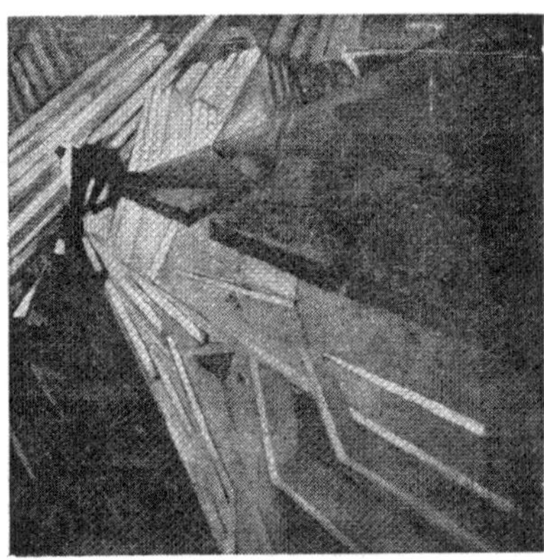

'Temptation of St. Anthony'

as 'invisiblism' ⟨અદૃશ્યનિઝમ⟩. After brutally demolishing the 'reality' in paintings in this way, if you then blame the spectator saying, "you can't understand the 'mystery' of our 'new style' and to understand it you need an 'expert' by your side," then what can this be called besides 'nonsensical' and 'baselessly argumentative'? In fact, these 'modernists' have taken on such an agonising pursuit, that the more difficult a painting is to understand, the more modern it is!

THREE ESSENTIAL ELEMENTS
OF AN ARTWORK

Any expressive or attractive work of literature or art has to, in some measure, have these three elements: 1. Clarity, 2. Power, and 3. Melody. Upon hearing this word 'clarity', modernists get instigated. The meaning of 'clarity' should not be considered merely the 'lack of mystery'. Even in the most esoteric of such artworks, there has to be some suggestive clarity. However, in the absolute dearth of information, such extreme levels of ambiguity can only be compared to the scribbles of a small child's stumbling hands on a slate. All discerning art viewers have this basic understanding that 'art' never reveals itself by shouting out: it speaks, but more than speaking, it suggests. Without a doubt, there is space for such suggestive clarity in an artwork.

The second element is 'power'. It gives life to an artwork. This 'power' emerges from within the artist's innermost feelings and naturally extends into their work. However, the artist must use the force of these feelings according to their own pace. 'Power' adds strength to the painting not by being extremely impulsive, but only by practising restraint; as required by the subject of the painting, the contents must be filled in frugally. These days in the world of art, the force of the winds of 'abstractionism' have crossed all limits in terms of content—it is as though the world of art has been made into an asylum of ridiculous images.

The third element is 'melody'. If artworks do not have rhythm, they become dull, barren, and dissonant. Just like the melody and tones of poems and songs have harmony, in the same way artworks too have harmony. This 'rhythm' presents before the eyes of the spectator, a fluidity of line, ferocity and a softness, darkness and radiance of colours that charms the viewers, making their heart feel energised and content; elevating their soul. However, if it is possible to find a needle in a haystack, then it is also possible to discern evocative harmony in paintings by today's modernists.

BLAME IT ON THE 'UNTRAINED EYES'

Modern artists repeatedly tell their critics, "the reason you cannot understand our new modern painting styles is due to the fact that your eyes are not habituated to do so. Just as those who enjoy film songs have no interest in classical music, and those ears attuned to Hindustani *ragas* will find Western music irritating, similarly you are being unnecessarily opinionated and are assuming that our 'new styles of painting' are lacking because your eyes are unhabituated. If you make an effort for four to six months and inspect our works abandoning bias, then your eyes will become habituated; you will then see how unique our modern style paintings are and how they offer such unprecedented joy!"

To which we respond: "yes, eyes should be habituated and an effort should be put into this, but is there anything fundamental to your new styles of painting upon which we can fix our gaze, put effort, train our eyes, and then get accustomed to? There are *ragas* in Hindustani classical music, and so despite your interest in film songs, there is scope to habituate novice ears and enjoy classical music with some effort. There is also a fixed method in the roots of Western music, as well as in the presence of *ragas*. However, just like the proverb *'khatle moti khod ke pratham payo j nahi'* ⟨which indicates that when the fundamentals of a structure are missing, what is the point in analysing its minor flaws⟩[5], if your 'modern' styles of painting don't even have the element of a foundational methodology, then on what basis can one make an effort?"

There is certainly an ingenuity in the new styles of these modern painters, but such bizarre styles seldom result in 'great' paintings which will be remembered for posterity. Oil can be extracted only from a sesame seed, not from sand! First and foremost, these newly christened novel styles 'intentionally' destroy what we call 'reality'. Entirely erasing reality is the pride and epic craftsmanship of these modernist painters! To avoid misunderstanding, it is important to note that we are not expecting absolute realism or explicitly clear meanings from the modernists; but shouldn't there be a hint of reality through which one can catch onto the expressive elements of their work of art?

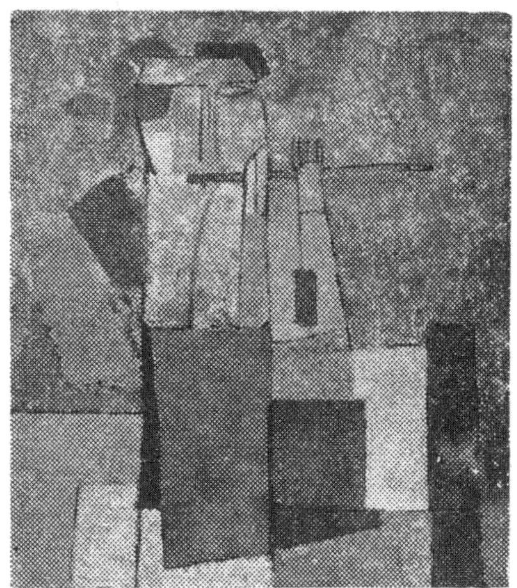

'Flute Player' · Artist: ⟨V.S.⟩ Gaitonde

ORIGINALITY OF ART

It is understandable that modern artists have pride and respect for their new style of art; however, it won't be out of context to bring into discussion this 'originality' of theirs. In actuality, there is nothing 'original' on this rotating planet or under the sun; even so, as far as literature and art are concerned, we do not hesitate in calling any new treatment, or freshness, 'original'. However, what is regrettable is that amongst today's modern artists, neither does the 'originality' of most touch the heart, nor does it even seem intellectually plausible. What is the value of such a half-baked originality, which says one thing but means another?

When a true artist ideates or draws a subject from their mind, they know very well that even if a painting has originality,

5 — Mehta has used the Gujarati proverb *'khatle moti khod ke pratham payo j nahi'*, which describes people finding faults with a cot without legs, when its existence as a cot itself can be questioned owing to the fact that a cot cannot be called so if it has no legs. Here the word *'payo'* is used as a pun, a word that means both the base of a cot, as well as something 'fundamental'.

the most important and final aspect of its ideation and drawing cannot only be the presence of originality, but also the presence of 'beauty'. Such art works that startle the viewers with 'forceful' uniqueness cannot be called 'original'. By seeing the artworks of so many emerging modernists of today, one regretfully learns that the more marked the ambiguity or ugliness of the work is for them, the more exceptionally 'original' it is. Such an attitude will result only in a crazy originality. The modernists of today, who are not only indifferent towards the presence of 'beauty', but are also defiant of it and are determinedly working to destroy 'beauty' in art by defending the notion of 'beauty in ugliness', seem to have forgotten the eternal truth that any kind of surprising originality is neither the essential result nor the end of an artwork. A meaningful end must be that of 'beauty', and 'originality' is but a means to achieve this end.

Within this show business of originality, the other sentiment of the modern artist which springs forth is: "because our artwork is unknown to the shortcomings of the 'usual', or in other words is 'unusual', the lay-spectator is in opposition to it." The fact is that the intentional twisting and contorting of the forms of nature, making them without any order, causing absolute destruction, and taking pride in the 'unusual' does not reflect the importance of the work or the artist. This is in fact a gross misuse of art.

The artists who monopolise today's countless new 'isms' are heard loudly and repeatedly criticising the famous artists of the past centuries by saying, "unlike the painters who came before us, we don't consider it crucial that a painting resembles the exaction offered by 'photography'. We are now less interested in the 'photographic' paintings from antiquated styles." However, if we observe the history of countless artworks and the long history of painting, then we very simply realise that even the artists of the past century have overturned the prevalent styles, and have brought about innovation. With the exception of a few hyper-realistic painters here and there, other pioneering artists riding on the wings of imagination, and in tune with their heart, mind, and eyes, have gifted the world paintings of landscapes, portraits, images from daily life, and historical and religious narratives, on the basis of the science of painting and composition. They too, being spontaneous and dreamy, have created artworks with new perspectives. However, unlike the modernists of today, never have they been vainly whimsical and uncontrolled, and presented a 'novelty' that distorts the figure beyond its limits!

SOME DIRECT OPEN QUESTIONS

To the many great emerging modern artists who brush aside the painting styles of the past century as 'antiquated', one can politely pose the questions: "Through your modern artworks, have you managed to show the epitome of talent, profound expressiveness, and wondrous richness, like Leonardo da Vinci? Have you conjured an intense radiance like Rubens? Have you managed exquisite colour compositions and arrangements of the beauty of human figures that excite the senses like Titian? Have you presented effective compositions and skillfully used intense darkness like the 'master of light and shadow', Rembrandt? Have you managed to present imaginative visualisations like the great landscape painter Turner, that resounds melodiously in the heart of the spectator, and is *music to their eyes*? Have you managed to evoke flawless compositions, unmistakable originality, and seductive forms like those of Raphael's? Have you shown the immense force of imagination and a mastery over anatomy like Michelangelo? Have you managed to depict a pure, delightful, tranquil, and attractive beauty like the female forms of Giorgione and Bouguereau that make one want to worship at the altar of 'beauty'? Have you shown the balance and delicacy of colour like Veronese? Have you made luminously coloured paintings that soothe the eyes like those by Tintoretto?..."

On seeing the attitude of young, emerging, modern artists of today—those who have rarely created an artwork that the viewer never tires of seeing, that never quenches the heart, and is a memory that one will never forget; those who have rarely honoured, glorified, established as necessary, and furthered the name of 'art'; those who are referring to the artists of the past century (as if they never brought imagination, originality, novelty, or wonder) as 'photographic' or 'camera artists'; and those who consider

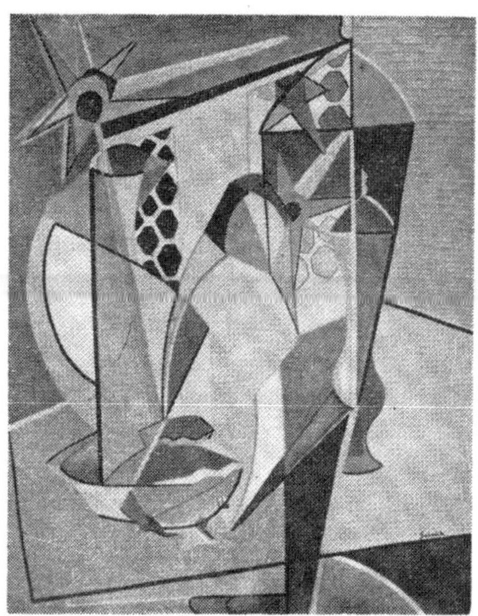

'Objects Composed' · Artist: Jehangir Sabavala

themselves forward and advanced—we are reminded of the popular idiomatic comparison between Raja Bhoj and Gangu Teli![6]

PABLO PICASSO

To assure that all this criticism does not result in a misunderstanding, it should be made loud and clear that not all paintings by all 'modernist' painters of today are to be rebuked or ridiculed. For example, the artist Pablo Picasso—who is now at the peak of his fame—had in the beginning of his career received great appreciation and applause for his wondrous paintings created during the Blue Period* and the Pink Period* between 1901 and 1906; but after receiving such relentless fame till the year 1912, his mind gradually took a turn and a strong negative disharmony crept into his works. Following many 'cubistic' styles such as Analytic, Synthetic, and Rococo, his paintings adopted a 'Surrealist' style, and eventually upon arriving at the 'Abstract' style, became whimsical and fantastic—in fact, they took on an ugly form.

[*In the time between 1901 to 1904, blue ⟨નીલો⟩ was a prominent colour, and between 1905 to 1906, pink ⟨ગુલાબી⟩ was abundant in Picasso's paintings.]

Picasso is considered among the pioneers of 'Cubism'. We do not oppose Cubism or any other 'isms'—and why should we? There is also no issue with the fact that as time passes, these 'isms' transform. The problem in fact, is only when this transformation turns into unscrupulous behaviour. For example, 'Cubism', which was at first pure Cubism, turned into 'Analytical Cubism' ⟨પૃથ્ક્કરણીય ક્યુબિઝમ⟩ and 'Curvilinear Cubism' ⟨વક્રાત્મક

6 — Mehta has used the proverb *'kyan Raja Bhoj ne kyan Gangu Teli!'*, which is a popular idiom referring to futile comparison of power between a King (Bhoj) and a commoner (Gangu Teli). The proverb, though without a clear historical context (due to different versions of the story in circulation), seems to have been derived from a situational relationship between two protagonists of varying status. Over a period of time, the idiom began to be used colloquially with its origin story becoming seemingly irrelevant.

કયુબિઝમ〉, and so on. Alright, but because of this, these cubist experts have created totally abnormal and disgusting paintings, and so it will not be wrong to call this the '*kachumbarism*[7] of Cubism' 〈કયુબિઝમ નું કચુમ્બરિઝમ〉. It is understandable when Picasso's dearest and most loyal admirers, who consider him atop the 'seventh heaven' and give him the title of 'the greatest artist of the present half-century', promptly reject the criticisms of Picasso as 'unforgivable insolence'. However, in such a short article, without courting controversy, can we politely ask if Picasso's brush has created any painting of such 'great' levels, which can be included amongst the remarkable, eternally memorable works of art gifted to the world by the numerous acclaimed expert artists of the last century? Those who unabashedly celebrate Picasso and his followers, should know that the world is not in dearth of other intelligent artists and art critics who also hold this opinion.

Not just Picasso, but there are numerous other Western 'modern' painters who follow in his footsteps to create a few good, but mostly maddening paintings, including French, German, Italian, British, and American 'modernists' such as Balla, Boccioni, Carrà, Villon, Sutherland, Miró, Dalí, Magnelli, van Doesburg, Rouault, Gris, Duchamp, Magritte, Delaunay, Kirchner, Léger, etc. How can one include all the detailed facts about all these modern artists and their artworks in this very brief explanation? For that one would need another book and a half.

IN OUR COUNTRY

Many artists in our country too have blindly started to imitate these painters of the West. In the painting exhibitions in capital cities like Mumbai, Delhi, Madras, Calcutta, Karachi, etc., such bizarre and absurd paintings are perpetually on display, and to inaugurate these shows, some either important or not-so-important minister or 'celebrity' (as if they also have some sort of an understanding of the subject)—the kinds who have the world in the palm of their hands[8]—are called, and keeping with the winds and trends of the time, they superficially praise these artists and their works to save face. The very next day, upon reading reviews in the papers, they 〈the artists〉 feel a major sense of accomplishment! And yet, at the same time

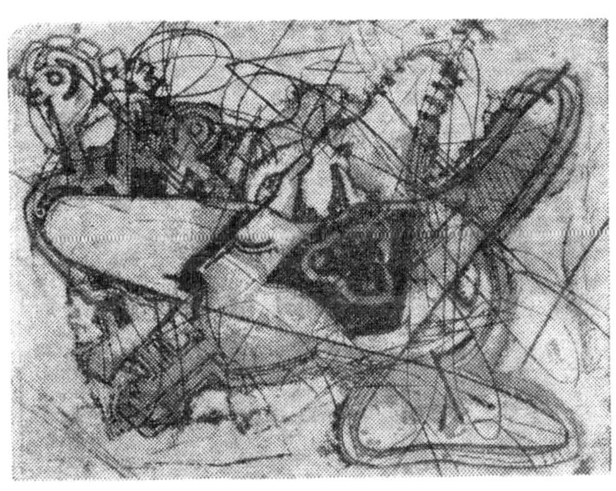

'Abstract Composition' · Artist: 〈Kaiko〉 Moti

7 — Here, the word '*kachumbarism*' consists of the Gujarati word '*kachumbar*' with the English suffix 'ism'. *Kachumbar* is a salad preparation where vegetables are cut into fine small pieces and garnished with some salt, chilli powder/black pepper, lemon, and coriander. *Kachumbar* is also often used to refer to a salad that is made by throwing together 'whatever is handy', owing to which Mehta satirically uses the word to comment on the 'recipe' of Cubism.

8 — Here, Mehta has originally used '*duniya jhukti hai jhukane wala chahiye*', a popular idiom that has found connections to Hindi film songs and *shayaris*. The idiom translates to 'the world does bow, all you need is the one to make it happen'.

and in the same place, one also gets to hear a few other exclamations: 'trashy', 'child's play', 'unnatural', 'crazy', 'madness', etc.

OPINIONS WORTH KNOWING

Initially, modernist paintings received a fair share of publicity and praise for their shock value and competitiveness. Even now, there is no shortage of those who sing its praise. But as and when these non-artistic, unnatural, and absurd paintings begin appearing in the public domain in larger numbers, presenting their strangeness and ugliness, the seasoned viewers' disinterest and dislike towards them also starts becoming especially visible. Seasoned connoisseurs have for a while now been bearing with this storm that has been wreaking havoc in the name of 'art'; but with every rising day, from the respected art experts as well as in the writings in papers of the East and West, in tabloids and caricatures, these have clearly become a laughing stock; and it seems that if this art-frenzy of today continues as it is, then as time goes by, it will become disagreeable to the viewers and eventually, become weak and rootless. Finally, it will be its unnaturalness that will bring it down to the ground or show it its place.

Several experts of the West and East, and artists themselves, have voiced their disapproval of it. For the readers' reference, some such opinions are presented here:

(1)

A quotation from 'Great Works of Art and What Makes Them Great' (pp 203–204) by F. W. Ruckstull (Member, National Institute of Arts and Letters; Organiser, National Sculpture Society; First Chief of Sculptors St. Louis' World Fair):

"...The modernists had now achieved their aim: the substitution of license 'in artistry' for a rational liberty in art. And with a bewildering rapidity there sprung up all sorts of 'leaders' of little movements and fads, each *a little more revolutionary* than the other, each inspired by the essence of the modernistic movement: the parading of individual technique and 'personal' mannerism, instead of the creation of beauty.

"Gradually, as one fad displaced the other, some of which died still-born, modernism slowly *veered away* from the original bold, vulgar *'realism'* of the founders of modernism, Manet, Degas, Lola, Rodin, Mirabeau, etc., towards a 'new idealism' that is, away from the realities of truth in art and life. The public had become tired of this so-called, but false, realism. For, after realistic 'impressionism', came the much less real post-impressionism; and then came still less real 'neo-post-impressionism'. Then came 'cubism'; then futurism. Then came the weirdest avalanche of increasingly unreal and insane 'isms', during which the painters and sculptors ran a sack-race with the dressmakers of the Rue de la Paix to see which could invent the greatest quantity of novelties— never mind about their sanity—and all to be 'put over' on the gullible rich morons of the art-world...

"This veering away, step by step, from the real to *their* 'ideal', gradually reached the absolutely unreal fantastic forms of 'abstract art' in which all semblance to human, or natural, forms has disappeared, and the contemplation of which will force any *normal* man to say: 'Either those artists are crazy, or I am!'

"...but the so-called serious press gives not only space, but a left-handed support to the 'aesthetics', as well as to the products, of this latest fad of 'abstract' art. This would not be so reprehensible and so dangerous socially if, in the propaganda in favour of this newest aberration, they did not try to *undermine the foundations* of all sane, healthy, and enduring art, by saying that *'representation'* has no place in art, even idealized art; that sanely stylized *'representation'* has no place in art means that the abstraction from the truth of nature should be so extreme that a man is made to look like a wheelbarrow and a woman like a monkey-wrench!

"And this topsy-turveying is defended by such glib, metaphysical-bunco reasoning, so plausibly done, so well done to capture the nouveau-rich morons in the art world, and so many of them as to become dangerous, that we feel it a duty to once for all show the fallacy of the doctrine, that *representation* should not be the basis of all art, especially since the speculators, who have loaded up a stock of this art junk, are now making herculean efforts to *force* our museums to *buy more and more of these aberrations*, to show to future generations the *'Zeitgeist'*, the spirit of the age, which prevailed in the world, from 1865 onward!"

(2)

From Giorgio de Chirico, a well-known 'surrealist' artist of that time:

"London, May 20th: Modern Art can be seen in asylum, according to former surrealist painter Giorgio de Chirico, who gave a lecture on the subject recently at the Royal Society of Arts in London.

"'Today one can no longer speak of decadence so much as of a complete artistic collapse,' he said. 'The practice of camouflaging lack of talent arose from this, as did those innumerable theories formulated both by painters and by those who were to a greater or lesser extent interested in painting. Cubism, Fauvism, Expressionism, and later on Abstractionism and Surrealism, were all vomited up by this so-called revolution. (...) Many men of science point out how the most characteristic side of modern art is the pathological one. They assert that this kind of art is no novelty to psychiatrists. In hospitals for mental diseases similar expressions are only too well-known.'" (Source: From the report on the speech given at 'Royal Society of Arts')

(3)

From the main article 'Freedom of the Brush' in 'Times of India':

"In art, modernity is coming increasingly to mean something that passes comprehension; the less intelligible a picture is, the more modern it is supposed to be. That, at least, is the common man's impression; and not all common men, it might be added, are blind to beauty of art...... But, of course, if artists insist on taking excessive pains to acquire the ability to draw the shaky and uncertain lines which a child of four is able to draw from sheer genius, no one can stop them......We are all in favor of letting the artists draw as many crazy lines as they like—in the hope that someday they will of their own accord draw the line somewhere and return to sanity."

(4)

Opinion of famous Pakistani artist ⟨Samuel⟩ Fyzee Rahamin:

"Mr. Fyzee Rahamin, Pakistan's noted painter, has deplored the tendency in a section of painters in Pakistan to imitate the West blindly in their paintings. He said in a press interview: 'The depressing aspect of the present day condition of the art of painting in Pakistan needs no explanation or demonstration. The degeneration in quality is impossible to exaggerate. Paintings ostentiously shown at art exhibitions reveal the extent to which the artists have fallen in degradation. The Western influence in design and execution are a travesty and mockery of their former selves. Backed by European teaching, one innovation after another is introduced, breaking the spell of their own tradition and bringing rapid deterioration in the system of the great historical arts of the Muslim. Perhaps the most glaring example is the replacement of the beautiful Moghul Miniature by the most horrible imitation of the 'Futurist' art of Europe—rightly termed in Europe the degenerate or the addled art of the 20th century. To this must be added the characteristic vulgarity in the style unsuited to the Oriental temperament and nature.'

"He said: 'Apart from individuals, there are several art-societies which have further helped to misguide the public. These societies display great interest in art and each one of them asserts that it is the only recognised body that can claim the attention towards art, and in the misdirected enthusiasm, more harm is being done to art than they realise. Therefore such organizations should not be taken seriously where the question of art proper is concerned.'" (Source: U.P.P., from 'Dawn' of 17th March 1957)

(5)

"Betsy, a seven-year-old chimpanzee residing at the Baltimore Zoo, has entered the world of art with a bang. A couple of months ago, just for laughs, a Baltimore News-Post printed photos of three modernist paintings. One was by a grown up artist, one by a six-year-old child, and the third by Betsy—who, the zoo had discovered, could produce modern-looking oil paintings with her fingers, toes, elbows, tongue, etc. The newspaper's readers were to guess which artist painted which picture: answer on another page.

"Well, the zoo since then has sold 17 of Betsy's pictures for a total of $145.00, and hopes for an eventual $600, which would buy the chimp a (shall we say) husband. If this isn't a footnote—or, better, a paw-note—on Modern Art as 90% racket and 10% sheer idiocy, what is it?" (Source: From an English newspaper)

(6)

Opinion of Mr. Kanaiyalal M. Munshi, the respected Governor of Uttar Pradesh:

"Mr. K. M. Munshi's View (by a Staff Reporter)

"Mr. K. M. Munshi said in Bombay on Monday that some of the modern trends in painting were 'without form or substance' and were symptomatic of the 'chaotic mind of the younger generation'.

"Mr. Munshi who was declaring open the first annual art exhibition of the Mukulkulam, a students' organisation, said that such a trend was only a 'passing phase' and advised the students not to stick to such a phase.

"'A thing of beauty is a thing in itself,' he said, and 'did not need any explanation for its appreciation,' whereas, some of the paintings of the modern variety, were to his mind, 'obscure and confusing.'" (Source: From the report of a speech published in the 'Times of India')

During and after the two dreaded and terrible World Wars, there has been an incredible flip in everything in the whole world. Being a part of society, the artists' mind has also been deeply affected. Faith in God, and in the belief systems of humans, has also been threatened and injured in some or the other way. Traces of their reactions towards hope and despair have manifested in their art as well. So, it is only natural for their creative minds to be involved in the search for new forms. However, these new forms cannot result in revelation of new styles where forms transgress all bounds of meaning. We can also accept that the forms in nature and the forms in art cannot be alike. It is this dis-similarity and variance between nature and art that creatively brings forward the eligibility and aptness (creative role of art) in works of art. However, while creating such forms, the one thing that must be borne in mind is that the artist does not obsess over the new forms and get possessed by it.

Here, a question that can emerge is, how can one examine if such forms have crossed these boundaries or not? The one and only way of testing this, which can be presented to both the viewers and the artists themselves,

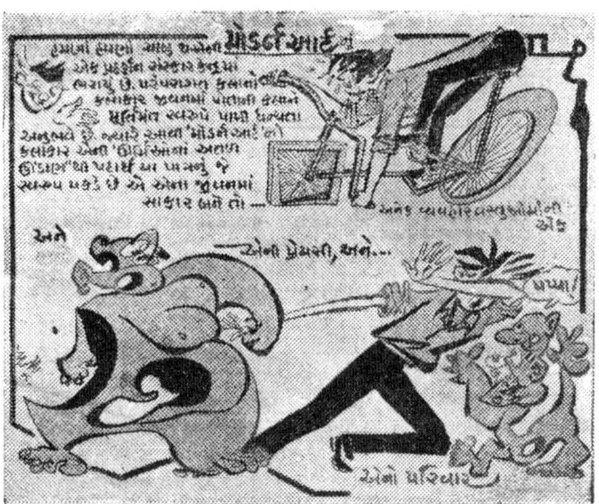

⟨Cartoon reads: "Currently, an exhibition of Modern Art is ongoing at Sanskar Kendra. The artist of traditional art feels grateful and satisfied upon finding their life embodied in their art form. ⟨But⟩ when the 'modern artist' captures the form of an object or its character through their 'flights of whims and imaginations', and if these forms were to materialise in real life, then here is how many day-to-day objects, his lover, and his family ⟨would appear⟩" ⟩

is: "The only test to judge a form of art is to find out how far it is appropriate to the meaning it seeks to express." (Excerpt from an article in 'Times of India' 25-9-58)

By reading the presented opinions, readers will be able to infer that the individuals putting forth these opinions are no ordinary people.

A habit of criticising things and people in all and sundry matters on the one hand, and simultaneously of overly praising on the other—for example, being 'stunned' by them—seems to be plaguing our society. When artworks by some deceptively famous western artists are bought from an American billionare ⟨*Kuber bhandaari*⟩ for lakhs of dollars, or from a wealthy European ⟨*Lakshmi na ladila*⟩ for thousands of pounds[9], exhibited, enshrined in special 'museums', and zealously publicised by newspapers, then being stunned by, or mindlessly following this one-sided and overt praise for such a painter (or painters) should not be appreciated. As much as there is a difference between piety and sacrilege, such can be the difference between artistry and the betrayal of the same. What is regrettable is that often this betrayal of art is given a name and is framed as skillful, and in the public eye it is legitimised, much like how fake currency gets passed off in the market. Alongside its appropriate use, we also see today's modernists deeply misusing the phrase 'art for art's sake', just as we repeatedly witness the wrongdoing of fresh grass being burnt with the dry.

Just as the memorable phrase 'Meden Agan' (Nothing in Excess), engraved by the ancient Greeks on the marble slab above the main entrance of the Temple of Apollo at the holy site of 'Delphi' is good for all humans, imbibing and practising this must be understood as beneficial for artists as well.

9 — In Hindu mythology, Kuber and Lakshmi are the god and goddess of wealth respectively. In this sentence, Mehta uses the words *'Kuber bhandaari'* to refer to a 'treasurer of great wealth' and *'Lakshmi na ladila'* to refer to one that is 'pampered by Lakshmi', suggesting rich American and European art collectors.

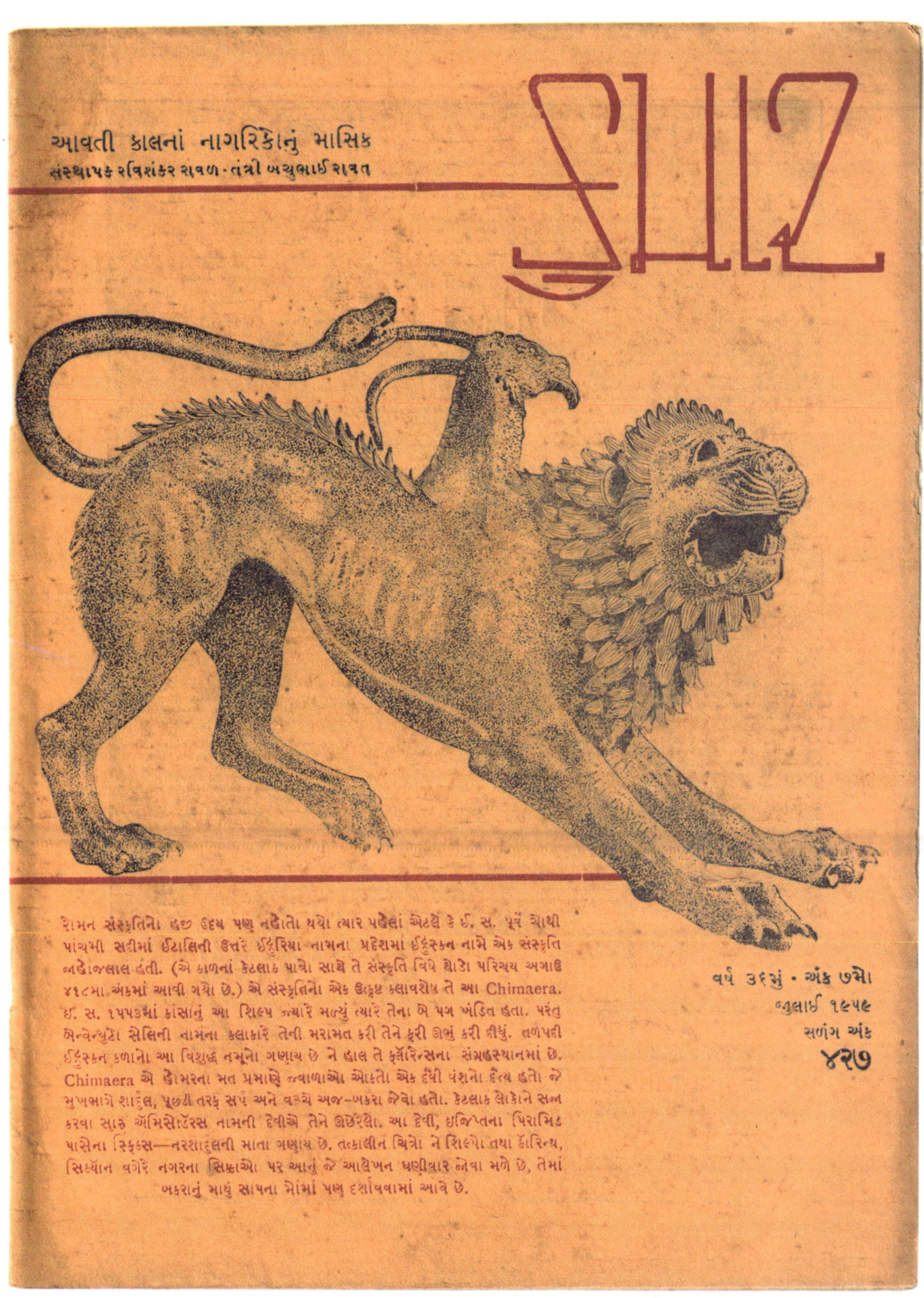

કુમાર

આવતી કાલનાં નાગરિકોનું માસિક
સંસ્થાપક રવિશંકર રાવળ · તંત્રી બચુભાઈ રાવત

રોમન સંસ્કૃતિનો હજી ઉદય પણ નહોતો થયો ત્યાર પહેલાં એટલે કે ઈ. સ. પૂર્વે ચોથી પાંચમી સદીમાં ઈટાલિની ઉત્તરે ઈટ્રુરિયા નામના પ્રદેશમાં ઈટ્રસ્કન નામે એક સંસ્કૃતિ નહોજલાલ હતી. (એ કાળનાં કેટલાક ચાચો સાથે તે સંસ્કૃતિ વિષે થોડો પરિચય અગાઉ ૪૧૮મા અંકમાં આવી ગયો છે.) એ સંસ્કૃતિનો એક ઉત્કૃષ્ટ કલાવશેષ તે આ Chimaera. ઈ. સ. ૧૫૫૩માં કાંસાનું આ શિલ્પ જ્યારે મળ્યું ત્યારે તેના બે પગ ખંડિત હતા. પરંતુ બેન્વેન્યુટો સેલિનિ નામના કલાકારે તેની મરામત કરી તેને ફરી આખું કરી દીધું. તળપદી ઈટ્રસ્કન કળાનો આ વિશુદ્ધ નમૂનો ગણાય છે ને હાલ તે ફ્લૉરેન્સના સંગ્રહસ્થાનમાં છે. Chimaera એ હોમરના મત પ્રમાણે જ્વાળાઓ ઓકતો એક દૈવી વંશનો દૈત્ય હતો જે મુખભાગે શાર્દૂલ, પૂછડી તરફ સર્પ અને વચ્ચે અજ-બકરા જેવો હતો. કેટલાક લોકોને સજા કરવા સારુ ઍમિસેન્ડૉરસ નામની દેવીએ તેને ઊછેરેલો. આ દેવી, ઇજિપ્તના પિરામિડ પાસેના સ્ફિંક્સ—નરશાર્દૂલની માતા ગણાય છે. તત્કાલીન ચિત્રો ને શિલ્પો તથા કૉરિન્થ, સિક્યોન વગેરે નગરના સિક્કાઓ પર આનું જે આલેખન ઘણીવાર જોવા મળે છે, તેમાં બકરાનું માથું સાપના મોંમાં પણ દર્શાવવામાં આવે છે.

વર્ષ ૩૬મું · અંક ૭મો
જુલાઈ ૧૯૫૯
સળંગ અંક
૪૨૭

Readers Write

I felt satisfied after reading the article on 'Modern Art' in the June ⟨1959⟩ issue of Kumar. For a long time my fellow artist friends and I were discussing the modern, intellectual experiments happening in the field of Indian art, and were hoping that some authoritative critic would flash a red light on this mindless imitation.

There was a time when we used to criticise Raja Ravi Varma for being indifferent to the Indian painting styles and imitating the Western realistic style. While his paintings had achieved popularity amongst the masses, today, desiring novelty, we praise some artists who baffle the public by imitating the absurd Western modern style which alienates one from art; and we see a majority of our emerging artists leaning towards this oversimplified and flippant modern style. The reason for this is not because they have understood some vital elements of the modernist art styles, but because it takes a rigorous study of line, composition, and colour arrangements to establish one's practice in even one of the ancient Indian painting styles. It is not possible to achieve the originality of Abanindranath Tagore, Jamini Roy, or Amrita Sher-Gil all of a sudden; whereas there is no headache of any kind in modern styles and all the shortcomings due to the lack of persevered practice are accommodated in it. Not only that, but instead of considering these as incomplete experiments, they have been considered as complete works of art, and have been receiving awards worth Rs. 2000 and gold medals too. As a result, our emerging artists have naturally been leaning towards the lucrative direction of cheap fame, and thus a trend of bizzare, ambiguous, and ugly artworks has come about, which disturbs the human thirst for beauty instead of trying to quench it. It is high time we think whether the initiation of this kind of art is taking us on the path of development or destruction.

There should be room for new experiments in the field of art, however they should only be given the importance of incomplete experiments.

—*Himmatbhai Mehta (Rajkot)*

The following is an excerpt from the article titled 'Arya Sangeet' on page 49 of ⟨Dattatreya Balkrishna⟩ Kalelkar's 'Jeevansanskriti': "Music originates through the desire to express the heart's sentiments. So initially the music is aligned with the poem; but when the sentiments become extreme and the literary words are unable to express them, then the music independently attempts to exert its power. In the Upanishads there is a description that whenever the sages get enlightened after resolving their doubts, then they sing by making the sound *ha aa aa aa vu*."

This statement can be applied to the modern style of painting. When it becomes impossible to express internal feelings through lines and colours, then the only mode of representing art that remains is modern obscure art, which seems rigid at first glance. Which ⟨Modern Art⟩, despite its seeming obscurity ⟨like that of the sound *ha aa aa aa vu*⟩, represents *everything*. 'Popular

Art' ⟨લોકભોગ્ય કળા⟩ and this 'Modern Art' can be respectively compared to 'light music' and 'classical music'.

This is about ideal art and music. Most often, popular music has been appreciated more than classical music. The case of popular art is similar. That is why both the words have 'popular' as a prefix. In the end, it can be concluded that just as art (all forms) has two facets (classical and popular), similarly there should be two categories for all those who create and those who appreciate art. Only then will both of them get their due respect. Then criticism regarding one's aptitude won't take place, as it happens nowadays.

—*Rameshchandra Shah (Mumbai)*

In general, there are very few people who know Modern Art; however if the artist and the viewers try to understand and explain this art, then this number can be increased. For example, along with the painting, if the artist can provide a short text about the characteristics and limitations of it, and the viewers can attain elementary knowledge to understand it, then the complaint against Modern Art can be eliminated.

Humans have a tendency to be innovative and to do things differently from the current traditions and norms. Restrictions of any kind are not desired by humans. The flowing water of a spring is pure, but stagnant water isn't. Similarly, art that flows and is devoid of any rules, flourishes.

Humans have worked towards breaking shackles in various art forms. An example is our poet Nanalal's experiment of breaking the rules of verse in poetry. I consider modern paintings as one such experiment. The difference between modern painting and academic painting is best understood through what Narsinh Mehta says:

Ved to em vade, shrutismruti saakh de,
Kanak kundal vishe bhed nhoye;

Ghat ghadiya pachhi naam rup jujva;
Ante toh hemnu hem hoye.
⟨The Vedas speak: listen, remember, and bear witness,
In the matter of golden earrings there can be no difference;
Only after you mold it, do you give it name and form;
In the end gold is but gold.⟩

—*Madhusudan N. Vyas (Surat)*

Shri Pherozeshah Rustomji Mehta has been lauding the arts and artists of the world by writing well-researched and reflective articles on painting and sculpture for about 25 years now. His article in the 426th issue ⟨June 1959⟩, accompanied by opinions of well known personalities about the adverse effects of such non-art on the world, has managed to clear many readers' doubts and has generated substantial interest amongst art-enthusiasts.

Today, after hundreds of years, India's architecture, paintings, and sculptures have come to hold a special place in the world, but despite that, if Indian artists continue displaying their lack of skill by misleading the people with absurdity under the garb of such current art, it will end up like cinema tunes. Today lakhs of cinema tunes have come and gone, yet classical music and its variety and originality still hold a very high position. This current style of art might result in lakhs of paintings but it will be short-lived, like cinema tunes, and will definitely not find a permanent place in museums in the future.

—*Maganlal Trivedi (Rajkot)*

I got to hear *shayaris* by two *shayars* through a friend who loves poetry. I'm sending its lines hoping it will be of interest. This is a good jibe at Modern Art.

Agar apna kaha tum, aap hi samjhe to kya samjhe,

Maza kahneka hay jab ek kahe aur dusra
samjhe;
Kalame 'Mir' samjhe aur zabane 'Mirza'
samjhe;
Magar inka kaha ye aap samjhe ya khuda
samjhe.
⟨What is understood at all, if only you
understand what you have said,
The joy of speech is then, when one says,
and the other understands;
Understood is the verse of 'Mir', and so are
the words of 'Mirza';
But what they say is understood either by
them or by God.⟩

—*Ramnik Meghani (Calcutta)*

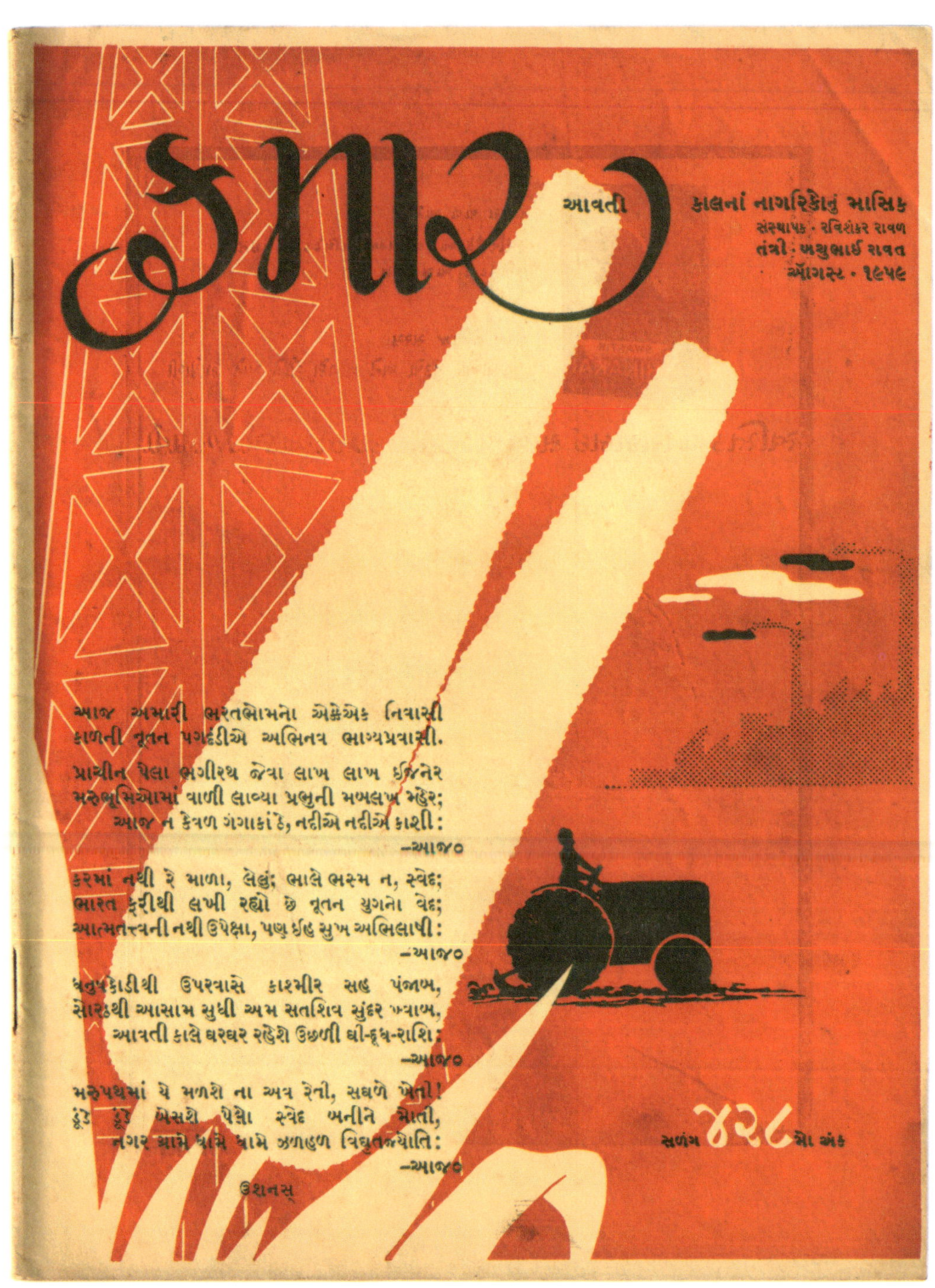

KUMAR #428 · AUGUST 1959

NEGRO BOXER હબસી મુક્કાબાજ

Jyoti Bhatt

We welcome this creative response to Shri Pherozeshah Mehta's article (Modern Art) published in the June ⟨1959⟩ issue. The readers of Kumar know the author of this piece Jyoti Bhatt from his painting 'Kaliyadaman' (issue 385) ⟨January 1956⟩ that was awarded Rs. 1000 by the Delhi Government at the National Art Exhibition in 1956 and from his painting 'Dampati' in the 400th issue ⟨April 1957⟩. While being felicitated for 'Kaliyadaman', he had expressed his desire to develop his art practice based on the Modern Art style rather than the Indian artistic tradition (like in this painting). Having passed the last exam of the Faculty of Fine Arts of Vadodara University (an institution that also lays heavy emphasis on such a style) with distinction, Bhatt has whole-heartedly attempted to explain his honest opinion with illustrations in this article. On the basis of this, the hope is that the readers, after understanding the mysteries of this painting ⟨'Negro Boxer' by Henri Matisse⟩, will share with us how their thoughts have changed.

Because of the title 'Modern Art' of Shri Pherozeshah's article, there seems to be some misunderstanding based on readers' letters that Mehta opposes all Modern Art styles. However, as specified in the lines ⟨5–10⟩, in the second column on page ⟨38 in this book⟩, his objection is against the obscure nature of abstract ⟨વસ્તુવિલોપન⟩ art where there seems to be no communication—no effort to demystify.

—Editor

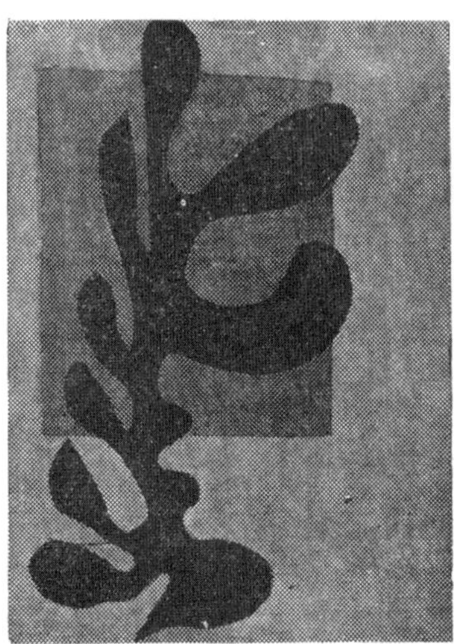

'Negro Boxer' (Habsi Mukkabaj) · Henri Matisse · Cut-out

In the article on Modern Art in the 426th issue of Kumar ⟨June 1959⟩, the above image was published and several allegations were also made against Modern Art. I feel that this effort of mine will prove helpful in reducing—if not erasing—the misunderstanding that has emerged from that article.

One must always remember that before forming any opinions about the original painting, one should have seen the painting. One does not get a complete idea by even seeing a colour reproduction of the original. Then how at all can a reproduction in monochrome (black and white) of insufficient quality provide the true perspective?

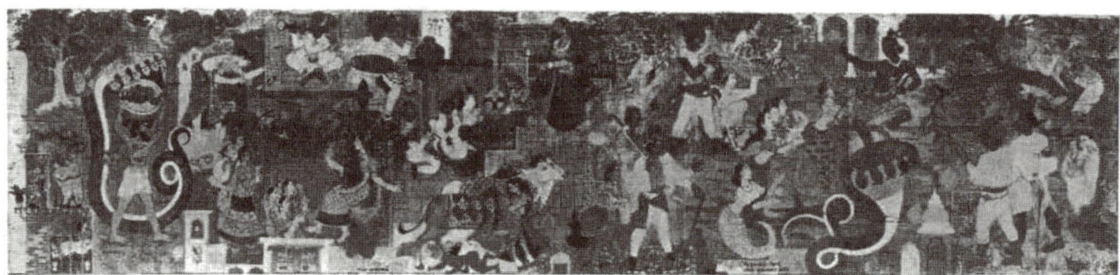

'Krishna-Lila' ⟨referred to by the editor as 'Kaliyadaman'⟩ · Artist: Jyoti Bhatt · ⟨The original caption states that along with a gold medal, Rs. 1,000 was awarded to this painting.⟩

⟨Published in Kumar #385 · January 1956⟩

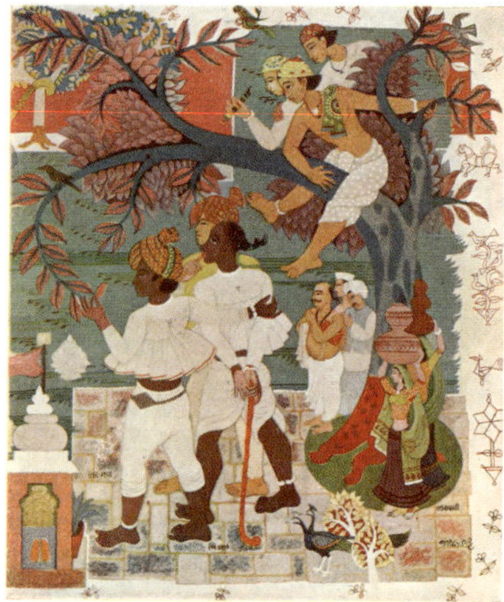

⟨Detail from 'Krishna-Lila', published in the Lalit Kala Akademi's catalogue of the National Exhibition of Art, 1956, p. 5⟩

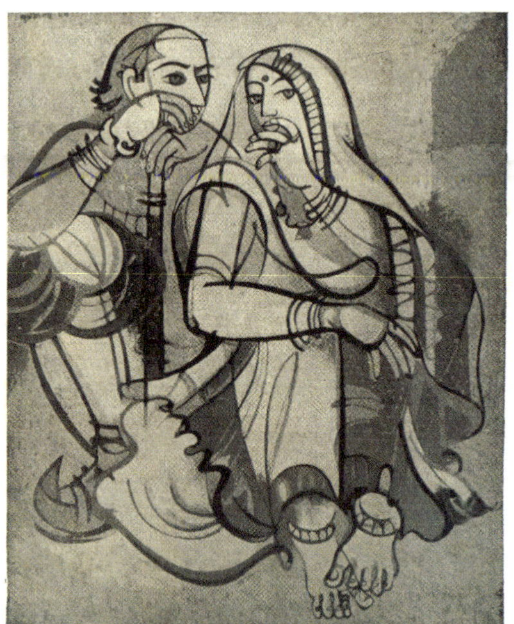

'Yugal' ⟨Couple⟩ ⟨referred to by the editor as 'Dampati'⟩ · Artist: Jyoti Bhatt · Courtesy of Air India International

⟨Published in Kumar #400 · April 1957⟩

It has been suggested in that article that desirable elements such as harmony, beautiful colours, and un-distorted—or less distorted—forms are not seen in today's paintings, and the implied meaning is not revealed. To the author of the article, today's paintings seem like a rotten, wandering, four-legged dog (dogs obviously have four legs—why this fact is stressed upon is unclear). Moreover, what the viewer sees seems to be an 'absurd' sight; entirely the opposite of what was suggested by the artist. For now, let us mull over only the painting that was at the start of that article. Before taking up the design of that painting, let us look at what design itself is (here, design does not mean 'pattern', but instead it refers to a beautiful composition made of colour, form, and line).

DESIGN

In any painting, design is one of the most important elements. How a mason uses bricks, lime, cement, water, etc. to erect a building, in exactly the same way, an artist uses colour, line, form, etc. to create a design. Be it geometrical forms (see below Illustration અ) or an organic depiction of flowers and leaves (see Illustration A), be it Matisse's 'Negro Boxer' or a painting of Radha-Krishna in the Kangra style, they are first and foremost design.

In any empty space (see ક, ખ, ગ, ધ in Illustration અ) when you draw a triangle, that space gets divided into parts and the eye is drawn to the middle. That same triangle gets divided further, resulting in many more smaller and bigger triangles. Although each one of them is positioned differently, after a point it becomes tiresome to look at. It does not have anything special that can hold the eye. There is great monotony in all the shapes. If one divides this illustration vertically into two, it appears symmetrical on both sides.

Right in the middle there is a triangle made of three tiny triangles. Three more triangles of similar size surround this. The four of them together make one triangle and around this there are pairs of triangles making three more triangles. All of these combined form the big outer triangle. However, looking at this monotony causes as much boredom as reading this description does, doesn't it? Here, another important thing to note is that after drawing the triangle in the 'ક, ખ, ગ, ધ' square, the remaining space of the square gets divided into three different parts. Two symmetrical shapes (which are more or less identical) on the left and right of the triangle, and one below the triangle—which is different from the first two. On the left side of the triangle, an imaginary triangle 'ક, છ, ધ' gets created. Although there is no line from the inside of the main triangle towards the outer border, the eyes are drawn towards the empty space between ચ and છ, similar to how an arrow sign like → draws the eyes ahead. As a result, an illusion is created with shapes such as 'ક, છ, ધ' and 'ચ, ખ, ગ' and as they are also triangles, the monotony of the design is further emphasised.

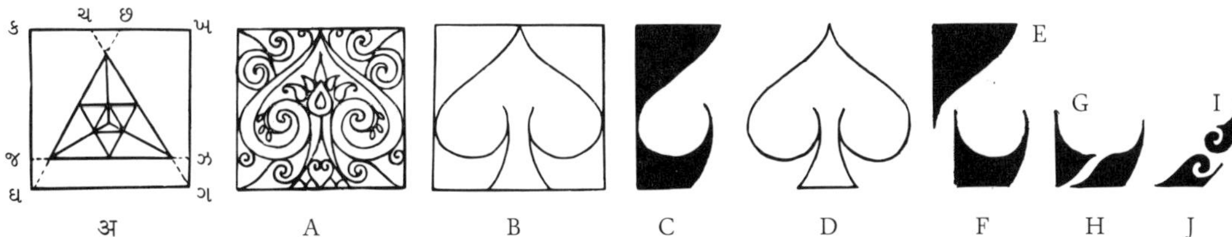

Now, let's take A, the second design. It has many more shapes, they are diverse, and are not made of just straight lines (like triangles, squares, etc.). This is also divided into two main parts (Illustration B), as a result of which shapes like Illustrations C and D are formed. C is divided into two parts—E and F, and F is divided into G and H. H is further divided into I and J. Here, each and every shape has its own independent appearance. They can be distinctly separated from each other, but at the same time they have a similarity (unity in variety). And just like this in Illustration D, many such big and small parts are created. Thus, when this design A is compared to design અ, it appears to be more attractive and holds the attention of the viewer for longer. Although it is definitely symmetrical, in comparison to અ it is less so; only when divided vertically down the middle. In અ however, merely joining any corner of the triangle to its corresponding base results in symmetry.

This symmetry can be considered as the simple first step to design. However, this (symmetry) also enhances the rigidity of the object or the shape. In nature such highly symmetrical objects are scarcely seen.*

[*It is said that very rarely is a person's (man or a woman's) face absolutely symmetrical. There is also an opinion that as a person ages, one side of their face changes more and the other side resembles their childhood visage.]

It is true that there is symmetry in man-made objects (architecture or fabricated objects for example) as well, but we do not consider them alive. Besides, our eyes prefer asymmetrical shapes, perhaps because more diversity is seen in them. For instance, let's look at these examples from our own everyday lives—a turban, its plume, a stole ⟨ખભા નો ખેસ⟩, the fastener of a tunic ⟨કેડિયાની કસ⟩, hair parted to one side, a handkerchief in a coat pocket on one side, a flower on the collar also tucked on just one side, a tattoo on the cheek, or as per today's fashion, a drawn on beauty spot.

To clarify, I am not trying to say that something is good only if it is asymmetrical, but all that I wish to say is that compositions of this kind are pleasing to the eye and can also be used in good design (and many artists today do so).

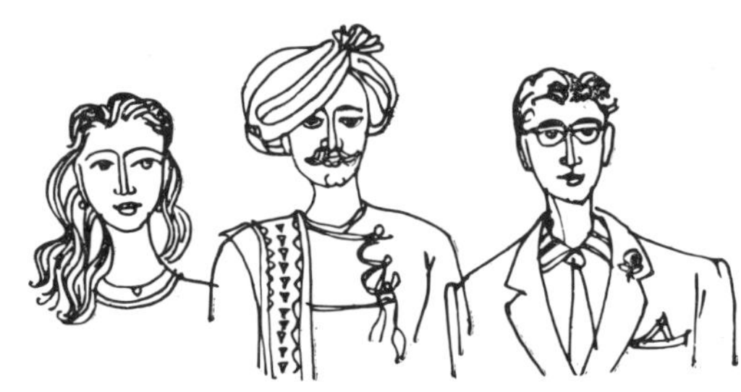

Now let's get to the main painting 'Negro Boxer' (Illustration 11). Before discussing its design, let me give you some introduction. It is not a painting in the conventional sense (painted with colours and a brush) but is a paper cut-out. The outermost rectangle, which marks the boundaries of the painting, is green in colour: a very garish green, like the wings of a parakeet (bright green). If you are familiar with the names, then somewhere between emerald green and green bice, more or less. The second smaller square inside it is a stark red: not like blood, but like a rose, an intense red like that of the wrapping paper a goldsmith would use to wrap jewellery—crimson lake. And the dynamic shape on top of both of these is black in colour: pitch black as *kajal*—lampblack.

These colours are of such a primary nature that they will appeal to and be identifiable by anyone who sees them. By no means can this be compared to a mangy dog. The shapes are also sufficiently clear. The essential quality—a speciality of paper-cutting

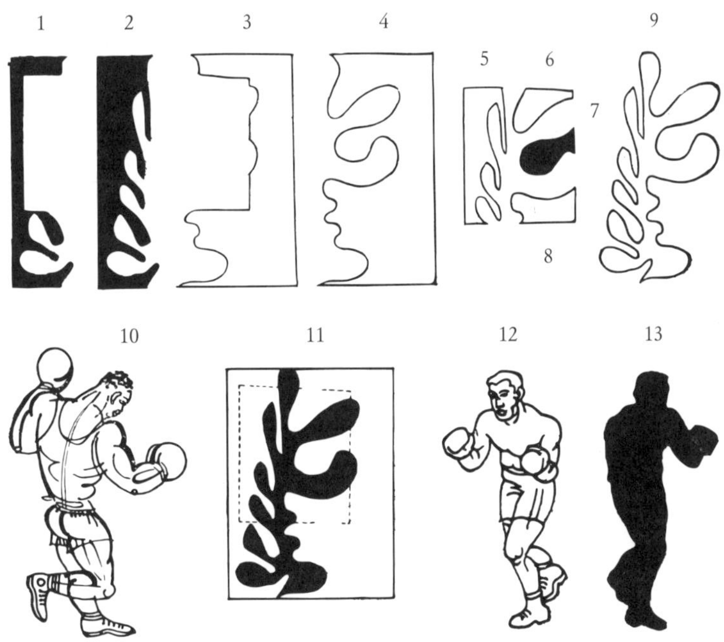

Illustrations explaining the artwork 'Negro Boxer'. (See text for detailed explanation.)

itself—is in the fact that one can obtain through it such clear shapes, something that cannot be achieved even through painting. Here too, because of the main shape (Illustration 9), the background gets divided into Illustrations 2 and 4. While observing carefully, one can also see Illustrations 1 and 3, as well as Illustrations 5-6-7-8 within the inner red square.

The small square is placed inside the outer rectangle in such a way that the remaining spaces on its four sides are each separate. Also, not a single line is parallel to the outer boundary.

This composition is also planned cleverly. It is not symmetrical at all. All the shapes are of different kinds. If one divides the painting vertically into two, the left side of it covers most of the image, and yet the right side does not seem empty: visual balance.

Without doubt, there is also rhythm. The flow of a river, the swaying of crops in the breeze, a snake slithering by, etc., are all considered by us as rhythmic movements. A line or composition over which our eyes can move with ease, accounts for rhythm in painting. In our Indian sculptures as well, *tribhanga*[10] (see ⟨overleaf⟩) is a stellar example of rhythm, and this rhythm can be seen in the main shape in Illustration 9. The outline is shown in Illustration 9 whereas the whole shape is shown in Illustration 11. Its overall rhythm is also like the shape of the English letter 'S'; moreover, this also reminds one of a growing thorny-sprouting plant, which when seen in colour presents a delightful atmosphere. Viewing it this way also prevents the comparison with a 'mangy dog'.

Now let's get to the 'title'. The title is not to provide the meaning or the explanation

---

10 — *Tribhanga* is formed from the Sanskrit words *'tri'* (three) and *'bhanga'* (bent) to indicate a body bent in three places. In classical Indian dances and sculpture, it refers to a counterpoise with the body bent at the knee, hip and neck, forming an 'S'-like shape.

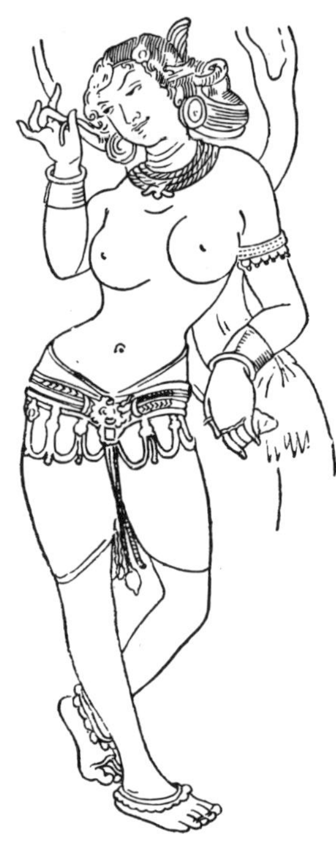

'Tribhanga' is a stellar example of rhythm in Indian sculpture.

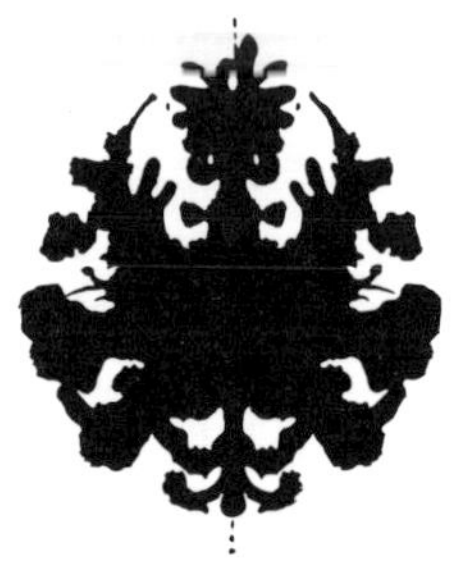

Beauty of symmetry—here, on a paper; before a blotch of ink on the left side can dry, the paper is folded and an impression is taken on the right side, and despite this shape not being indicative of any particular object (it is entirely coincidental if it resembles any object), it makes a beautiful pattern. Even within a kaleidoscope the irregular looking shape creates a 'pattern' when reflected six times, which is also pleasing to the eye; this is because the uniform regularity of repetition (order and discipline) brings out the beauty of the geometric composition.

of the painting (though sometimes this is also how titles are given). It is afterall just a name. It is not a necessity that it ⟨ the painting ⟩ should always carry the characteristics of the name. The title of a painting functions just like the proverb, *'Lakshmidas bhikh mange, Amarsing maran pame, toh Thanthanpal shu khota?'* ⟨If a person named Lakshmidas, a devotee of the goddess of wealth, could be a beggar; Amarsing, a person whose name means immortal, could be dying; then what is wrong with the name Thanthanpal, given by a mother to her child, after hearing the sound of a pot rolling down a hill?⟩ These days many artists don't even give titles, and if they do, they are like 'Painting No. 1' or 'Composition' or 'An Arrangement in Yellow'. Many times, the artist gives the title only for a personal reason. If a painting is made upon witnessing a public, noisy, chaotic area of a city, the effect of that chaos is shown with 'vigorous brush strokes and splashes of colour' ⟨ લપેટા ઝપેટા ને ડાઘા ડબકાં ⟩ (possibly even without showing the road, the people, buses, buildings, or street lights), and then can also be titled after the place that inspired it (for example, 'Chandni Chowk' or 'Times Square'). Refer to Severini's painting 'Le Boulevard' published in Kumar issue 426 ⟨ June 1959 ⟩, page number 230 ⟨ page 33 in this book ⟩.

I do not know why this painting is titled 'Negro Boxer', but in my understanding the following can be a reason:

Illustration 12 is a drawing based on the photograph of the undefeated 'World Heavyweight Boxing Champion' Rocky Marciano from three years ago, which depicts an action from the sport of boxing. Illustration 13 is the inverted image of it, but as a silhouette ⟨ છાયા ચિત્ર ⟩.

The protagonist of our discussions, the main shape in the painting, is black in colour. We also know that Europeans and Americans associate 'black' with a race. Moreover, by looking at the shape, one is reminded of boxing (look at the similarity between Illustrations 10 and 11): especially to people in places where boxing is a popular sport. Also, the realistically drawn Illustration 13 seems too rigid, motionless, and lifeless, doesn't it? Whereas, in spite of being entirely abstract (that which is not a representation or copy of an object) Illustration 11 succeeds in offering an impression of a black boxer at play: an impression not of his hands and legs, or his eyes, nose, and ears, but of the spirit of the sport, of its vigour, and of the quick successive motions of the strong arms. The swift back and forth movement of the boxer does not allow the eye to fix itself at any one point. Similarly, here too ⟨in this painting⟩, our eyes, as they shuttle from left to right, keep moving from the top to the bottom and to the top again. Do you experience this in Illustration 13? Speak the truth okay, with your hand on your heart. Also anyone will accept that the letters in the title at the beginning of this article resemble a true, living boxer more than just printed letters. The moment we read these letters, an image of a boxer appears in front of our eyes. Those who take interest in boxing may see ⟨resemblances of⟩ well-built Black champions such as Joe Louis or Floyd Patterson. But in actuality, there is no similarity between his (the boxer's) 'appearance' and that of the letters. Letters: they are absolutely 'abstract' symbols. And yet, out of 'habit' we are able to see the various visuals that emerge from them. Similarly, by seeing—or getting habituated to seeing—abstract paintings or paintings with some abstracted 'distorted' shapes, one will begin to find beauty in them and understand what the painter intends to say. With such a pessimistic mindset as *'khatle moti khod ke paya j na made'* ⟨refer to footnote 5 on page 36⟩ one cannot be hopeful of any results.

Of Illustration 9 and 11, the first is made with only lines; the second is filled in black colour. From the apparent difference in the two and the varying impact that they have, the importance of colour in shapes can be understood.

Since the main painting could not be printed in colour, we haven't delved deeper; but (as far as I know) just like a boxing ring (square platform) is elevated—raised from the ground, with a stretched canvas atop its surface—the red square ring is elevated on the green ground and it comes forward because of the inherent strength of the colour: its property. And considering all these reasons, the painting may have been titled 'Negro Boxer'.

A writer or a poet not only describes a beautiful object, but also compares it to other beautiful objects. For example, the meaning of *'kamal-nayan'* ⟨lotus-like eyes⟩ is understood by us. When we say eyes like a lotus or like a fish, we compare only their shapes (of lotus or fish) with the eyes, right? Let alone their colour, we also forget their other properties. When we say arms like the trunk of an elephant, we do not imply the trunk's thick skin, its ability to curl, or the fact that the arms are the colour of rain clouds, but only that the arms are large, and of such shape. When we read similes that compare braided hair with a snake and thighs with a banana stem, we do not literally compare the body with these objects, but instead consider what is written by the writer, and the way in which it has been written. As a result, our appreciation for the writing is greater, even more than the woman being described. Similarly when we see 'distorted' shapes in a painting, it is out of place to think of how terrible a woman or man of this shape will look in real life; but instead we must consider how the artist has painted, what is the relationship between the colours used, what effect does it have, how 'harmonious' it is, etc. Why all this has been done, is exactly what we need to see and understand. What about when we compare a beautiful woman's face to the moon? What if we imagine a face shaped absolutely round like the moon, with a few spots, and even without the nose-eyes-lips? How strange is that? There we only keep in mind the bright white colour. We call this a simile ⟨ઉપમા અલંકાર⟩. Furthermore, when the poet's heart soars higher, instead of comparing the face to the moon, they refer to the face as the moon itself: 'on sighting this moon of the Earth, the moon of the sky hid behind the clouds', etc. We call this a metaphor ⟨રૂપક અલંકાર⟩. Painters, poets, actors, and dancers are all artists—there is sentiment and emotion in all their hearts which they are able to express, differentiating them from the layperson. The only difference is that their mediums differ: colours, words, acting, gestures, etc. But when the same artist (here, Matisse) uses language to title a painting, revealing his poetic heart, then there is no need to be surprised. We have accorded a very high position to exactly this in literature.

I make no claims that after reading this article the reader will relish Modern Art—like the swish of a magic wand would draw the curtains from one's eyes, opening them to divine vision; but here I have only attempted to show that which I am deeply interested in, seeing which brings me great satisfaction, and how and what I see in the same. If this helps someone find their way then I will consider my efforts successful.

Notes on the paintings printed on the adjacent page:

I. 'Composition' · Artist: ⟨Sonia⟩ Delaunay · This 'Composition' is made of different geometric shapes and colours. The title of the painting (Composition) does not mean anything else.

II. 'Landscape' · Artist: ⟨Leopold⟩ Survage · The leaf in the foreground of the painting, a dark shape of the ground indicating the horizon, a triangular shape indicating the roof of a building, and the three dots on it resembling windows, a flying bird against a blue ⟨ભૂરો⟩ circle (which also indicates the sky and its symbols—like the shape of the sun or the full moon) is all that there is to this painting. That is why it has been titled 'Landscape'. As this isn't a painting of any particular place but has elements that are seen in any natural scenery, it is titled 'Landscape'.

III. 'Gouache' · Artist: ⟨Sophie⟩ Taeuber-Arp · The title 'Gouache' does not indicate the form of any objects in the painting, it only indicates the medium of the painting. The way Matisse's 'Negro Boxer' is made from paper cut-outs, similarly this is made in 'Gouache', that is watercolour mixed with white paint. This results in a different effect: the colours gain body, and the painting can be made on any paper other than white as well. Hence, when required, transparent or translucent colours can also be used to reveal the colour of the paper below. The colour of the paper can also be left as is.

IV. 'A Person Looking at the Sun' · Artist: ⟨Joan⟩ Miró · The shape at the bottom right of the painting is in black, hinting at a figure looking upwards, and the round shape above it is red in colour. Because of its shape, colour, and placement (at a height and suspended without support), it resembles the sun. Hence the painting is titled so. As a matter of fact it is similar to Matisse's 'Negro Boxer', except that it is 'painted'. The colours are also somewhat similar. This too has circular shapes from the smallest to the largest size, and a few slender lines. With the help of these two, a beautiful design has been composed. Additionally, unlike in Matisse's painting, an ash-like ⟨રાખોડિયો⟩ or neutral ⟨મુંજરો⟩ colour is used in the background, resulting in the colourful shapes being foregrounded and emphasised, and also creating a sense of space.

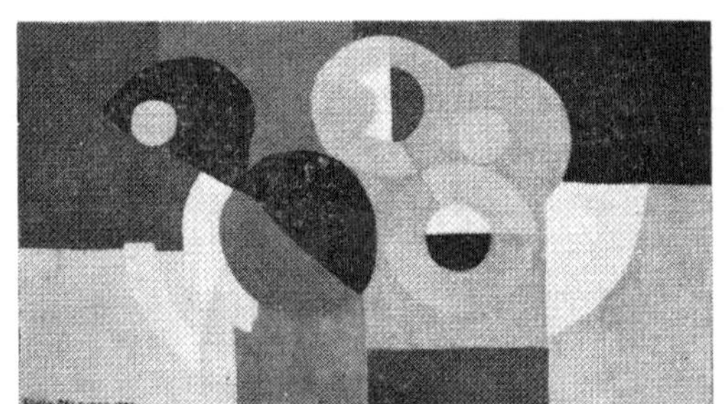

I

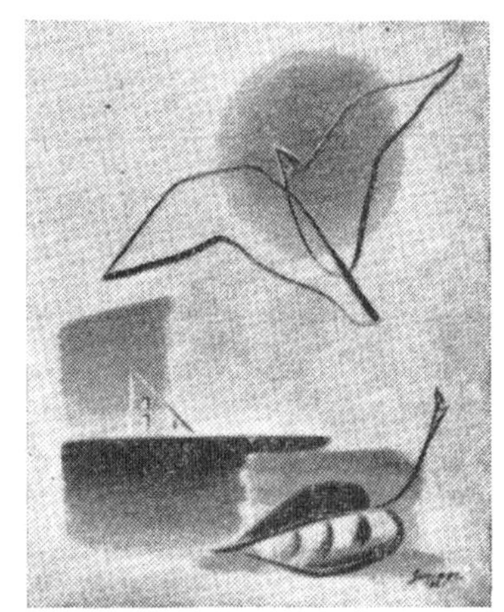

II

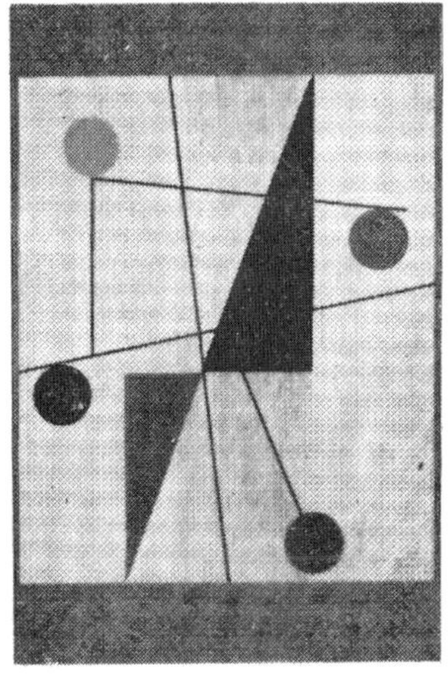

III

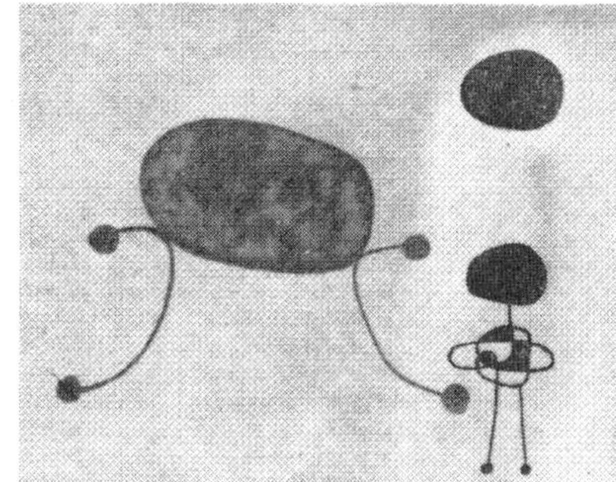

IV

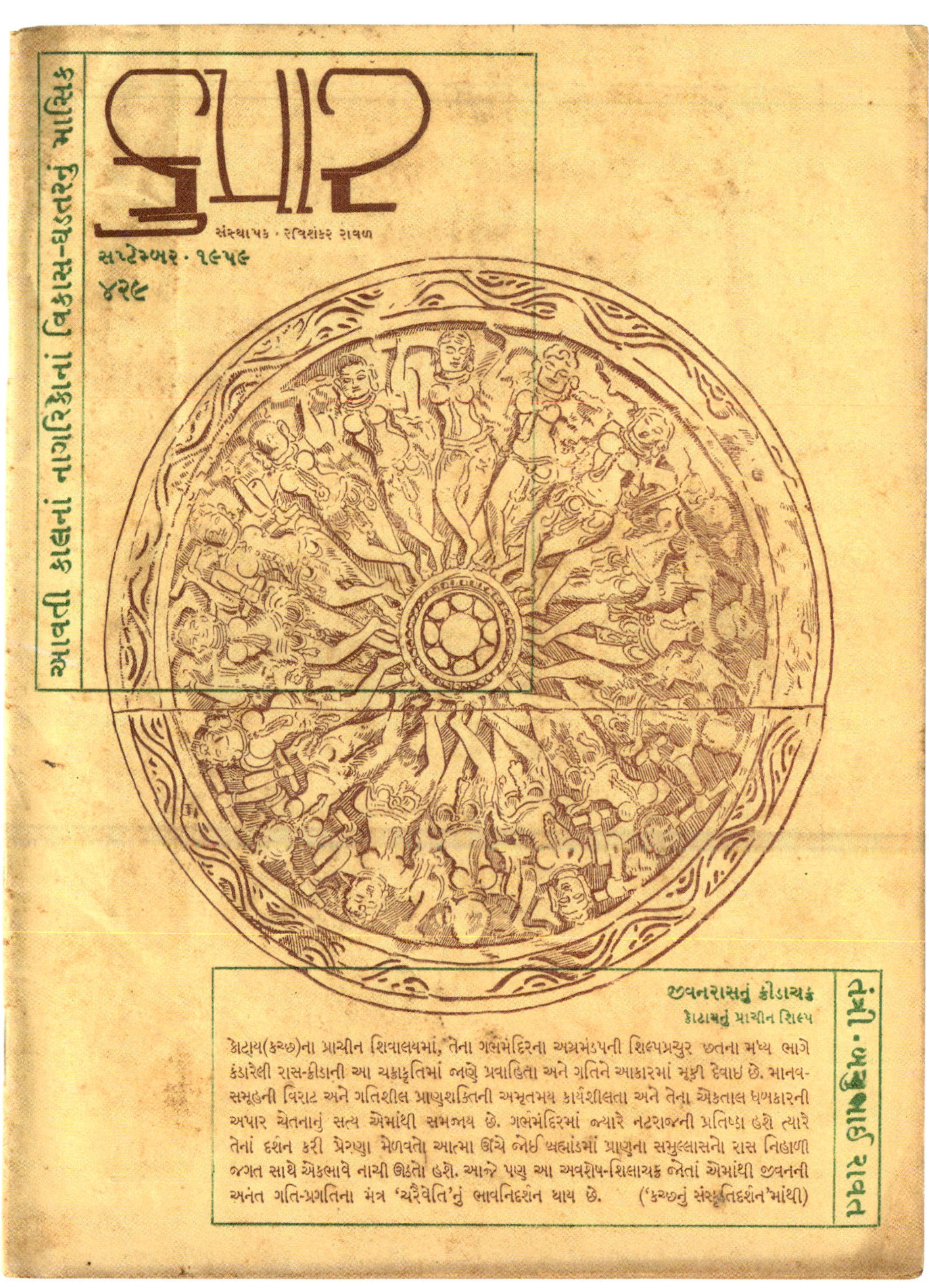

જીવનરાસનું ક્રીડાચક્ર
કોઠારાનું પ્રાચીન શિલ્પ

કોટાય(કચ્છ)ના પ્રાચીન શિવાલયમાં, તેના ગર્ભમંદિરના અગ્રમંડપની શિલ્પપ્રચુર છતના મધ્ય ભાગે કંડારેલી રાસ-ક્રીડાની આ ચક્રાકૃતિમાં જાણે પ્રવાહિતા અને ગતિને આકારમાં મૂકી દેવાઈ છે. માનવ-સમૂહની વિરાટ અને ગતિશીલ પ્રાણશક્તિની અમૃતમય કાર્યશીલતા અને તેના એકતાલ ઘબકારની અપાર ચેતનાનું સત્ય એમાંથી સમજાય છે. ગર્ભમંદિરમાં જ્યારે નટરાજની પ્રતિષ્ઠા હશે ત્યારે તેનાં દર્શન કરી પ્રેરણા મેળવતો આત્મા જાણે જોઈ વ્રહ્માંડમાં પ્રાણના સમુલ્લાસનો રાસ નિહાળી જગત સાથે એકભાવે નાચી ઊઠતો હશે. આજે પણ આ અવશેષ-શિલાચક્ર જોતાં એમાંથી જીવનની અનંત ગતિ-પ્રગતિના મંત્ર 'ચરૈવેતિ'નું ભાવનિદર્શન થાય છે. ('કચ્છનું સંસ્કૃતિદર્શન'માંથી)

KUMAR #429 · SEPTEMBER 1959

Readers Write

New art is that of the 20th century; and as always is an expression of life, ideas, and the spirit of the time—neither merely a play of beauty, nor a sign of incompleteness. These days various branches of all kinds of art, literature, and science and technology are spreading at a constant speed. They flourish by breaking old beliefs, limitations, or rules. This is a distinct characteristic of the current time. To understand this we too will have to catch up with its pace. The armchair-critics of aesthetics should give up trying to understand this. It is an expression created by the most experienced of artists. Like a giant force, it has taken control of—and will continue to control—every aspect of art and life. No one will be able to stop this force. One point remains however, that due to people's misunderstanding and the artist's immaturity, this trend—which is in its transitional stage—has hence been at the receiving end of disadvantage, but it is a mistake if someone thinks this is art from the West. This art is a wonderful expression of the entire world, human civilisation, and life.

—*Kirit Bhatt (Rajkot)*

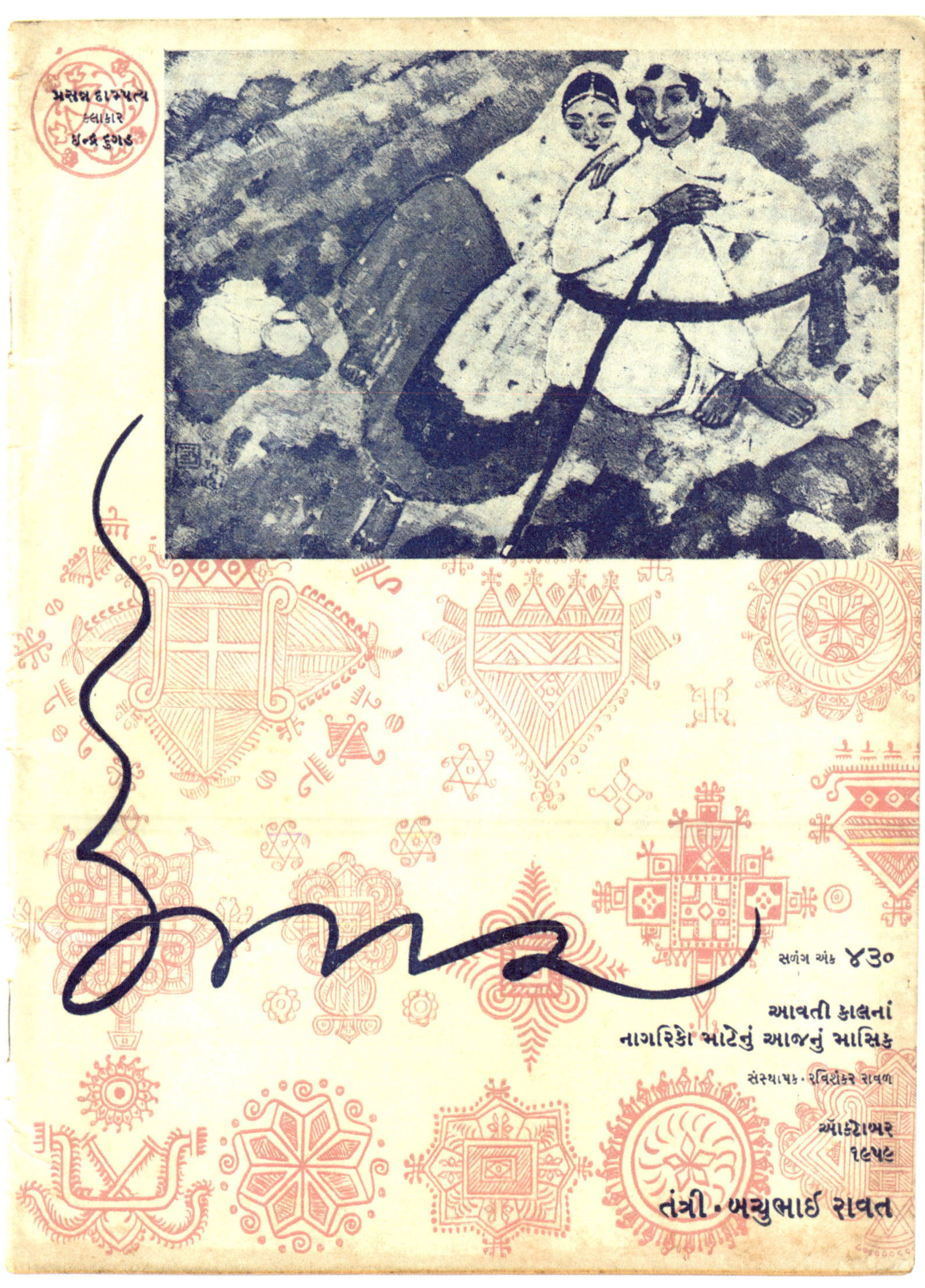

KUMAR #430 · OCTOBER 1959

Readers Write

I read the article explaining the features of 'Negro Boxer'. Such efforts have been made, and continue to be made, here and abroad, but mostly, these articles are also as obscure as the 'modern paintings' themselves. Language is a means of communicating thoughts, and art that of exchanging emotions. This implies that where the empire of language gets defeated, art has to take the reins.

In the art of music, only a melodious tune when sung in the voice of a trained vocalist can evoke the whole essence and sweetness of a *raga* to the listener's ears; it is impossible to offer such an introduction through language. Moreover, even attempting something like that will be equal to ridiculing the art of music. Similarly, if the painting is unable to convey what it is supposed to, then even if any scholar writes a very long article, it will not help.

I am reminded of a statement made by Tolstoy years ago about modern incomprehensible art: "'Some artists are great, but no one can understand their art, and even though the art is good, many people are not able to understand it'; such a foolish opinion has become so commonplace and it has rooted itself so deeply into our minds, that we are unable to see its absurdity."

—*Himmatbhai Mehta (Rajkot)*

I found Shri Jyoti Bhatt's article to be very useful. My gratitude to the author for such an informative article. Upon reading it, I was able to understand paintings from the Picasso-school to a certain extent.

Shri Chandrakant Bakshi's story is also interesting. Only in his writing I saw the art of commentary through the form of a story. It seems like he has mastered the art of bringing effectiveness of matter through depicting a situation.

—*Dr. Shivprasad Trivedi (Umreth)*

I read the commentary on 'Negro Boxer' with interest. From now on, if in every issue a proper explanatory commentary on the best paintings of Modern Art gets published, then I believe that Kumar will be instrumental in more or less removing the misconceptions associated with Modern Art and in offering inspiration to the aspiring young artists taking a step in the direction of the aforementioned style.

—*Labhshankar R. Pandya (Bhiloda)*

I read Mr. Mehta's interesting article on 'Modern Art' in the June ⟨1959⟩ issue. The entire article clearly opposes modernism and in that sense the article seems one-sided and biased. Like you have mentioned in the editor's note, there is another side to it as well. A description or critique presenting the characteristics of Modern Art can only be given by a practitioner of Modern Art. However, I would like to draw the attention of the readers of Kumar, who are interested in this subject, to one or two books. At the time of reading this article, I was also reading 'Enjoying Modern Art' (writer Sarah Newmeyer) and 'The Painter's Eye' (writer

Maurice Grosser). Both the books showcase the progress of Modern Art over the last 100 years. After reading both books, even a curious layperson will at least realise that 'Modern Art' is not merely a hoax!

—Jyotish Jani (Goregaon)

A painting by Pradyumna Tanna titled 'Khuno' ⟨Corner⟩ was printed in the July ⟨1959⟩ issue. What is so special about it that it received a prize of Rs. 1000 in the art exhibition? I am not jealous of Mr. Tanna, just surprised.

—Jinaram M. Danidhariya (Chiroda)

*[*The colour palette of that painting, patterns formed by the arrangement, and its ability to present the atmosphere with absolute simplicity and clarity, was considered praiseworthy. Since we printed it in monochrome, it does not show the above-mentioned effects. It has been printed as per its original colours in 'The Illustrated Weekly of India', which may seem more exemplary. The reader may be especially surprised to know that the Maharaja of Gwalior has bought this painting at a high price. From time to time, we have been offering assessments of the value of such creations based on our capacity and resources, and shall continue to give special attention to it.]*

⟨*—Editor*⟩

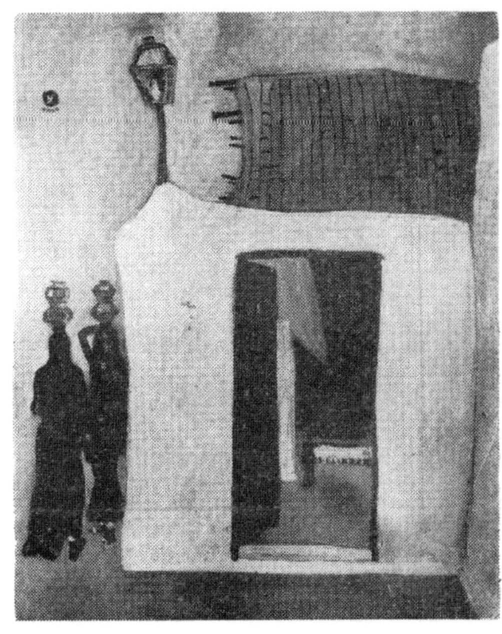

'Khuno' ⟨Corner⟩ · Pradyumna Tanna's painting that won the prize of Rs. 1000 at the Mumbai State Art Exhibition of 1959.

⟨Published in Kumar #427 · July 1959⟩

A RESPONSE TO THE DEBATE ON

MODERN ART

Pherozeshah Rustomji Mehta

I have read with much interest the article 'Habsi Mukkabaj' by the artist Jyoti Bhatt, published in the August ⟨1959⟩ issue of Kumar. It needs to be clarified here that the reproduced image of 'Negro Boxer' that was printed along with my article was not given by me; however, the literature-loving Gujarati public who is interested in art, will be thankful to him for providing a scholarly and appreciative analysis of that painting, and his humble and honest purpose behind it. Normally, and based on my personal copy of the colour reproduction of 'Negro Boxer', my opinion aligns with Shri Bhatt that to completely understand any painting, it has to be seen in its original colours.

To substantiate his views, Shri Bhatt has quoted the saying, *'Lakshmidas bhikh mange, Amarsing maran pame, toh Thanthanpal shu khota?'* ⟨refer to page 54, second column, lines 5–14 for the translation⟩; but when there is an explosive outbreak of absolutely distorted, mutilated, and destructive paintings in the abstract style, Bhatt's opinion that it is alright to not title them, proves to be odd and of little help to the viewers; it is like getting further stuck in the modern darkness of non-art that is being propagated in the name of 'art'. This samaritan too, has in his youth, seen many boxing competitions, and yet I must say that if such a title was not read below the painting, then I too would have certainly believed this 'Negro Boxer' to have been—in the words of Shri Jyoti Bhatt—'a wild plant'. Instead of not titling the painting at all, or naming them 'Painting No.1', or 'Composition', or 'An Arrangement in Yellow', and such names in the new scheme, isn't it better for the public that the painting be titled based on its subject?

This painting is of the type that we call dynamic-painting ⟨ગતિ-ચિત્ર⟩. The unique feature of such dynamic paintings is the vigour seen in them. Matisse has shown this vigour so impactfully, that it leaves an impression. Moreover, this painting is definitely more appealing with its simple colour arrangements, apt elaboration, and with its vigour-evoking curved lines. Even so, when compared with the same artist Matisse's other sophisticated artistic paintings such as 'The Dessert', 'Red Studio', 'Open Window', etc., for some strong reasons, this 'Negro Boxer' can be considered inferior in the world of painting. Moreover, there is an abundance of such vigorous, superior works in the field of painting. The French painter Nicolas Poussin's 'The Rape of the Sabines', Dutch artist ⟨William⟩ van de Velde's 'A Gale', English painter John Charlton's 'Balaclava', British artist Solomon J. Solomon's 'Samson'—these and many other such paintings can be said to be of a higher standard for these reasons: (1) that there is no intentional destruction of the human form or other forms of nature; (2) they are free of 'pushy artistry' ⟨ધક્કામાર કલાબાજ⟩ or what in the English vocabulary we call 'shock tactics'; and (3) most importantly they all

64

inherently carry many such eternal truths and treasures by which they themselves hold a higher position in the world of painting. The enjoyment derived from dynamic-paintings of such a high standard too, is of a higher order; whereas works of pushy artistry, despite being mysterious, can offer us little more than smart witticism.

This does not mean paintings like the 'Negro Boxer' are not worthy of respect or a place of their own. Every category or type of painting has the right to find its place in the vast world of art; but at the same time, it must be thought of and decided whether that place is superior, average, or inferior.

To avoid any misunderstandings, it is important to note that measuring the artistic worth of Henri Matisse based only on the work 'Negro Boxer' does injustice to such a well-known painter. As a humble writer, I have derived great joy from the reproductions of Henri Matisse's sophisticated and beautiful paintings influenced and inspired by Islamic, African, and ancient Greek Art, and so to say with regards to the modern artist, this writer's opinion is that all that is good should be certainly accepted and praised (despite a difference of opinion), but at the same time, one must not hesitate to ignore those obviously formless, distorted paintings (which cannot be identified by any indication) that bring dishonour or cause hurt to the prestige of art.

Shri Bhatt in his article says that what we need to see and understand in painting is the use of colours, the relationship between them, the effect this has, its 'harmony', and the artists' intention behind it all; but he also says, "it is out of place to think of how terrible a woman or man of this shape will look in real life." As such the truthfulness in the lines and colours of a painting are observed, its 'harmony' is observed, but why is it that only the truthfulness of the human figures is considered 'out of place' to think about? Such

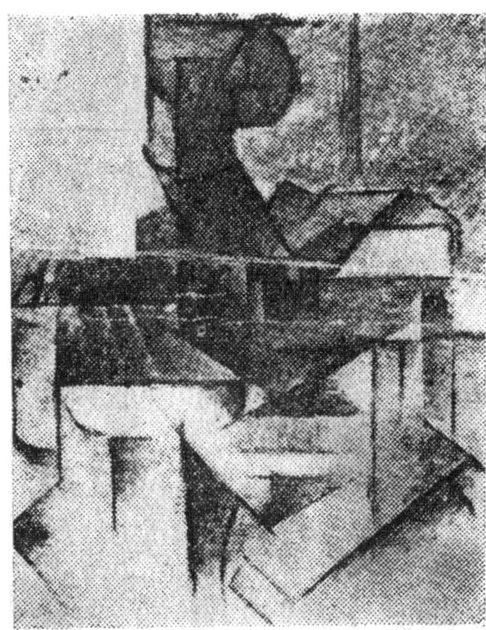

'Portrait' · Artist: ⟨Pablo⟩ Picasso

strange thought processes are why we continue to see the intentional, rampant, morbid disappearance, and mutilation (something or the other in the name of 'modern style') of the God-given human form in the heaps and piles of today's paintings, even where not required.

To make this narrative convincing, a painting by the well-known artist of this new style, Pablo Picasso, titled 'Portrait', and the artist ⟨Marcel⟩ Duchamp's painting, 'King and Queen' are presented here. Keeping with the subject, there is no objection to presenting the human figure in its distorted form as needed in the painting, but when something as absurd as a 'coal chute' is presented in the name of a 'Portrait' (as the famous artist ⟨Frederick Wellington⟩ Ruckstull says about this painting), and there is no sign of the King or Queen in 'King and Queen'—with not even as much as a hint—then what is wrong if the public interested in art has a 'pessimistic attitude' of *'khatle moti khod ke*

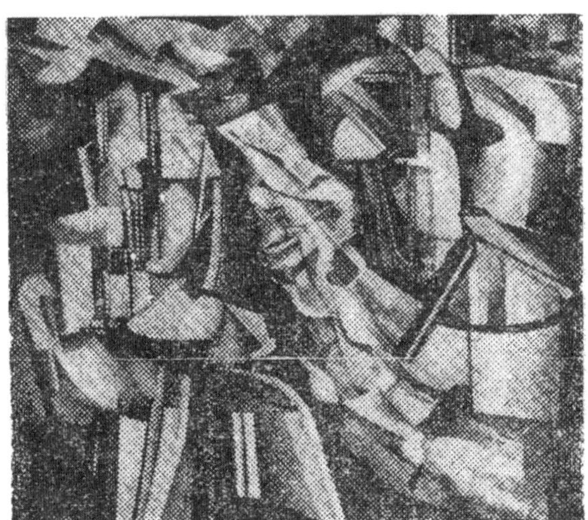

'King and Queen' · Artist: ⟨Marcel⟩ Duchamp

payo j na made' ⟨refer to footnote 5 on page 36⟩ when they see such completely abstracted paintings? Paintings are not only for artists or connoisseurs, they are for the public too; they are to nurture the aesthetics of human society further, to encourage and direct people on the path of advancement and progress—this truth should not be erased and forgotten, as is being done increasingly today in the name of 'Modern Art'.

Finally, to end this article, presented here, in his own words, is what Henri Matisse—whose 'Negro Boxer', Shri Jyoti Bhatt has done a commendable job at explaining at great length—has to say about how art must be, who it is for, how it should impact the spectator, and what he thinks about it all: "What I dream of is an art of balance, purity, and serenity, devoid of troubling or depressing subject-matter, an art which might be for every mental worker, he be businessman or writer, like an appeasing influence, like a mental soother, something like a good arm-chair in which to rest from physical fatigue." ('Modern French Painting' by Sam Hunter, p.176)

'PASSION' OR 'INSANITY'?

Some advocates of the modern painting style tell us that, "it is when an artist's feelings are roused that it becomes impossible to express their inner feelings in lines and colours, and then the medium that remains to represent art seems to be the surfacially rigid, modern obscure art". Everyone knows that the impassioned internal emotions are essential to art as well as the artist. This cannot be denied. But the complaint ⟨in my previous article⟩ wasn't with this internal 'passion' of the artist but with their 'insane' emotions. What factors cause a deep impact on the present day artist's psyche were also explained in that. While reading about the lives of the numerous Western modernist painters of today, the mention of their highly delirious nature is found very evidently. The difference between internal 'passion' and 'insanity' in the field of painting can instantly be identified when seeing the many paintings of today's modernist art style. Look at the two paintings presented ⟨overleaf⟩. Which of the two is a result of the artist's 'inner passion' and which is merely a fruit of their inner 'insanity' is such that it can be very easily ascertained. One is the famous historic Italian painter Caravaggio's painting of 'Saint Jerome'; the second is the modern French painter Jean Dubuffet's oil painting, 'Eyes Closed', painted in 1954. In the first: in the dark quarter of an isolated chapel, the aged, frail-bodied priest, Saint Jerome is seen facing a human skull in deep contemplation. On his powerful face is the glow of the radiance of his wisdom and piety. This painting by Caravaggio, that one is enticed to look at again and again, clearly expresses the artist's inner passion fully. Antithetical to this, is the French artist Dubuffet's modern style painting, which too is of a human figure—but even so, how distorted! Look, is there any trace of the 'closed eyes' or parts such as lips, ears, nose,

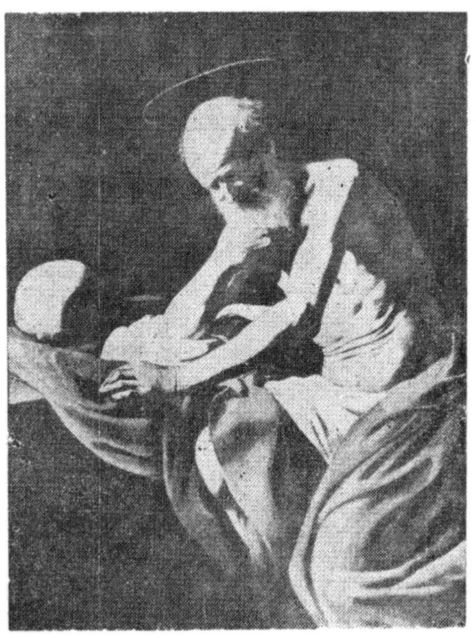

'Saint Jerome' · Artist: ⟨Michelangelo Merisi da⟩ Caravaggio

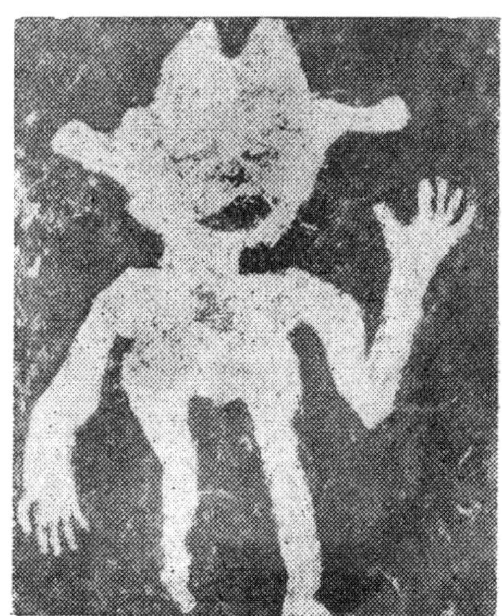

'Eyes Closed' · Artist: ⟨Jean⟩ Dubuffet

hands, legs, etc.? Even if someone wishes to justify the 'mystery' of this distortion in whatever way, it will still only seem that this, and the other numerous distorted paintings of today, are a symbol not of the maker's 'passion', but of their 'insanity'.

That 'Modern Art' paintings appear 'rigid and obscure' on the surface is accepted by its advocates. Its only defence is that its technique is similar to that of 'classical music' (a superior form of music). It isn't like 'light music', and for the same reason it cannot be 'for popular consumption' ⟨લોક-ભોગ્ય⟩. Like how only a sage can understand the scriptures, these 'rigid and obscure' paintings can only be understood by connoisseurs, such is the rebuttal of the opposition.

In response, we ask with all due respect, leave aside the complete existence of 'classical music' in modern painting techniques and modern painting, is there even a faint glimmer of the same seen here? The traces and intonation of *ragas* are present in the mere *aa...aa...aa...* of maestros of classical music. But here though, there seems to be a complete dearth of any such elements in relation to painting.

Similar to how singers and musicians create music that has words inspired by intense emotions, has an arrangement of *ragas*, and is free-spirited, even painters should have some such freedom of expression; such thinking prompted a group of Western artists of the early nineteenth century to start making non-figurative or abstract ⟨અમૂર્ત⟩ paintings. What form (or deformity) this initiation has eventually resulted in, we are clearly witnessing right now! In this context, it will be better that we acquaint ourselves with the thoughts of some qualified officials and celebrated artists, before we ordinary 'art-appreciators', who only understand art meant 'for popular consumption', say something. The famous British artist Sir William Orpen

K.B.E., R.A., R.I., in his book 'Outline of Art', discusses this subject and writes:

"In theory it seems plausible enough that if a musician is free to weave melodies without reference to natural sounds, a painter should be free to construct compositions without reference to natural forms. It is also true that the emotional pleasure we derive from the stained-glass windows of an old cathedral does not depend on the subject painted. We are enchanted with the radiant beauty of the pattern of colour. So far so good, but now comes the point that no artist living or dead has yet succeeded in convincing the world that these stained-glass windows would give us any keener or purer emotional pleasure if they had no subjects, or been able himself to produce an abstract painting more beautiful in colour and pattern than paintings based on concrete forms."

Like in its politics, France in the latter half of the nineteenth century saw the mobilisation of new agitations even in the art world. At that time, a certain group of artists broke free from the traditional customs of the then prevalent culture, and enthusiastically welcomed the simplicity of life. They believed that modern life has in a way become diseased—"If modern life is diseased, modern art must be diseased also. We can only restore art to health by starting it afresh like children or savages." (The Outline of Art, p. 362)

To begin painting like a child or a forest-dweller, they rallied against the 'complex' style of 'Neo-Impressionism' which was popular at that time. This new group of artists came to be known as the 'Fauves'—meaning 'Wild Beasts'—in Paris. For as long as these 'Fauvists' tried to simplify and keep the painting technique as less complicated as possible, they yielded a decent crop of paintings in the art world. But owing to their contempt and anger towards the present cultural tradition, midway, they changed course away from the right direction. Naturally, it resulted in the opposite, and since then, like the green burning along with the dry, it was the beginning of the end of the tasteful art of an era.

That which has been referred to as 'childish art' and 'mad people's art' by the scholars of veteran art institutes such as the Royal Academy and many art critics, and which in the end has been compared to 'chimpanzee's art', has crossed all bounds of extremism and anarchy, and cannot even be defended by cheeky arguments based on the 'ha aa aa aa vu' of ancient sages, or by the 'experimental free verse' poetry of the poet Nanalal, or even the couplet from Narsinh Mehta's poem *'Ante toh hemnu hem j hoye'* ⟨In the end gold is but gold⟩.*

[*With this response, we are ending the debate around the main article.]

⟨—Editor⟩

કુમાર

આવતી કાલનાં નાગરિકોનું માસિક

સંસ્થાપક · રવિશંકર રાવળ

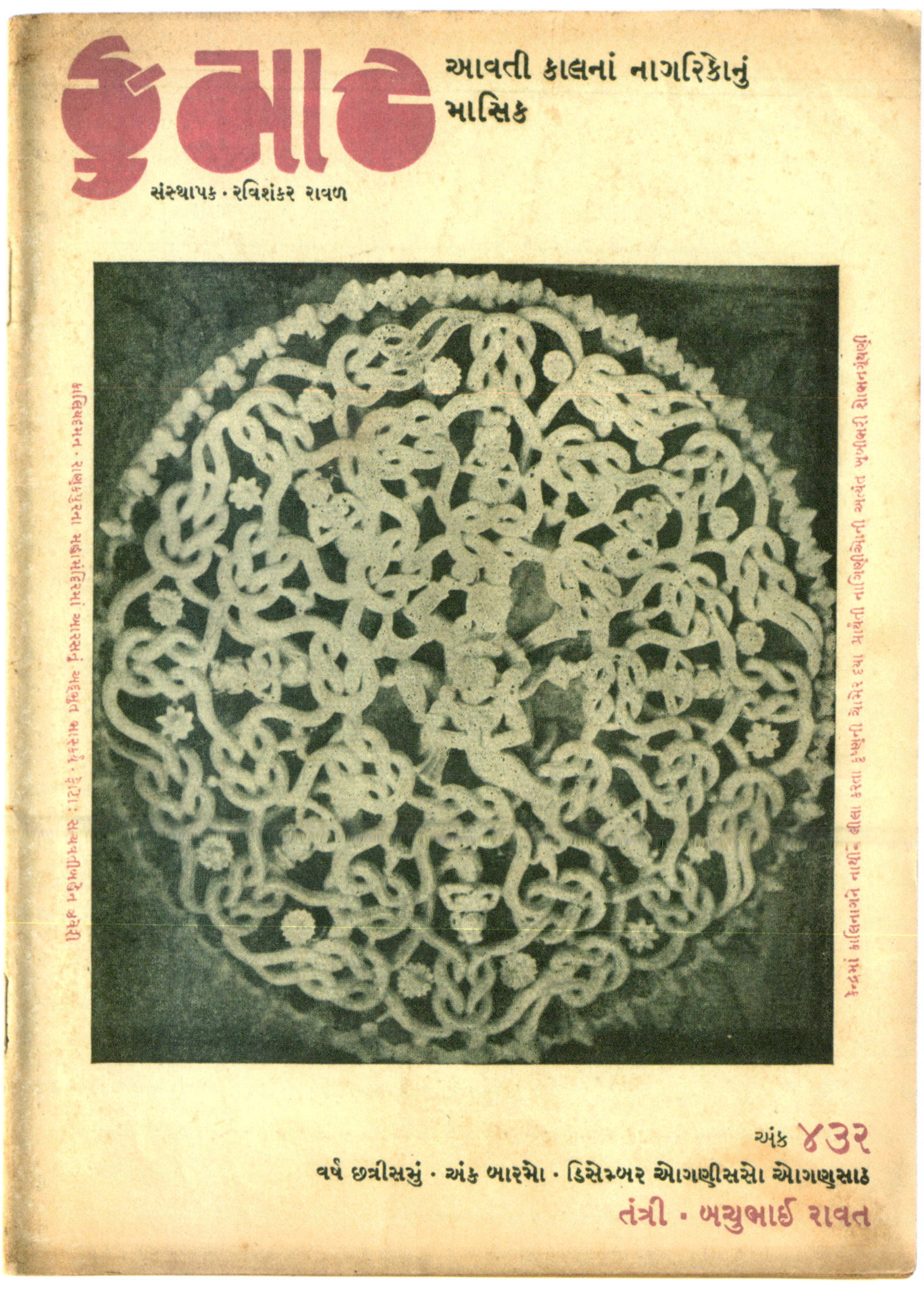

અંક ૪૩૨

વર્ષ છત્રીસમું · અંક બારમો · ડિસેમ્બર ઓગણીસસો ઓગણુસાઠ

તંત્રી · બચુભાઈ રાવત

KUMAR #432 · DECEMBER 1959

DISTORTION IN ART

AN ARTICLE EXPLAINING THE REASONS BEHIND THE STRANGENESS OF, AND DISTORTION IN, 'MODERN ART' WITH CLEAR EXAMPLES AND ILLUSTRATIONS

Jyoti Bhatt

Oftentimes in Modern Art (painting and sculpture) one gets to see distorted human figures and other forms of common household objects. On the basis of this, naturally, we are compelled to ask if humans can even appear so?

Such distortion results from several different reasons. One of these is 'representation' ⟨રજૂઆત⟩: how the maximum number of characteristics of the original object can be represented.

Whenever we see an object, we determine its appearance based on the positions we are looking at it from (see Illustration 1). In the Figure क, a vase is placed on a table, and at points अ, ब, क, ड eyes are drawn, indicating different vantage points. As seen from each of these points, the vase and table resemble Figures अ, ब, क, and ड respectively. Thus, when the object is seen from many different vantage points, the shapes it will be perceived as will differ as well. However, one thing that draws special attention here is that some shapes are more helpful in identifying the object, such as क, whereas some are less helpful, such as अ.

Similar is the case with the human figure. When viewed from any of the different perspectives from top to bottom, only its image seen exactly from the front resembles the original human figure most closely, and

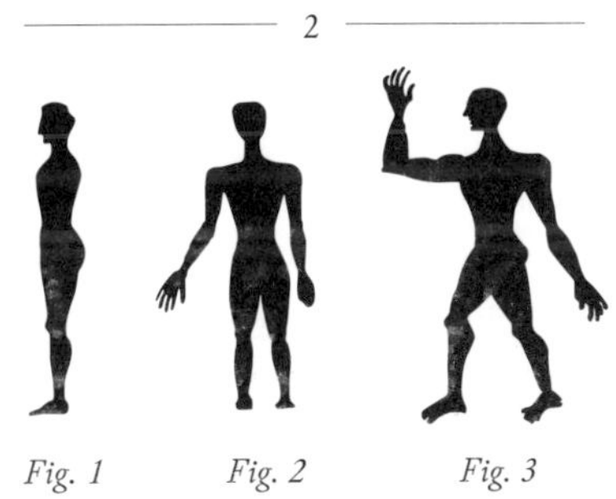

Fig. 1   Fig. 2   Fig. 3

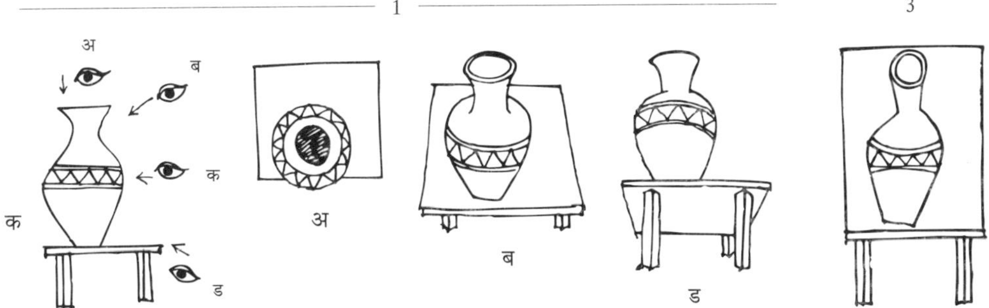

is the most easily recognisable form. But the human form is not symmetrical from all four sides, like a vase. The human figure looks different from its side and front. Additionally, though it is a single unit, it is made up of many different parts and subparts. For example, hands, legs, and then the nose, ears, eyes, fingers, etc. (see Illustration 2).

When a human figure is viewed from the side ⟨ Figure 1 ⟩, its other leg, both the arms, and the space in between the arms and the waist is not visible. But here, the shape of the face is clearer than in Figure 2. Particular features of the body like the eyes and ears are not seen in both, and yet, we can tell for certain that the first figure clearly depicts a human face whereas in the second figure, if we separate the head from the body, it will not be possible to confirm with surety if it is a face at all. It may resemble the key-hole of a lock, or an upside down vase, or some such thing. The shape of the leg is clear in the first figure, whereas it isn't as clear in the second figure. Still, in it we see two legs instead of one. Hence, it is more successful in representing the whole (human) figure. In the hand too, the palm with separate fingers assures clarity.

And so, all that was considered appropriate and of greater clarity has been combined to make the third figure, which carries the maximum detail. But this happens only with regards to the shape—which resembles a silhouette.

Now in Illustration 3, the vase and table are drawn in such a way that a maximum number of both their characteristics can be represented. When seeing अ in Illustration 1, one gets a complete sense of the top of the table, and in क one gets the full sense of its width and legs. In Illustration 3, both of these are represented together. Similarly, the vase has been drawn as seen from the side; but while in क it is not clear if it is a solid, spherical object or a cardboard cut-

out of that shape, in Illustration 3, when we see the circular opening of its mouth, then this confusion is resolved. It is also easier to understand where on the table the vase is placed.

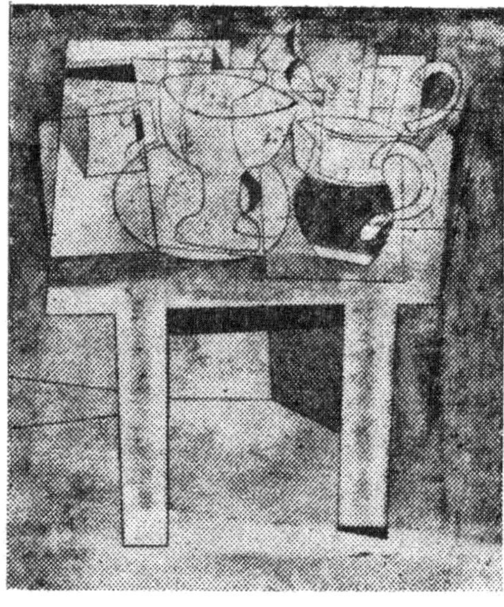

'Objects on a Table' · Artist: Ben Nicholson

From prehistoric times until today, this kind of distortion has very much existed (perhaps for many different reasons). Examples of this have been given here. While viewing these images, one must bear in mind that apart from distortion of this kind, there are several other facets which together make up the whole image. But, our discussion at this point is limited only to distortion.

But what is the need for such kinds of distortion?

Painting is a flat object, while sculpture is voluminous. In a sculpture, the sculpted form can be seen by us from all four sides, and so the sections and parts not visible from one side are visible from another; but in painting there isn't a possibility of viewing it from

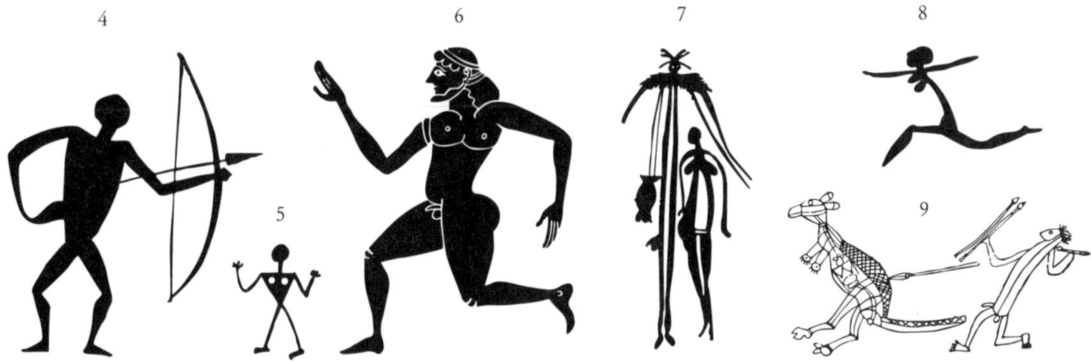

another side or the back. (If the painting is made on a translucent surface, then maybe a little bit may show, but it will be the same object or shape which is visible from the front. Unlike a sculpture, one cannot see the chest from the front and the spine from the back.)

When prehistoric humans began drawing, lines were unknown to them (we will look at what lines are at another time). They would use a colour or a charred piece of wood to draw shadow-like shapes, and from this—through the forms they made—they would try to express all that they wanted to say (see Illustration 4). When the question of female or male arose, then to show the distinction they would highlight the main difference in appearance between the two, like the shapes of genitals and breasts (see Illustration 5, 6, 7, 8, 9). Moreover, those (prehistoric) artists—whose observational skills were more cultivated—also observed that a man's chest is wider than his hips, and that a woman's hips are wider than her chest, because she must bear the weight of a child for nine months; such observations are also visible in some of their drawings (see Illustration 7).

But ever since these artists became aware of the line, their task became much easier. It became both feasible and easy for them to show the details of the body at their respective locations (see Illustration 6); but even so, they drew in a way where the original form was represented from both the side and the front (one after another). Additionally, their knowledge of these things was also essential to why they drew in such a way. The artist knew that there are two hands, two legs, and two eyes, and similarly two breasts—then how is it okay to not represent it! It really does not matter whether the one who drew this was a prehistoric human or Picasso (see Illustration 19).

Illustration 4 and 5 are made by tribals from India in today's time, not by prehistoric humans; yet there is an uncanny resemblance between both their arts.

Illustration 6 has been taken from Greek pottery. The drawing is from approximately 2000 years ago. Here, the human figure has been depicted with the least number of lines and detail. Illustration 7 is a sculpture made by a prehistoric human. In that too, the importance given to the genitals is understandable. Illustration 9 is an animal drawn by a prehistoric human. In that too, all the body parts of the original animal have been drawn with clear distinction.

The reasons owing to which prehistoric humans clearly portrayed each body part distinctly, is the same reason with which today's village artist—unburdened by so-

10

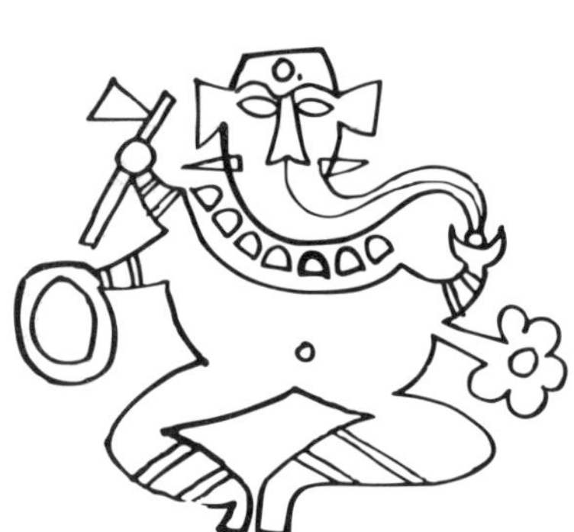

A Ganpati idol carved in wood on
the outer side of a doorsill of a home
in a village in Saurashtra.

11

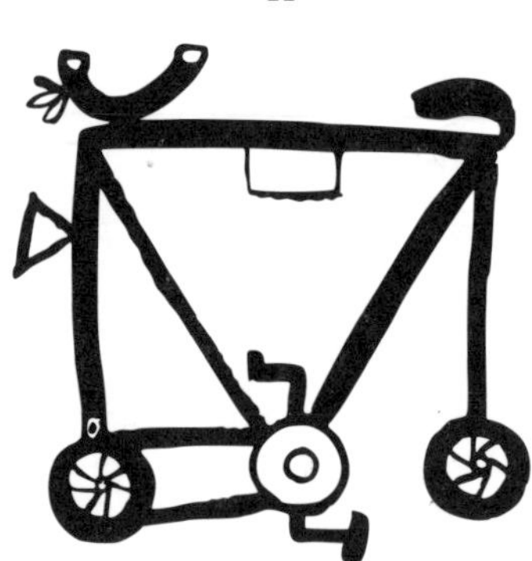

A drawing of a cycle on a stole of a
woman from the Bharwad community
of Saurashtra.

called education and the culture of the city—
draws or sculpts. Illustration 10 is the idol of
Gajanan ⟨also known as Ganpati⟩ with four
hands, carved on the doorsill of the entrance
gate of a house in a village of Saurashtra. Even
though it is a carved figure, it can in a way
be compared to a painting because it is an
embossed (relief) form; likewise, with the
least details and only outlines, the lotus, disc,
axe, *laddu*, etc. have been shown in his hands.
Illustration 11 is a print on a stole ⟨ઓઢણી⟩
belonging to a woman of the Bharwad
community from Saurashtra—a community
that is usually engrossed in their own culture.
The time in which they live and the objects
they see undoubtedly result in a resounding
echo in their minds. Here, a cycle is drawn
in a way that it is seen from the side, but its
handle is drawn as though it is seen from the
front—with both grips. Whether its 'chain' is
attached to the front or the rear wheel is not a
matter of concern for the artist (because they
don't want to drive it).

Illustrations 7, 8, 9 are examples of art
by Australian Aboriginals. In Illustration 7, a
woman and a man are drawn together. The
difference in their heights is clear. The male

figure is drawn in such a way that the body
and legs are viewed from the front, but to
emphasise that it is indeed a man, the genitals
are drawn on one side, and as viewed from
the side. In the female figure, it seems that
the artist has beautifully observed the rhythm
and grace with which she stands. Her waist is
drawn wide and her breasts are shown facing
outwards on either side, as it was not possible
to draw them where they should have been.
Additionally, drawing them distinctly ensures
that they receive more prominence, as our eyes
are drawn there owing to the colour-contrast
that is the result of the empty space on all four
sides. Here both breasts are parallel to the
ground (as it usually is), but in Illustration 8
the same is represented differently. There the
body is drawn as viewed from the side, where
one breast may be hidden behind the other.
But to avoid this, the artist has drawn one
above the other.

In Illustration 9, the running kangaroo's
face, body, and tail are shown as viewed from
the side as are the two back legs, and the two
front legs are shown as viewed from the front.
However, the position of the back legs is such
that they are seen from either the front or

the back—meaning that one leg (the front) doesn't overlap the other (the back).

Illustration 12 is an image of a relief carving from the Sanchi Stupa. Here the head, body, and legs are such that they are seen from the front, but the part of the legs below the knees are as if viewed from the side, and that too as if each foot is viewed separately from the left and right side respectively. However, how can the hands folded in *namaskar* be shown protruding forward and brought out of the flatness of the surface of the stone? Moreover, the hands are also foreshortened and so are rendered as seen from the side.

Illustration 12 A is also from Sanchi. Even here, to depict the characteristics of the bird, both its wings have been spread fully, the shape of its body has been shown as viewed from the side, and its tail has been shown as viewed from above or below.

Illustration 13 is a part of the table depicted in a 13th century Spanish painting 'The Holy Supper'. In that, both the table and the pattern of the tablecloth are shown as seen from above, whereas the vessels are shown as seen from the side; and as the open mouths of the vessels are drawn at least as halves, we can see that they have volume.

Here a doubt may arise—were those who drew all this conscious of these things? I feel the answer to this will surely be 'no'. These artists (except the painters of today, who have been imparted a modern art education) would have been unaware of the statements and reasons we have just given; yet they have represented everything naturally. They knew that a table is square in shape and that is why they have drawn a square; and that it needs legs, else how will it stand? Hence the legs are also drawn. And as this is very natural, a similarity can be seen in drawings done twenty-five thousand years ago (Altamira, Singhanpur, etc.) and those drawings done today by villagers and tribals (and likewise by little children).

12

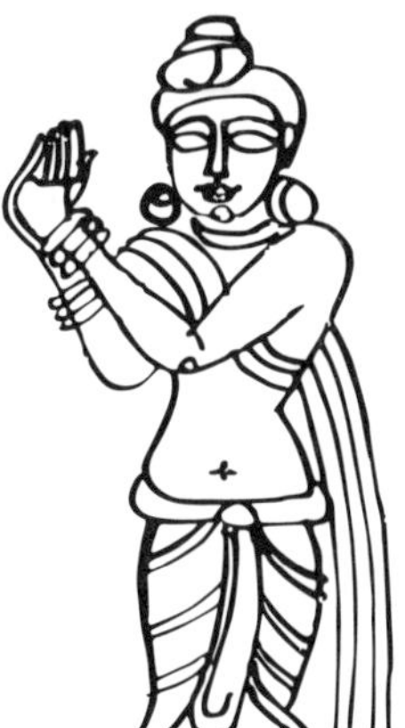

An idol with hands folded in *namaskar* from the sculptures of the Sanchi Stupa.

12 A

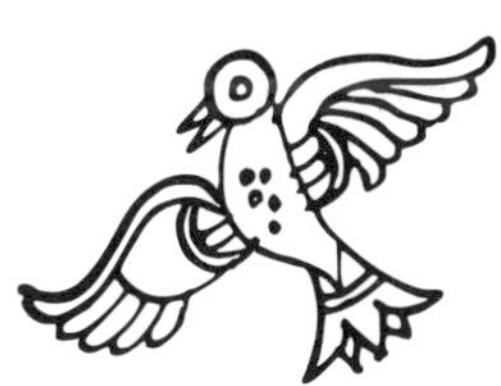

13

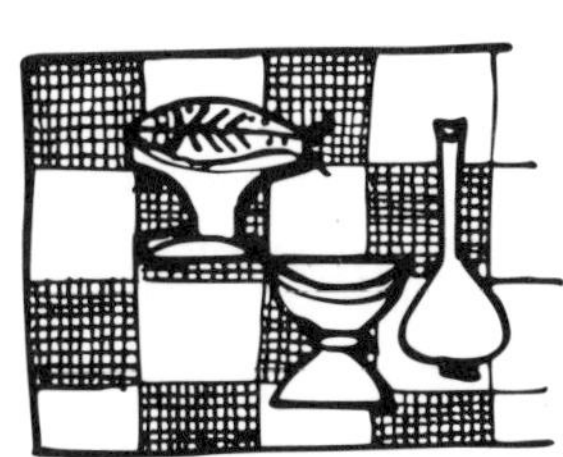

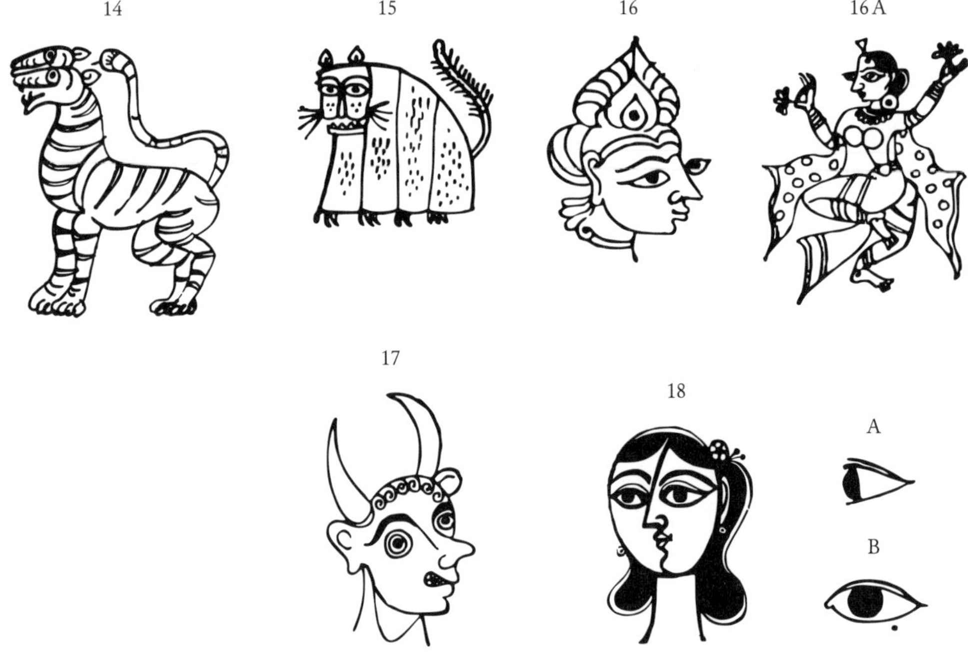

Illustration 14 is taken from a Jain manuscript. In spite of the tiger being drawn from the side, both its eyes are shown; the face has been drawn in a way that is a composite of a front view and a side view. We already know that the eyes take a place of great importance in the human body. It is only the eyes that facilitate the recognition of a person. And likewise, in Illustration 15 (from the walls of a home in a village of Saurashtra), the tiger is drawn in a manner that both its eyes are visible.

In Illustration 16 (from a Jain manuscript) despite the face being shown as seen from the side (in profile), the second eye is shown outside ⟨the face⟩. (In the Australian drawings as well, the body parts are shown from the outer side, like in this one). Also in the body of the dancing lady (in the Jain manuscript) ⟨Illustration 16 A⟩ there is a combination of three different perspectives—as seen from the front, the back, and the side.

Illustration 17 is from a (13th century) painting done in Spain. In this the top half of the face is shown as somewhat seen from the front (because of the two horns, two ears, and two eyes), and the bottom half is shown as seen from the side. The modern painters of today have discovered a slightly newer technique based on this, which is visible in Illustration 18. The face is represented as seen from the front, its features are also in their appropriate positions, yet it is shown in such a way that the side-view of the face also gets represented alongside this view. When the eye is shown as seen from the front (B), it seems to represent more characteristics than when the eye is shown as seen from the side (A), that is why both eyes are drawn as seen from the front. For this reason, in Rajput[11],

---

11 — The stylistic characteristics described here are technically seen in Western Indian Jain paintings, although Bhatt refers to this as Rajput.

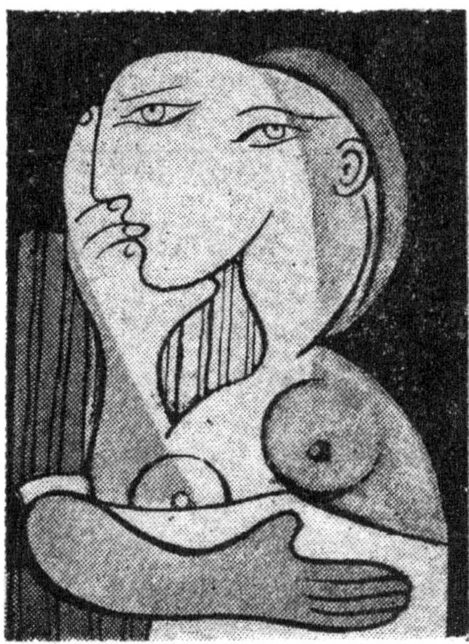

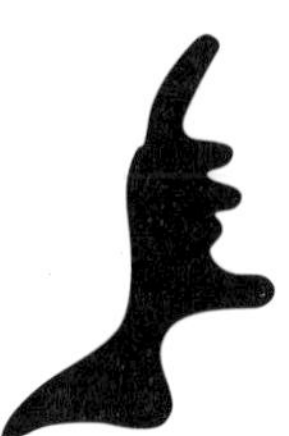

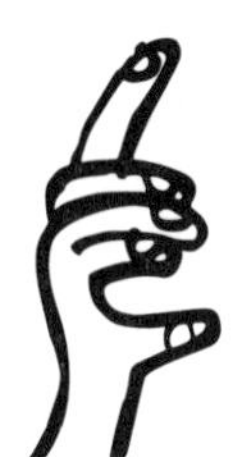

A work by Modern Art's most profoundly
whimsical artist ⟨Pablo⟩ Picasso.

Jain, and other similar paintings as well, even though the face is drawn from the side, the eyes are shown only as seen from the front.

In Illustration 19, a painting by Picasso, his use of all the things we read above, is clearly visible. But apart from these, there are many other elements in it. One thing that specifically draws our attention is that only a single line has been drawn to separate the face and the hand. Where the nose, lips, and chin end—at their edges—is where the fingers of the hand begin! Thus the same line serves as the contour for both. To a certain extent, this can be called polysemy ⟨શ્લેષ અલંકાર⟩[12]; although Picasso himself prefers that his paintings not be compared to literature. Here too, both eyes are shown; the face is such that it is seen from the side, yet both the eyes are as if seen from the front, and the space between them is also left in a similar manner.

When this strategy came to the modern artists, they started using it, and in doing so they saw that entirely new shapes emerged due to such distorted shapes (new shapes, their relationship to each other, and their design is explained in detail in the article 'Negro Boxer' in issue 428 ⟨August 1959⟩), and this they have put to good use in their own paintings as well. An example of this is given here: in Illustration 19 A, the shape of the hand of the lady resting her face on her palm is shown blackened out. Owing to the relationship of the forms adjacent to it, one can infer that it is a hand; but even if one does not understand it to be a hand, or forgets this fact, one will still have an idea about what this shape could be. Moreover, one must see this shape in relation to other shapes as well.

The meaning of the word distortion, according to the dictionary: "the forceful

12 — *Slesha alankara* refers to a type of *alankara* (embellishment, or figures of speech) in classical Indian poetry and dramaturgy where one word serves two purposes, replacing the need for another word to imply a secondary meaning.

twisting-turning, degrading of any object, substance, or of a story-fact-incident, etc.".". But in the language of painting the word distortion is not used only in this sense. When the shape of the original object, the geometrical relation between its outlines, and, in the same way, its proportions, are not depicted in their respective ratios, but are represented in another ratio, then we say that the original has been distorted. When there has been some manipulation to the original form (as seen by the eyes) it is called distortion, but this does not mean that the original has been 'deformed'.

According to the expert art critic Herbert Read, Greek sculptures (such as Venus, David, Apollo[13], etc.) that are considered entirely realistic, are also distorted, because they aren't copies of the form of a single living human; these have been imagined by collecting all that is ideal from numerous individuals' bodies (in a manner that an average can be arrived at), and then, based on the above idea of the best attributes of physical beauty, have been sculpted. The same can be said for Indian sculptures as well.

---

13 — Here, Jyoti Bhatt refers to Greco-Roman sculpture in general. While Venus (de Milo) is the only Greek sculpture of the three listed here, the classicism associated with Greco-Roman sculpture is seen in David and Apollo (Belvedere) as well.

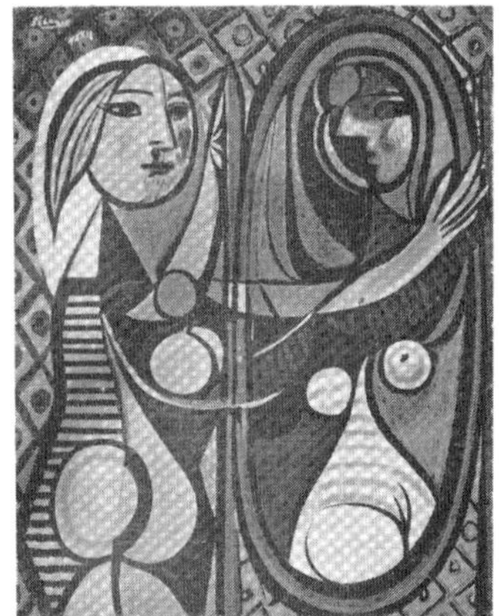

I

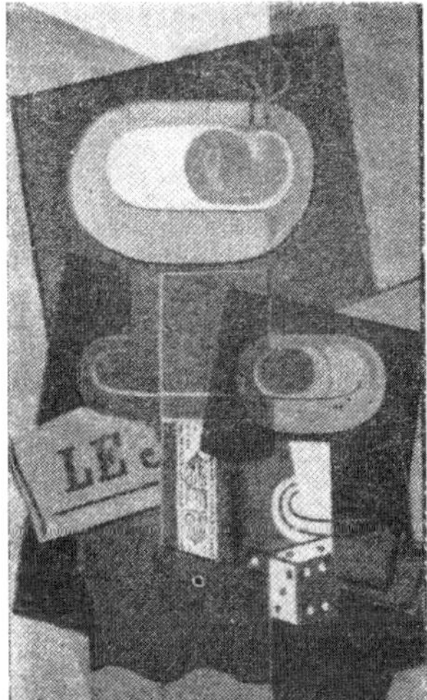

III

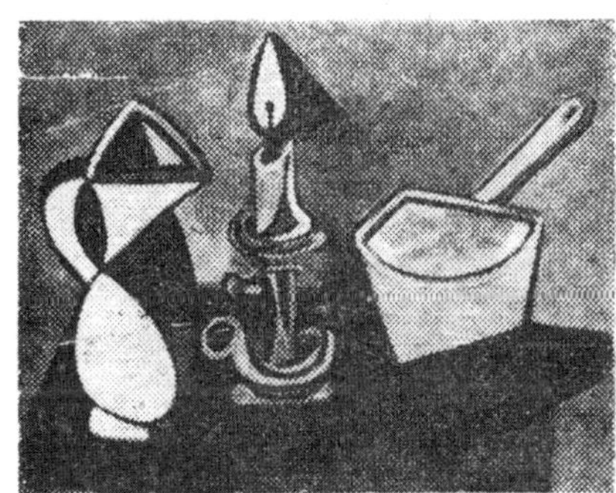

II

IV

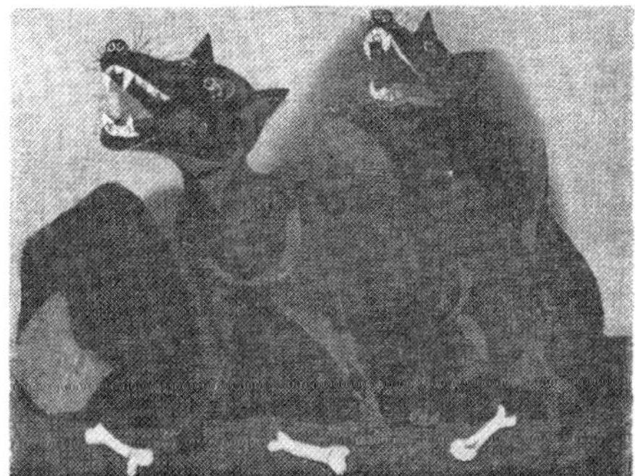

V

In the context of the article Distortion in Art, which explains distortion in Modern Art, some 'deeply distorted' artworks by some world-renowned artists are shown here.

I. 'Girl Before a Mirror' · Artist: Pablo Picasso
II. 'Woman at the Window' · Artist: Pablo Picasso
III. 'The Dice'—the beauty of non-living objects · Artist: Juan Gris
IV. ⟨Pablo⟩ Picasso's painting 'Jug, Candle and Enamel Pan', rendering characteristics of these objects.
V. Mexican artist ⟨Rufino⟩ Tamayo's aggressive painting 'Animals'

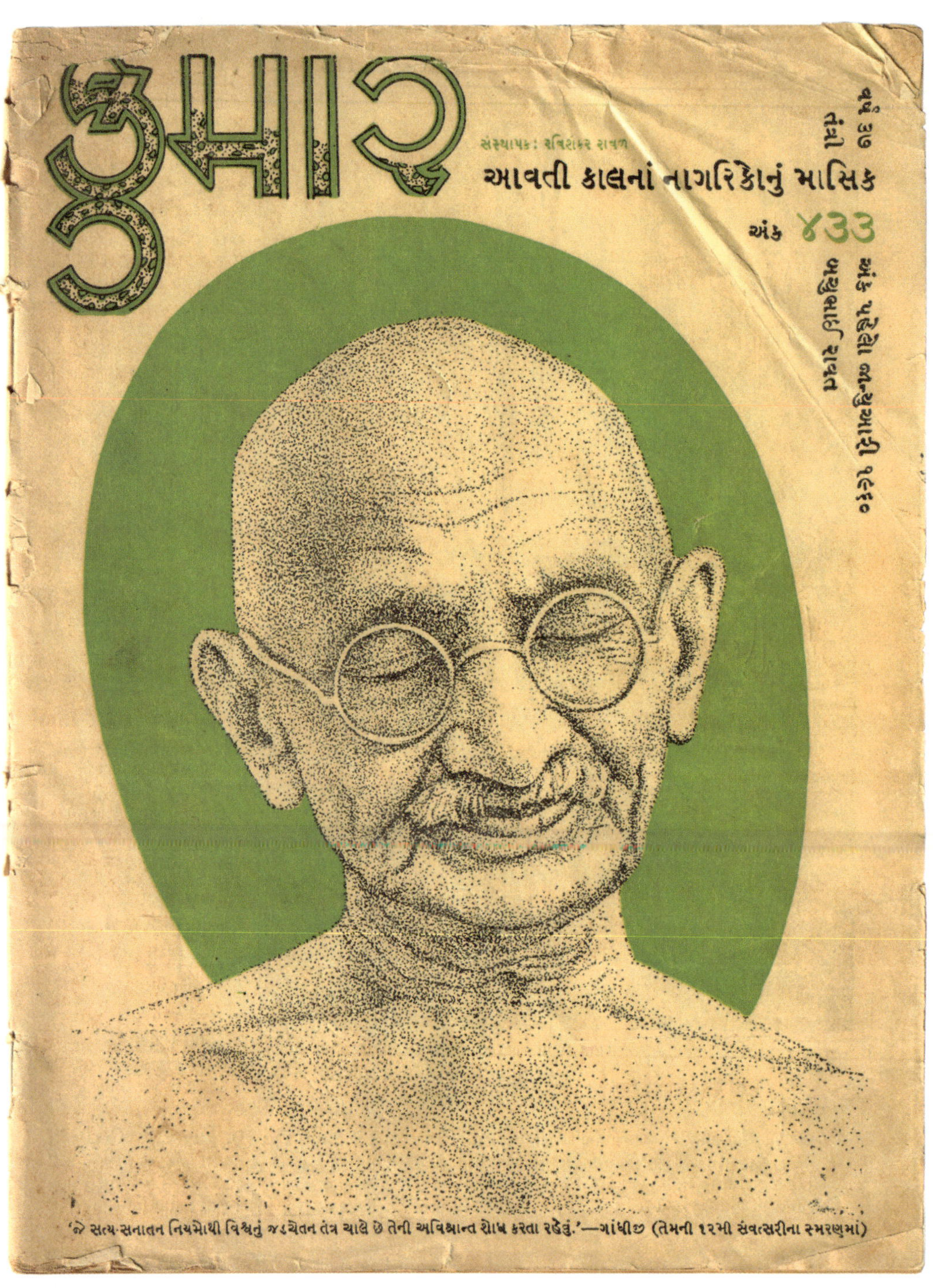

KUMAR #433 · JANUARY 1960

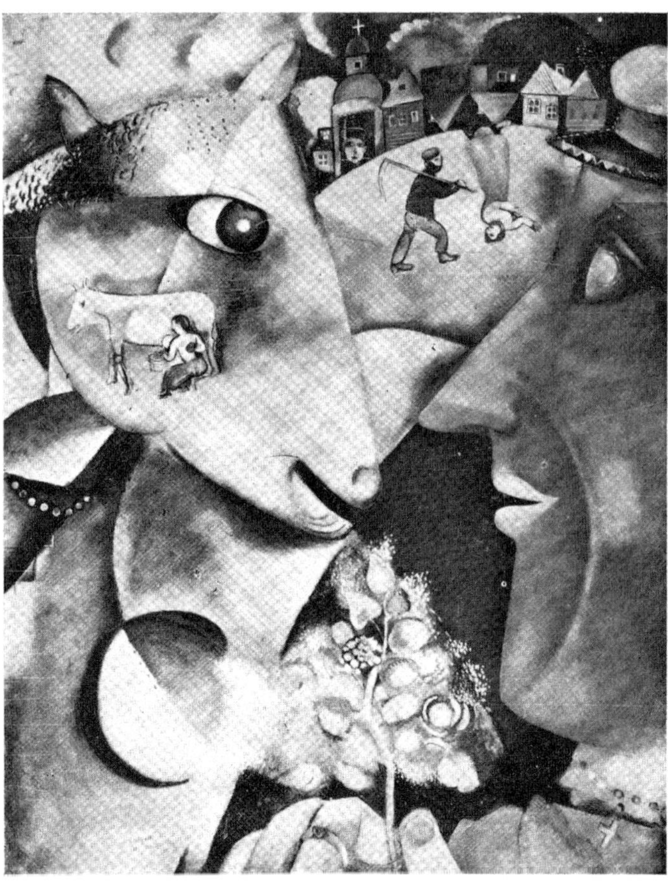

'I and the Village' · Artist: ⟨Marc⟩ Chagall

From time to time, different artists have used different modes of representation in accordance with what has been discussed in the article 'Distortion in Art' in this issue. 'Cubist' artists would break down the forms of the subject of their painting into triangular shapes and rearrange these shapes anew, proportionately. Inspired by this method, the French artist Chagall has taken impressions of all the characters, animals, and incidents from the village where he was born—which were etched in his memory—and has whimsically arranged them in this painting. In doing so, neither have the relative proportions of the figures been maintained accurately nor are the colours true to nature; and behold, it also seems that all rules of gravity have been done away with! This painting, measuring approximately 6 x 5 ft, is in the collection of America's renowned Guggenheim Museum.[14] ⟨—Editor⟩

14 — The mentioned painting is in the permanent collection of the MoMA. However, the painting was acquired with the help of the Mrs. Simon Guggenheim Fund. It might have been exhibited at the Guggenheim when the editor saw it, but the Guggenheim is not in the line of provenance.

AN ARTICLE FURTHER EXPLAINING
DISTORTION IN ART

Jyoti Bhatt

Last time, we saw examples of one of the many reasons which leads to distortion in an image (the need for solutions through which key characteristics of an object can be used so that the object can be represented in a discernible manner). There are other reasons as well.

The image itself is the first step to distortion. Even in images that are direct copies of nature, the elements of nature (which along with length and breadth, have the third dimension of depth as well) only carry the first two dimensions when represented; the third dimension is present as merely an illusion. Actually its existence remains absent. In other words, 'a majority of paintings' represent three-dimensional objects from nature by converting them—distorting them—into two-dimensional objects. I say 'a majority of paintings' because not all paintings are made with the intention of representing the objects of nature; but for each and every painting made with such intention, this statement holds entirely true.

Any line drawing can be referred to as an example of distortion; because even the efforts made in painting—to render the original object's colour and maintain the effect of light and shade—is absent in drawing. There is also a prevalent opinion that lines are entirely an invention of humans. There is something akin to lines in nature, but objectively these are not lines. They are either extremely thin yet solid, three-dimensional objects—for example, a wire, the thin branch of a creeper, a thread, etc.—or the gap between two objects that lie very close to each other, which in actuality is nothing. For example, the gap between the wooden frame and the pane of a window or a door (see Illustration 1).

Similarly, when we look at an object in reality, we cannot see what is behind it—unless it is transparent. However, what happens when we make a line drawing of it? What we see within its outlines is the same paper and the very same colour that is seen outside of the outlines as well. Hence, two dimensional objects, or those whose third dimension is negligible (paper or cardboard toys, leaves, etc.) are represented only through their outlines in line drawings, and apart from this everything else is left aside—or as we would say, they get 'distorted'.

There are other reasons for such distortion as well. Such as, to represent an imagined version of an object instead of its physical appearance; or a particular characteristic of it which cannot be seen when viewed from only one side; or to represent features which cannot be seen with our eyes. When a god or goddess is painted, then behind them a circle is drawn. This circle of light cannot be seen with our eyes (though some people claim to have seen such a light). In the same way, consider four hands instead of two, three eyes (Lord Shiva is imagined as having three eyes), and even a human torso with the head of an animal, for example, Varaha, Narasimha, Ganesha, etc.

From time to time, there are paintings where both the mother and her unborn child in the womb are painted together; some monstrous creature having eaten the other small life-form is also shown; or even a well painted with the water inside it. On the basis of their knowledge about the object being painted and the reality, the artist attempts to visualise things that can be seen and understood (although this includes that which cannot normally be seen with the naked eye).

Moreover, there is no end to paintings that depict the tides of imagination, daydreams, or the untamed steed of the mind. These are all things that cannot be seen with the naked eye, but even so can be imagined or 'seen' with the inner eye.

Because of all the reasons stated above, we find paintings with shapes of distorted objects in Modern Art.

Additionally, another thing that draws our attention in some such paintings, is that an object that lies behind another is also depicted fully—even if it is arranged in a manner that the object in front is blocking it. In such paintings, there is definitely an intention to show both objects in their complete, full, and original individual forms, but in doing so, the parts of both objects which block each other (overlap with each other), and the parts outside this overlap then come into existence as new shapes. This, in spite of their relationship with the original form, also gives rise to unique new forms, which in turn result in new designs as well (refer to 'Negro Boxer' in Kumar issue 428; and the painting by Pablo Picasso attached here as Illustration 8).

Now we shall look at the images given ⟨below⟩. In Illustration 1, small pieces of black paper are arranged next to each other in such a way that they give an illusion of a white line drawing. What we really see as the white line is the space between two unconnected pieces. The originally drawn (or cut-out) parts are actually black.

In Figure अ of Illustration 2, the meshed screen pattern that we see within the shape of the vessel, is also visible outside it. In other words, the vessel is drawn with black lines on a paper—the background—with such a pattern. Moreover, it looks transparent, as though made of glass. Or, as shown in Figure क, it also looks as if it is open from the middle—a shape made with thin wire through which something can be passed. In Figure ब, the form of the object becomes even more clear and evident as the pattern inside it and outside it are not the same. Such a pattern functions as a colour being filled in an image.

In अ of Illustration 3, the drawing of the table, the objects on top of it, and its

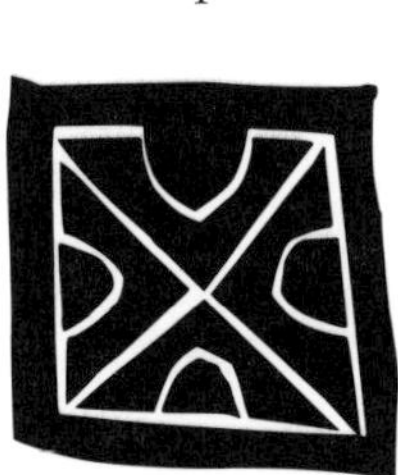

1

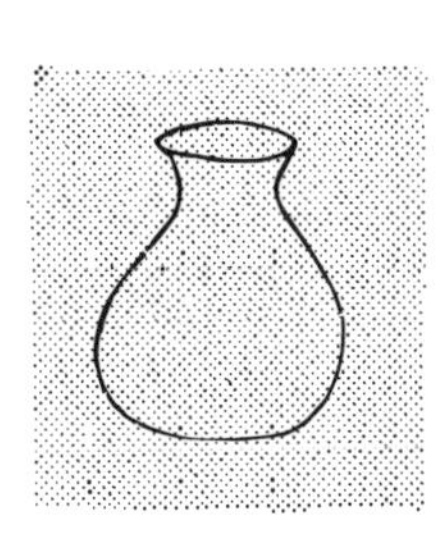

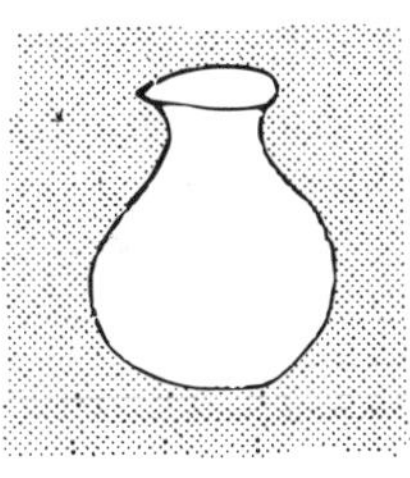

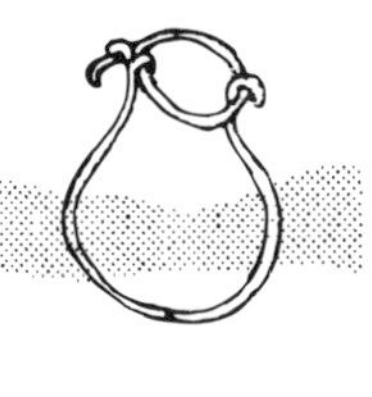

2

अ

ब

क

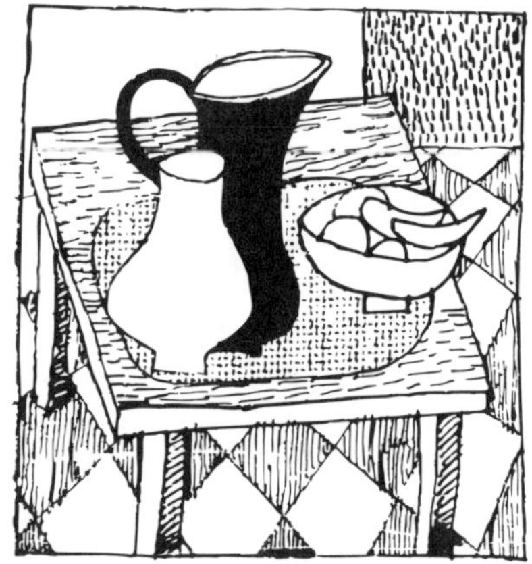

3 अ

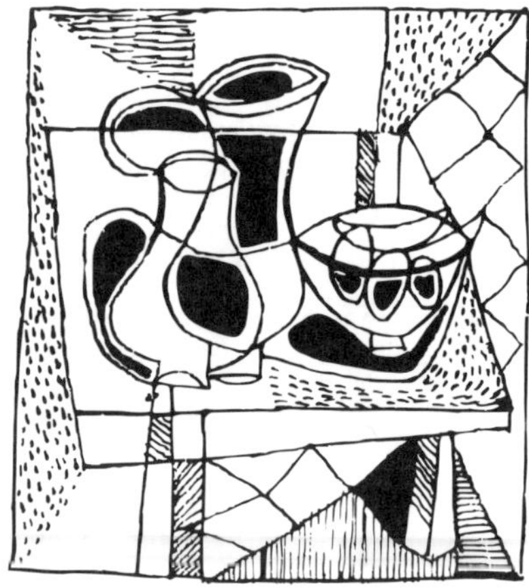

3 ब

background can be considered more realistic in comparison to ब. The black vessel with the handle is partially hidden by the vessel that appears white, and similarly it is clearly visible that the objects have been arranged in front of (and behind) each other. The design of Figure ब is very similar to that of Figure अ, but instead of the objects being hidden behind each other, all the objects at the back appear as if fully visible. Because of this, a new type of variation in shapes comes into existence. Additionally, owing to the relation of these objects with each other, one also gets an idea of the form of the original objects. Moreover, in Figure अ, the colour scheme (though here, instead of the original colours, only black has been used to symbolically indicate colour) is used in a slightly different manner; because whether the painting is a pictorial representation of the visual elements of nature, or a reflection of the artist's imagination, it holds its own individual appearance as an image. An artist's task is to design and compose all that is inside its ⟨the frame's⟩ outer boundaries (be that a square, rectangle, etc.). Here, the space occupied by the shapes is just as important as the space left outside of the shapes. Which is why the artist considers both of these while composing a painting, and it is only then that a good composition can be made.

We have seen that line is a human invention. So, for those artists who have

---

4

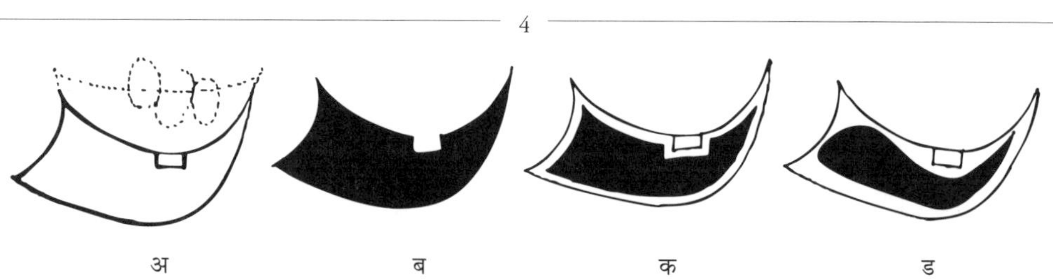

अ   ब   क   ड

faith in this opinion, or for those who can feel the beauty of line, it is natural to want the significance of lines to be preserved. In Illustration 4, a part from ब of Illustration 3 itself is drawn enlarged. In this, the shape drawn with lines in Figure अ is seen, and so are its lines. In Figure ब the shape remains exactly the same, but the line is not visible. For this reason, in Figure क a solution is sought to show line, shape, and colour at the same time. But here arises the dilemma of monotony. The shape made with line and the shape made with colour both seem the same (except for a difference in size). The white space between the line outside and the black shape inside (which somewhat resembles a thick white line) also seems uniform and runs parallely. Additionally, the original shape has many sharp corners, which hurts and unsettles the eye, and even appears twice (doubled) in

क. However in Figure ड, there has been an attempt to solve all these problems at once: the black shape inside this appears 'softer' than the black shape inside Figure क. In the same way, the shape inside takes up more space compared to the line outside it, which is why it catches one's attention more. Owing to this, the shape outside (that looks 'odd' to the eye) appears to be hidden. To make a painting more eye-catching, this method and technique has been used—and continues to be used—by many painters. Alongside, a few more examples of this have been printed. However it must be noted that one must not make the mistake of assuming that this ⟨the above mentioned technique⟩ is all that they have.

Illustrations 5 to 7 are line drawings made from a range of sculptures, but the intent of distortion here has not changed.

5

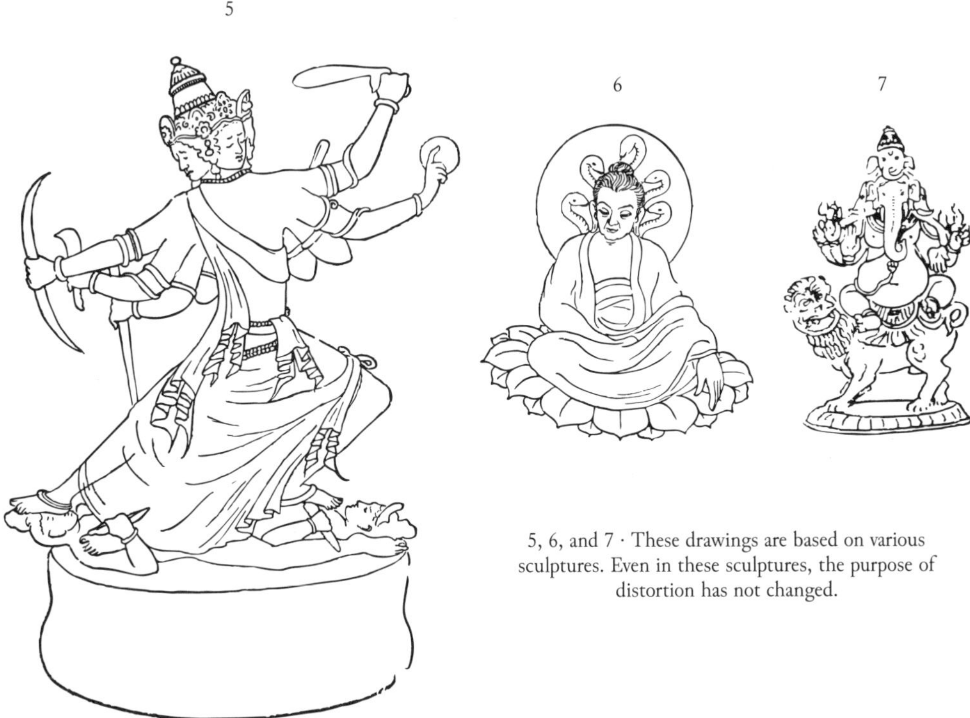

6

7

5, 6, and 7 · These drawings are based on various sculptures. Even in these sculptures, the purpose of distortion has not changed.

8

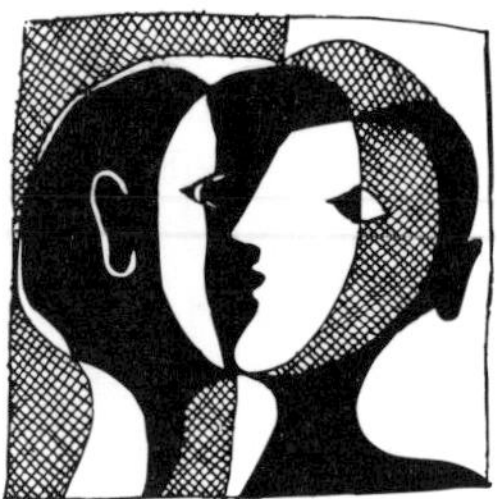

A drawing by ⟨Pablo⟩ Picasso

9

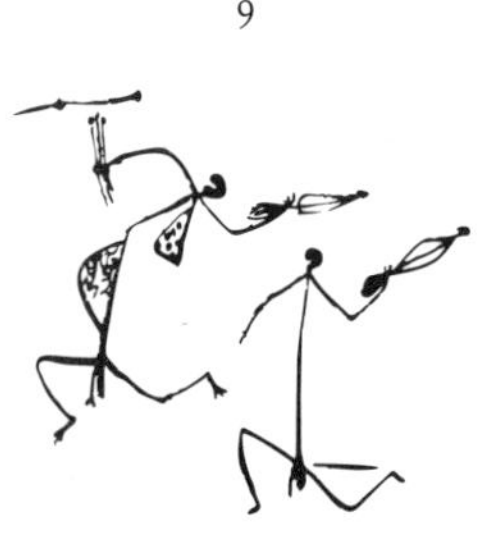

A drawing by Australian
Aboriginals

10

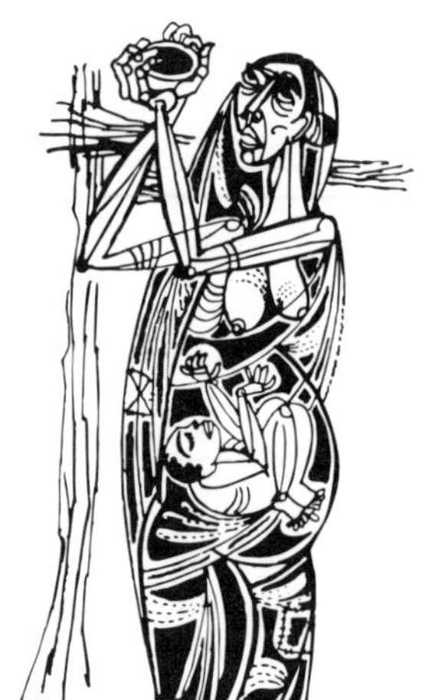

An artist is affected by all the
worldly forces of society, and
their reaction finds expression
in their art in the form of
lines, shapes, and designs.
To understand the reaction
experienced by the artist in this
painting (Illustration 10), read
this article.

Illustration 8 is a drawing by Picasso. Illustration 9 is a line drawing done by Australian Aboriginals. Here an Aboriginal person is shown chasing a ghost, and the spear thrown by this person seems to have missed its target. Also, there are people or children shown in the belly of the running ghost, which it would have devoured.

Illustration 10: I once heard a voice on the street—"O Bapa! At least show some mercy to the child in my belly!" This is the root of this drawing's inspiration. It is difficult to deduce the impact such a drawing will have on a viewer's mind. They may think that this is a red flag shown against the community of beggars, or a sarcastic comment on the evil practice of begging that passes down through generations; some may also possibly assume that there is a hidden intention of political propaganda or partisan support; some others may also think that this artist is an absolutely faithless cynic, one who has only seen the dark side of society and thus believes all of society (or the world) to be evil and difficult to digest.

Whether any of these reasons apply or not is not important. The artist exists within this society and is bound to be impacted by both the positive and negative aspects of worldly forces; and hence it is also understandable that it is impossible for these resultant reactions to not be seen in their art. And yet, for this, an artist uses only lines, shapes, and their designs—just as we have seen and understood before. One more thing has been added: how halos behind gods and goddesses, or a parasol above a king, adds more meaning and importance ⟨to those figures⟩, in the same way the black shapes used in this drawing—the face, hand, breast, and the child in the belly—are all helpful in the subject's clear depiction.

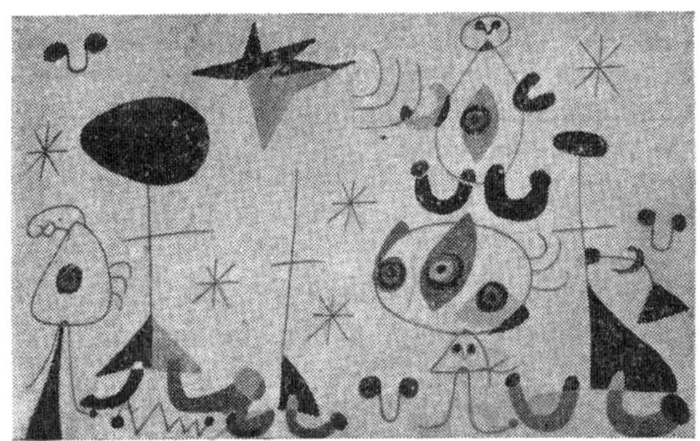

'Snob Party at the Princess's' · Artist: ⟨Joan⟩ Miró

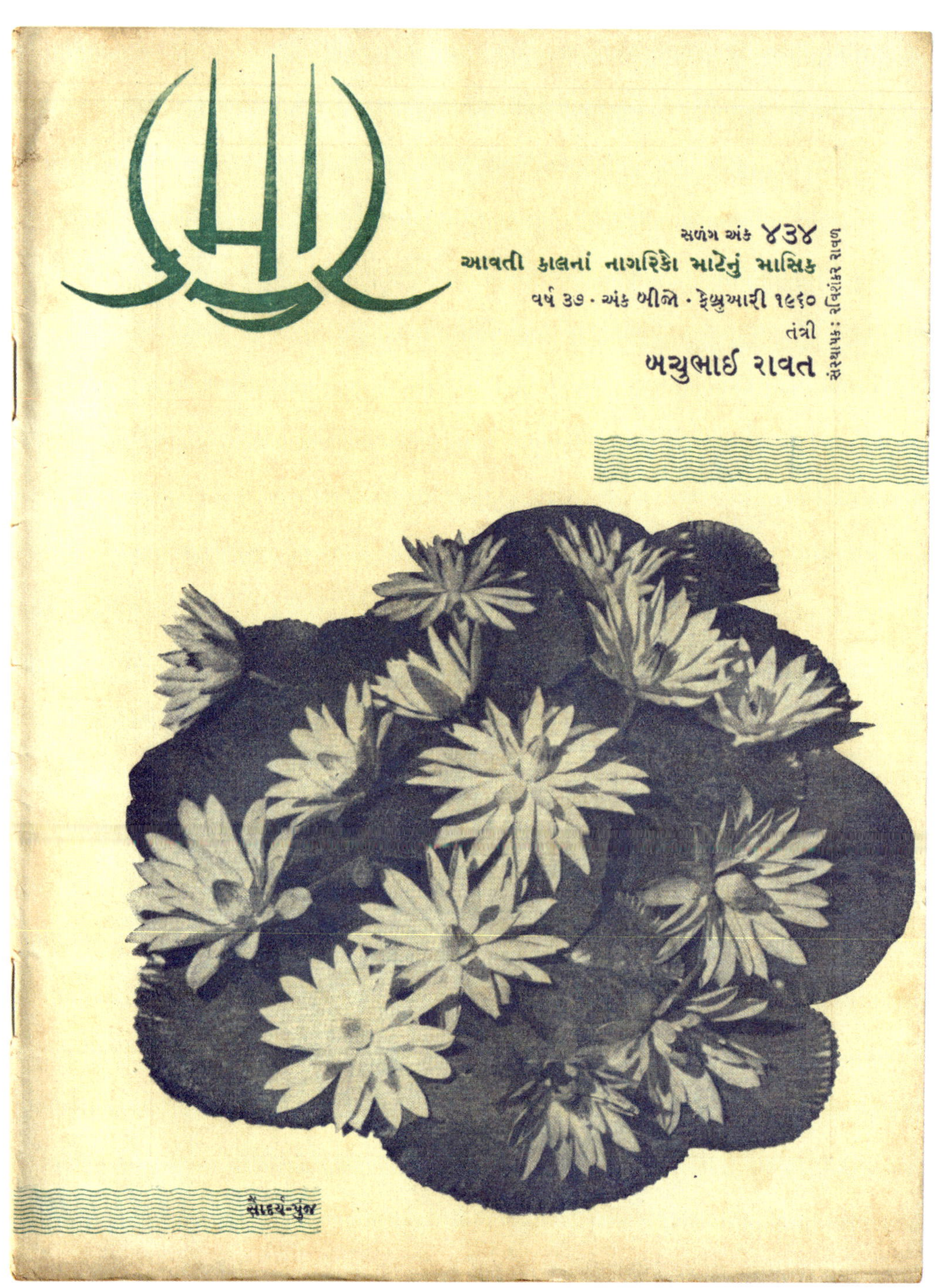

સળંગ અંક ૪૩૪
આવતી કાલનાં નાગરિકો માટેનું માસિક
વર્ષ ૩૭ · અંક બીજો · ફેબ્રુઆરી ૧૯૬૦
તંત્રી
બચુભાઈ રાવત

EXPLAINING THE REASONS FOR
DISTORTION IN ART

Jyoti Bhatt
shares well-researched information on an
important element of art—the 'symbol'

So far, we have seen that the distortion we either fail to understand or find ugly at first glance, is not only found in Modern Art, but has been taking place in art from prehistoric times up until today, every step of the way.

The 'symbol' is a significant element in art. One does not necessarily have to explain what a symbol is. Not only objects, forms, or shapes, but many a time even colours have been used as symbols in painting. For instance, while Krishna is painted blue ⟨નીલા, વાદળી⟩, skin of such a colour is never actually seen (except in the case of unusual lighting), and yet that colour helps us in identifying Krishna—something that the artist bears in mind while composing all the other colours (see the image printed in colour in this issue ⟨overleaf⟩). The colour of the skin of evil, cunning, and harmless people do not in actuality differ based on their countenance, yet ⟨for example⟩ in Kathakali, just as a dancer paints their face with different colours (such as green, black, and white) to depict the nature of the character they're playing, similarly at Ajanta, the paintings also employ different colours to depict distinct temperaments and classes of people, like green (for non-Aryans[15], demons, etc.), dusky, or fair. (Fairer tones to be used for gods, *yakshas*, and *apsaras*[16]; whiter tones for the oceans, the Himalayas, and the Ganges; and darker tones for Vasuki[17], demons, and monsters, etc. have been prescribed in Bharata's Natyashastra[18]. Even in the Vishnudharmottara Purana[19], detailing our ancient scriptures on painting, there are directives on the usage of colour for people from different regions, and similarly how *chandragaur* ⟨as fair as the moon⟩,

---

15 — Here, the word 'Aryan' implies 'civilised' or 'refined', and the word 'non-Aryan' implies 'outsiders'. It is an ethnocultural, self-designated word used by the early Indo-Iranians. In the historiography of the Indian context, 'non-Aryan' is understood as the 'Dravidian' civilisation, that largely consists of people now living in the southern part of the country.

16 — *Yakshas* and *apsaras* are celestial beings that appear in Indic mythology. *Yakshas* are often referred to as guardians of nature, while *apsaras* are nymphs of unsurpassable beauty, skilled in the arts of dance and music.

17 — A serpent king in Hinduism and Buddhism.

18 — A detailed treatise and handbook on dramatic art written between the 1st and 3rd century BCE, that deals with classical theatre, including music, dance, poetics, and aesthetics.

19 — A Hindu text which is encyclopaedic in nature (assumed to date back to the 7th century CE), the Vishnudharmottara Purana deals with subjects ranging from cosmology and genealogy, to medicine, politics, and food. Divided into three parts, the third deals specifically with image making, music, language, and other creative practices.

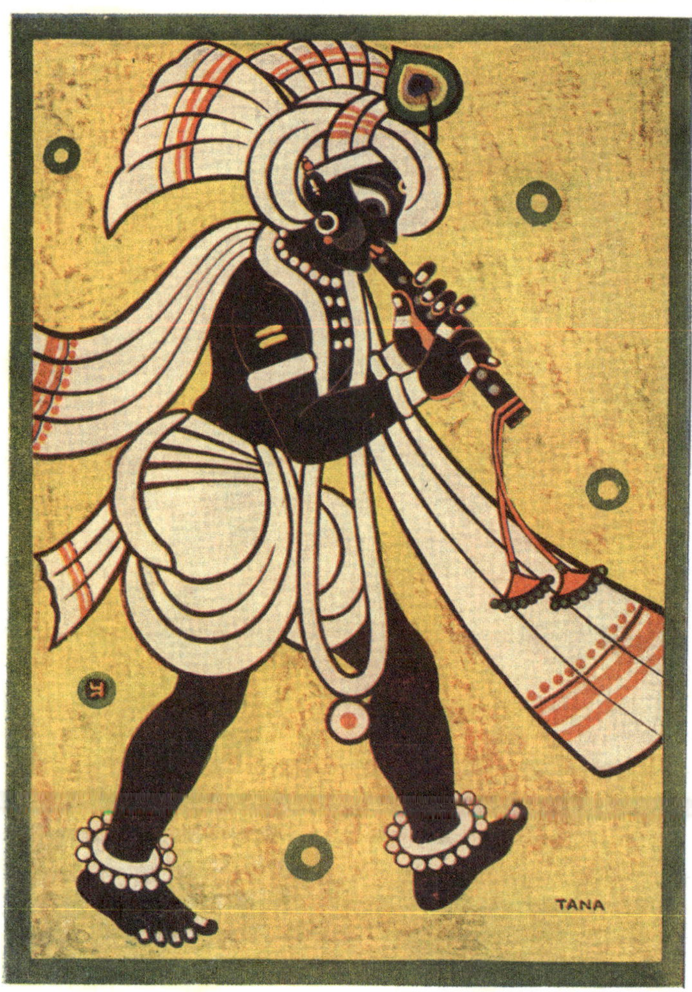

'Murlidhar' ⟨Flute Player⟩ · Artist: Pradyumna Tanna
⟨Published in Kumar #434 · February 1960⟩

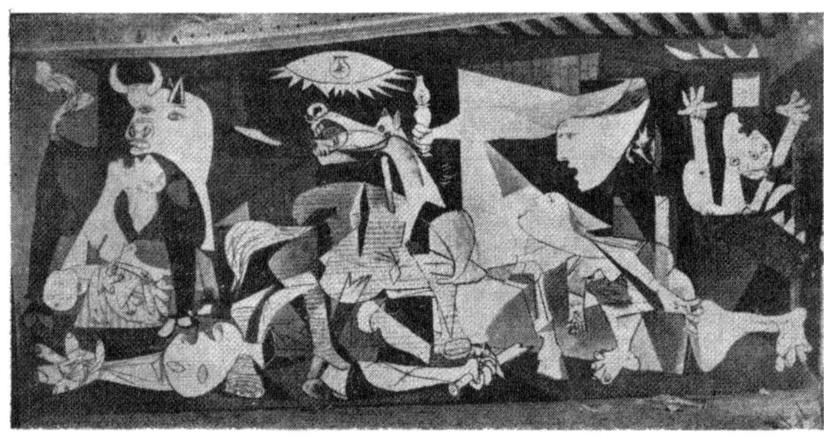

'Guernica' · In this huge painting by ⟨Pablo⟩ Picasso based on his internal pain emerging from anarchy created by the war on his motherland, the colours are used by him as symbols of post-war depression, pain, suffering, and hardship.

padmagaur ⟨as fair as a lotus⟩, *aapandur* ⟨as colourless as Pandu[20]⟩ or pale complexion, and *shyam* ⟨dark⟩ complexion should be used for *brahmins, kshatriyas, vaishyas*, and *shudras*, respectively.) In the Kathakali dance form, a green-coloured face is used to portray Arjuna, Krishna, Nala, and such characters of divine nature. But if a red shape—like a moustache—is painted on that green, then that character is antagonistic (characters of aristocratic nature like Duryodhana, Ravana, Jarasandha, etc.).

A white beard for monkeys and Hanuman, but a black beard for forest-dwellers and hunters—even for Shiva in the *kirata* form[21]. But when the beard is red, it represents a monstrous character, demon, etc.

No matter who may have decided these colour-symbols, once they have been decided and accepted by the public, they come to be used only through this connotation, where the symbols become a chain linking the inner feelings of the painter with that of the viewer. In today's times, the colour sky blue ⟨આસમાની⟩ is considered as a symbol of the distressed classes of society, and colours like deep-almond ⟨ઘેરો બદામી⟩, brown ⟨તપખીરી⟩, ash ⟨રાખોડી⟩, or grey ⟨મુંજડો⟩, etc. are seen in modern paintings as symbols of emotions such as sorrow, despair, or sentimentality. In the paintings created by the artist Picasso in the period between 1901 and 1905, the colour blue has been prominent and it has been used as a symbol for society in distress. This period of his works is known as the 'Blue Period'. Similarly, he has used colours as symbols in his painting titled 'Guernica' (Guernica is the name of the place that was ravaged during the First World War). Painted in 1937, this massive painting of approximately 14 x 31 feet can be considered different in its style (cubistic) from the 'Blue Period', but the colours used—black, grey, muddy brown ⟨ભૂખરો⟩, and light dull blue[22]—are very

20 — The father of the Pandavas, identified as having pale and colourless skin.

21 — A Shaivite iconography where Shiva takes the form of a hunter.

22 — While the description here is of the painting (which is painted in monochromatic greys), it is possible that the colours spoken of are based on the Guernica tapestry (commissioned by Nelson A. Rockefeller) which was also on display in New York at the time of Bhatt's visit in 1961.

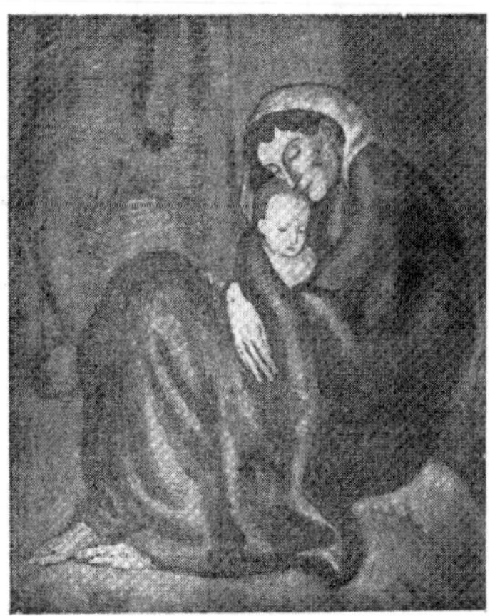

A painting from the artist ⟨Pablo⟩ Picasso's 'Blue Period'. The colour blue is considered as a symbol for the distressed class of the society. This colour has been prominently used by Picasso in the renderings of distressed society created during this period.

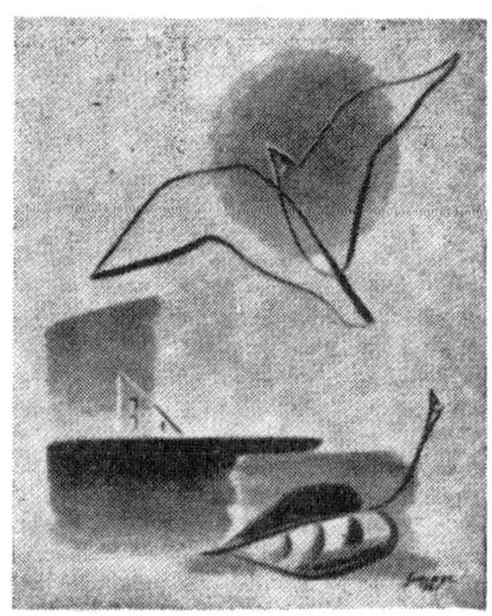

'Landscape' · Artist: ⟨Leopold⟩ Survage · Here the artist has used all objects as mere symbols.

successful in representing despair, suffering, torture, and hardship after the war. In this too, the colours have been used as symbols, and as the colours do not resemble the reality of everyday objects, this representation can be seen as distorted. However, there have been strong reasons behind such distortions. To believe that this is the result of the many untamed horses of the mind or of insanity would be hasty.

Due to printing and monetary limitations, it has not been possible to publish these paintings in their original colours or in multicolour, but from such experiments ⟨of using colours as symbols⟩ one gets to see that colours truly have the ability to evoke different emotions.

At different times, symbols and their meanings change too. Colours have been used as symbols in our Western Indian (Rajput) paintings as well. In a single painting, a house would be shown, along with what is happening both inside and outside it. Just the exterior shape of the house can be shown for such a depiction—avoiding all details like the façade, doors, windows—and to emphasise

the view inside the house, red would be used as a background for the human figures. Moreover, if one had to suggest the presence of both Radha and Krishna in the painting, as well as the many miles of separation between them, representing such distance in the painting literally is not possible; which is why, as a symbol to indicate them being in separate places, the trees and plants, as well as the backgrounds, are coloured differently— and hence what needs to be understood gets communicated. See the painting 'Krishna-Radha' on the first colour printed page of Kumar issue 307 ⟨July 1949⟩. Even if the distance between them is comparatively less than the height of their own bodies, we still have to believe they are very far from one another, and that they are suffering in bereavement because they cannot see each other. If one refuses to believe it, then one cannot be compelled to believe this forcefully or unwillingly, but only when we see the symbols and colours in the manner that the artist themselves have used, can we appreciate and take joy in the painting and experience its essence. On the theatre stage, in order

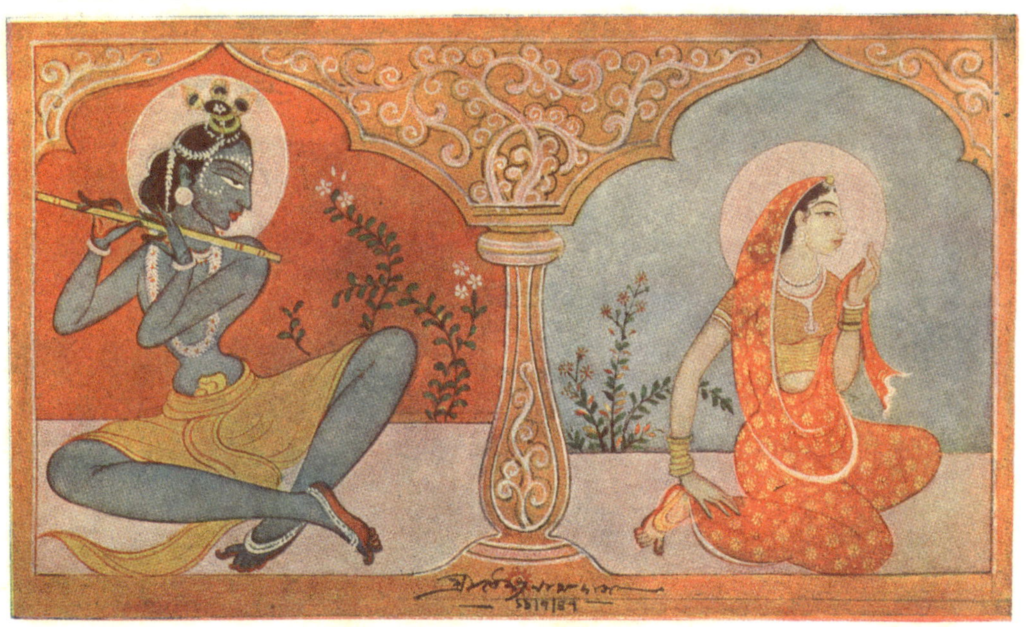

'Krishna-Radha' · Artist: Vaidhyanath Das

⟨Published in Kumar #307 · July 1949⟩

to portray that the performer is thinking of something, a monologue is performed. At that time they speak at such a high volume that even the audience sitting in the last row can hear them; however, in that moment, they themselves move a bit to the side, or the performer standing besides them moves just a little further away, and behaves (performs) as if they cannot hear the one who is speaking at all! And in spite of all this not being realistic and physically feasible, we are forced to believe that the voice we hear is in fact the thoughts of the first performer, while the person next to them is completely unaware of it.

Just as colour is used as a symbol to denote different locations and different feelings (joy, sorrow, etc.), in the same way it is used for time as well. When the sky is depicted absolutely black we understand that the incident in the painting is taking place at night. But painting every detail as it is seen in the darkness of night was not considered necessary by the painters of our country. People, their clothes and belongings, trees and plants, fruits and flowers, roads, etc., would be shown and painted as seen on a bright day, because the fact that it is night has already been established through the colour black. In this case, is it essential that just because we cannot see anything in the dark, we insist that it shouldn't be painted either? In some paintings, a small lamp would be shown burning, because that too can be helpful in showing the time (night); but they did not make an effort to show how the objects or humans all around look when they are lit by the light of the lamp (although there exist some examples of Indian paintings which are comparatively realistic and depict this kind of light-compositions as well). Owing to this, a viewer is sometimes confused—often has a

doubt—whether all this is the result of the artist's incompetence or lack of knowledge! But after one knows and understands the intention behind such a painting, one will be better able to enjoy other such works of art. Then such paintings that seemed like mere illustrations ⟨પ્રસંગચિત્રો⟩ will begin to seem poetic. Yes! In the beginning, one will definitely have to make an effort to decode the poem.

As *time* is the topic of discussion, let us also look at other symbols used to depict it. To show night, the moon (a full moon or the waxing moon on *beej*[23]), an owl, a lamp, etc., are used; for the start of the day, a rooster crowing at a height; and for daytime, the sun, etc. Also, to depict different seasons, symbols like peafowl, clouds, and bolts of lightning (for the month of monsoon, *ashaadh*[24]), a bonfire (for the chilling cold of the winters), a hand fan, garden, fountain, terrace, etc., (for the summer) are used. Although these are quite simple and easily understood, when they are used as symbols they need to be represented in a way that they are clearly visible, and so their proportions in comparison to other objects also need to be altered—and has been. The same is seen in the case of colours as well. In a painting of Govardhan Girdhari Krishna ⟨Krishna carrying the Mount Govardhan⟩, it is not possible to show the mountain enlarged, and it is also not possible to depict Krishna as small as he should be in comparison to the mountain; then how should this be shown?

These are but only paintings—not photographs that document the original scene as it is (or paintings with similar intents). That is why paintings have been, and continue to be, made using distortion, often at the cost of actual proportions. The painter definitely works toward ensuring that

---

23 — *'Beej'*, also referred to as *'dooj'* or *'dwitiya'*, is the second day in the lunar fortnight of the Hindu calendar.

24 — The month in the Hindu calendar that corresponds to the start of monsoon.

the painting looks beautiful when just viewed as a painting, but often their intent is also to have us recall the original incident. We would have definitely read or heard of these incidents (still in the context of 'Govardhan Girdhari' 〈Krishna〉) in elaborate detail, and since we are already aware of the size of the mountain and Indra's anger, we are reminded of all that while viewing the painting. To indicate that the Govardhan mountain is large, as symbols, forests, giant beasts, and sages performing penance are also shown on it; but even in this there is evidently a 'folly' in proportions! As the shapes (animal, bird, tree, etc.) are rendered large enough to include sufficient detail, the viewer can easily view, and upon viewing identify and understand. And yet, the painter is definitely mindful of how large the Govardhan mountain should be in accordance with the proportion of the painting and in what way it should be arranged to look good. Likewise, on that mountain—within its shape—where the trees and animals should be painted and how large they should be (as per the 'design') is also carefully considered. To further understand the thoughts above, let us look at a few examples.

DESCRIPTION OF ILLUSTRATIONS

In Illustration 1 and Illustration 2, a moon and sun have been drawn. In these, their outer circular shape is most definitely related to their original shape (the shape as seen from Earth, without the help of a telescope); additionally, there is also the shape of a crescent in the moon. But the deer inside the moon or the human-like face that has been given to the sun—with a moustache, etc.—is merely imagination. However, today they have become common shapes and symbols. When we see such a sun, a human face devoid of a body, with locks and waves of hair, is not what comes to mind.

In Illustration 3, three trees as seen in small paintings (miniatures) from Jain

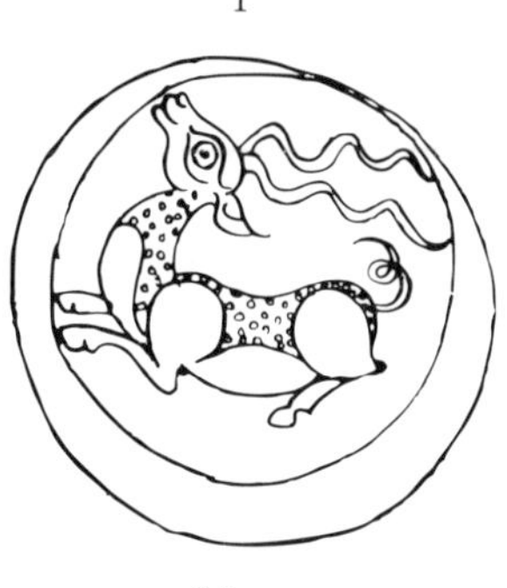

1

Moon

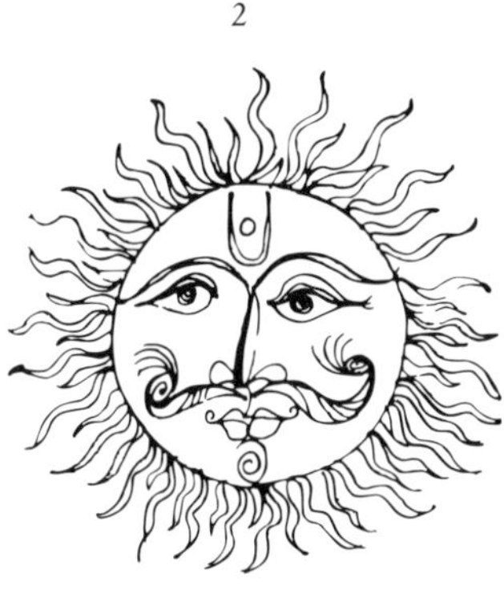

2

Sun

manuscripts have been shown. Behind the depiction of trees like these in the painting, there is definitely the intention of presenting a pleasing and eye-catching design; but along with this the trees are also used as symbols to show forests, parks, or orchards. Moreover, the artist has not attempted to show what trees these are; but the painted branches, leaves, and flowers act as symbols to further emphasise that this *is* a tree. The parrot seated on the right side is much larger than it should be in comparison to the tree, but here as well the bird remains one of the many symbols to represent the tree as a tree. This method of using such kinds of birds and leaves as symbols to represent a tree can be seen in the artworks of modern artists as well (see

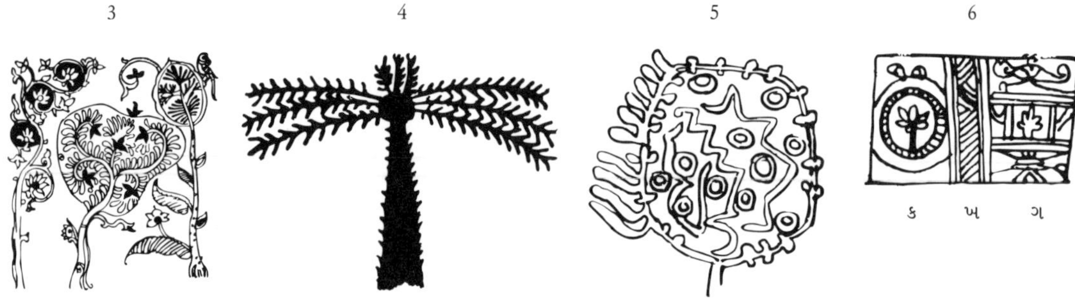

4 and 5 are both from ⟨Pablo⟩ Picasso's works

the image 'Landscape' by ⟨Leopold⟩ Survage, shown ⟨on page 90 in this book⟩).

Illustration 4 and 5 are two trees from ⟨Pablo⟩ Picasso's drawings: In these the first is a palm, and the second tree is from his symbolic painting, 'Peace'.

Illustration 6: It is said in Jain religious texts that "when Shraman Bhagwan Mahavira entered Devananda Brahmani's womb from *devlok* (the heavenly realm)... that night Devananda saw fourteen *mahaswapnas*[25] (great and auspicious dreams)". There are many visualisations of those fourteen dreams in Jain paintings, out of which three have been presented here. Visions seen in the dreams were mere symbols of other elements and emotions. Moreover, the forms used in these paintings to represent the visions from the dreams are symbols as well.

The descriptions found of those dreams are so— "Padmasarovar (ऽ in the Illustration): They saw the Padmasarovar (celestial lotus pond) as the tenth dream. The entire lake was filled with lotuses and aquatic fauna of several varieties and colours... The lake is an indicator of sanctity."

"Ksheerasamudra (ખ in the Illustration): Ksheerasamudra (ocean of milk) was seen by them as the eleventh dream. The brightness of the center of that ocean is comparable to that of the brightness of the rays of the moon. Its unfathomable waters were expanding in all directions."

"Devavimana (ગ in the Illustration): The twelfth dream was of a thousand and eight pillars from which hung garlands of heavenly flowers, atop which were inscribed fascinating images of wolves, oxen, horses, humans, birds, elephants, branches of the ashoka tree, and lotus stems; from within this emanated songs sung in melodious notes as well as sounds of instruments which spread a sense of contentment all around."

Now, how can the helpless artist accommodate all this in such a small space? (Even just this written description has occupied so much space!) Hence, the artist has used a circle as a symbol for the lake, and within it a single lotus has been painted as a symbol to represent the Padmasarovar. Here the intention is only to remind followers of the Jain religion of the fourteen auspicious dreams, and that seems to have been achieved.

Illustration 7: Here the image is divided into two registers. The upper register represents the ocean (the fish symbolises the ocean) and there is also a ship (that is symbolised by a mast, waving sail, and ropes).

---

25 — Mahavira, the 32nd Tirthankara of the Jain religious order (also called the Shraman Bhagwan), was a divine being who took form as a human in the mortal world. The birth of all *Mahapurushas* (Great Beings), as with Mahavira, is heralded by the appearance of fourteen auspicious visions (*mahaswapnas*) dreamt by the mother.

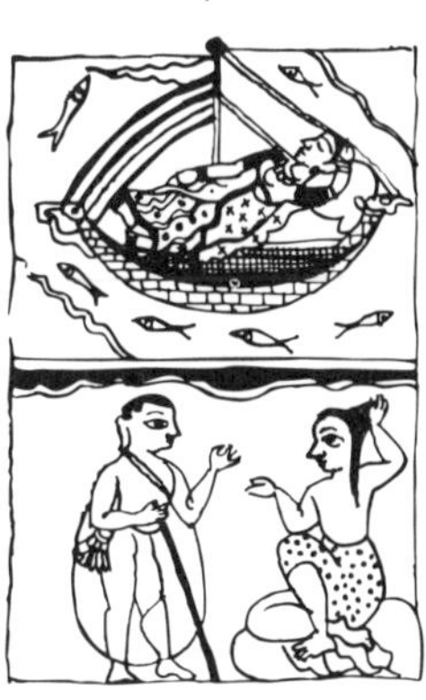

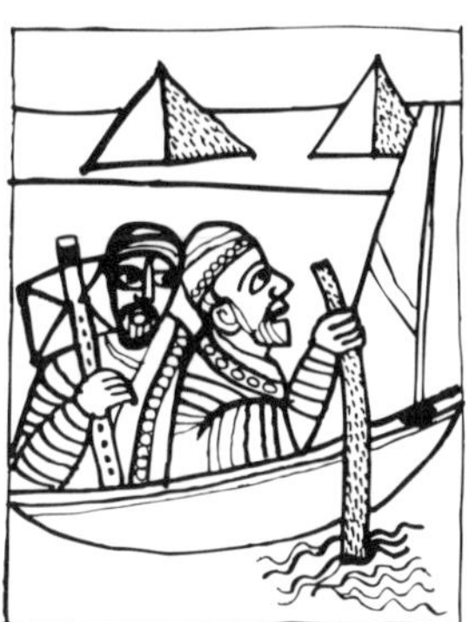

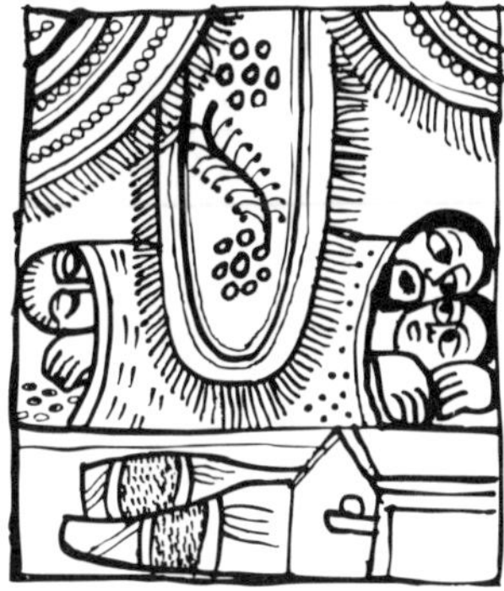

Two events from Jain religious scriptures have been shown in a single image.

Ethiopian Art

A woman is sleeping inside the ship. After reading all of this, one cannot still have questions such as: "How is it possible to see a whole ship even while it floats in the ocean?", "How can there be fish in the sky on all four sides of a ship?", and "How can the body of a woman cover the entire length of a ship?" This painting also represents a story from the Jain religion. The complete story is as follows:

Palit ⟨a character from Jain literature⟩ is seen here returning home by ship with his wife. It was upon this homeward journey that a child was born to them. The child was named Samudrapal, as he was born at sea (*samudra*). Growing up, Samudrapal turned out to be a fine young man. One day, upon seeing a thief being publicly shamed and paraded around the streets, he enters a state of introspection and becomes conscious of desire and materialism. Influenced by true abstinence, he detaches himself from worldly pleasures and becomes a hermit.

The woman seen sleeping in the ship is Palit's wife, and this scene in the upper register symbolises the birth of Samudrapal. Consequently, the lower register of the image refers to the part of the story where Samudrapal abandons worldly pleasures; pulling out locks of his hair, he is shown accepting monkhood in the presence of a hermit standing nearby. (This tale and the images are taken from the Jain Kalpadruma.[26])

Illustration 8 and 9 are both from a series of paintings from Ethiopia, depicting historical incidents. Made in the nineteenth century, these paintings depict foundation stories from the fourteenth century Bible. In the first image (Illustration 8) they have depicted two people seated, travelling in a ship. Similar to the ship shown in Illustration 7, its entire bottom-half is depicted, and additionally the people seated inside are so large that it cannot be discerned how their lower-half fits inside the ship. However the only intention here has been to depict an incident where some people are travelling along the Nile to reach Ethiopia. In this image it has been very clearly depicted as to how people seated inside the ship look from the outside, and how much of them will be visible. The ship, apart from being a symbol of their travel, is also a symbol of their migration ⟨હિજરત⟩; and

26 — A collection of Jain literature and stories.

10

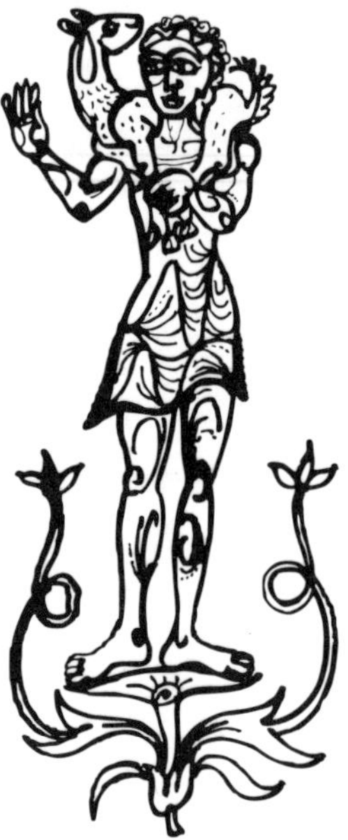

'Good Shepherd'

11

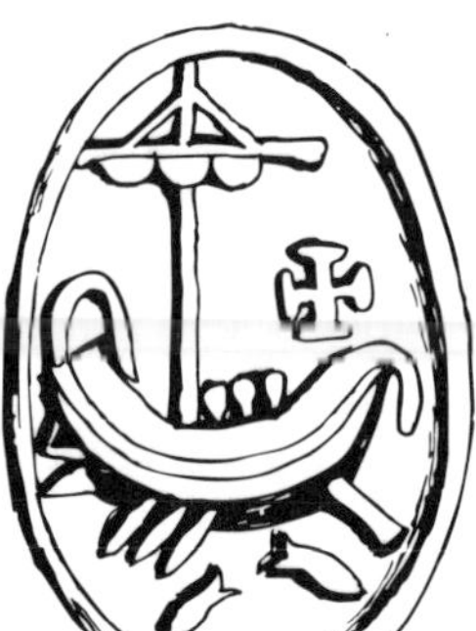

A symbol for Jesus Christ

12

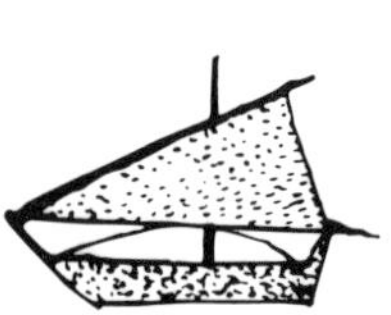

A ship as symbol by
⟨Pablo⟩ Picasso

a sail is depicted to show that it is a large ship, and not a boat. Moreover, to establish that the river is Nile and the place behind it is Egypt, two pyramids have been depicted as well. In other images from this series, a gathering of people is drawn in a ship of the same size, in which small faces and shoulders can be seen in the front, and in all the rows behind only face after face is seen.

The image beside it (Illustration 9) is not a drawing of a person with two faces and a person with a face in place of their legs, but instead shows what is happening in two places at once; and that is why the left and right of the image is separated by a curtain down the middle. In another drawing from the same series, the person sleeping on the left side in Illustration 9 takes the place of the person sleeping on the right, the person on the right is shown sleeping on the ground, and then the curtain in the middle is removed.

Illustration 10 shows a young man (without a beard or moustache) drawn standing with a goat on his shoulders as the 'good shepherd'—a symbol of Jesus Christ. Early Christian Art did not represent Jesus in the same way as is done today. Closer to home as well, in early Buddhist art, the Buddha was represented through symbols such as the *peepal* ⟨sacred fig⟩, *dharmachakra* ⟨Wheel of Dharma⟩, etc. In the Bible there appears the story of a shepherd who had rescued goats. Jesus too, saved the lives of humans who lived their life like herds of sheep and goats—rescuing them from an abyss—and this symbol would have originated from such a comparison.

Illustration 11 is also an example of the same Christian Art. Here too, as we have seen earlier, sails and poles have been used to represent the ship, and as the ship is in water, two fish have been shown frolicking to reiterate the water. All these symbols establish that this is a ship, but the fact that the ship here has been shown as a symbol of Jesus can

13

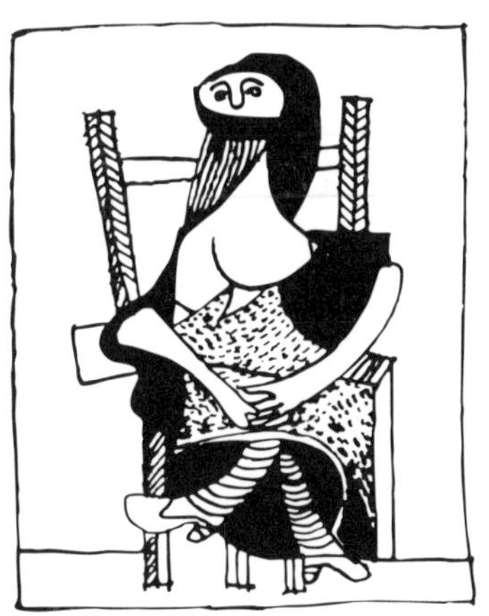

'Seated Woman' · This is a drawing
of a painting by ⟨Pablo⟩ Picasso. The
various body parts are mere symbols of
that woman.

14

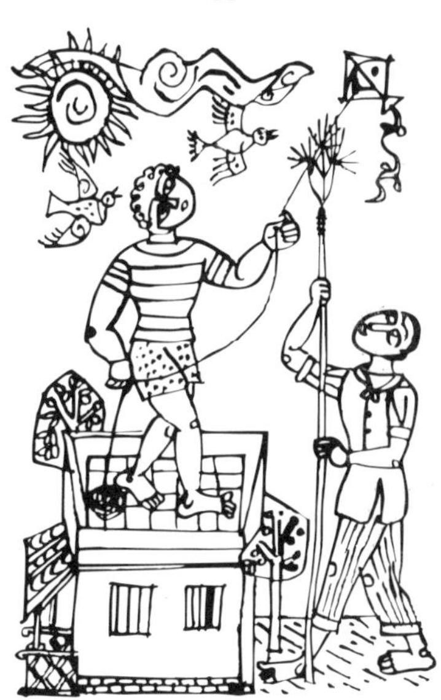

be understood by the cross placed beside it.
Just like in our part of the world there are
notions of the god that ferries one across the
time of life which is comparable to an ocean
⟨ભવસાગર⟩, similarly, I feel that this ⟨image⟩
too may be connected to some such belief.

Illustration 12: Here too is a tale about
a ship. The sail and mast in this image, taken
from a painting by Picasso, are both similar
to what we have seen before. But to show the
seashore in that painting, this ship is painted
as a symbol, representing the background
space as the tempestuous ocean.

Our original discussion has been on
distortion. Here, the effort or intention is not
to depict what the ship looks like (whether
it be a *kotiyo* or a *baglo*[27]), but to show
other aspects—the ocean, water, migration,
etc.—through the ship. And this is why the
distorted ship, its distorted proportions in
relation to other objects, and its incomplete
details, etc. can be seen.

Illustration 13: This is a line drawing
made from Picasso's painting titled, 'Seated
Woman'. In actuality, this painting doesn't
get counted as a symbolic painting, but if
we consider the body parts seen in it only
as symbols used to depict a woman, then it
is understood why Picasso has called this
painting 'Seated Woman'.

In Illustration 14, symbols have been
used even in this line drawing of the painting
titled, 'Patang' ⟨Kite⟩ (1952), done by the
writer of this article (Jyoti Bhatt). At the
risk of being repetitive, let me remind you,
that here, as explained in the previous issues
(432 and 433 ⟨December 1959 and January
1960⟩) of Kumar, the intention has been to
depict the characteristics of an object clearly,
through distortion. Additionally, shapes seen
from more than one vantage point are shown
together as one object. All of these are clearly
seen in lesser or greater degree in every image
shown with this ⟨article⟩.

27 — *Kotiyo* and *baglo* are Gujarati names for types of Arabian sailboats built in Gujarat. *Baglo* specifically refers to the
bagla, a type of Arabian *dhow* boat.

15

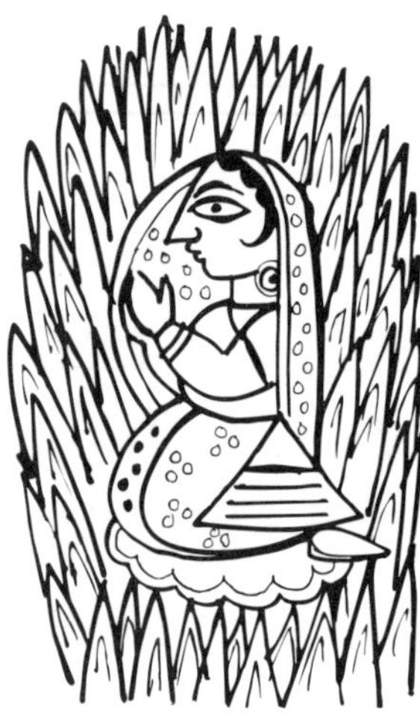

16

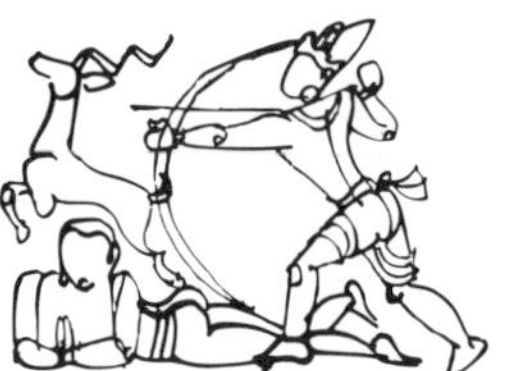

Drawing of a sculpture from Pattadakal, 'The Killing of Maarich'.

17

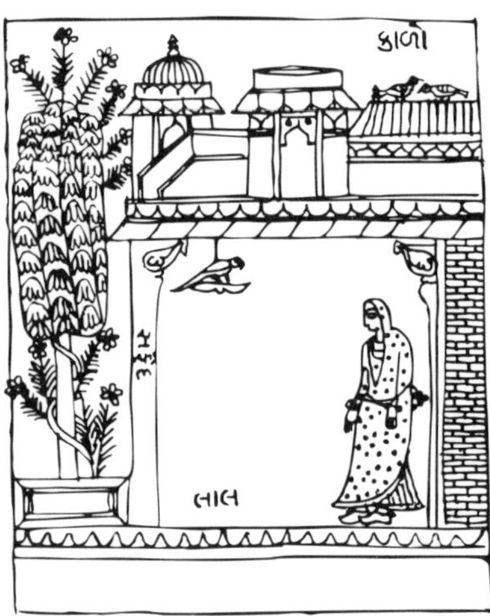

⟨Within the illustration, Bhatt has penned down the names of colours to help with visualisation. In the sky he writes '*kado*' (black), '*safed*' (white) in the pillar, and '*lal*' (red) in the interior of the house.⟩

Illustration 15: A line drawing from a part of Shri Jamini Roy's painting titled 'Sita no Agnipravesh'. Here, as we have seen earlier (like the sailing ship shown in its entirety), Sita is depicted whole in the fire, not even slightly hidden or cut off by the flames. Whether in reality the flames of the fire are of this shape or not, in this painting they are undoubtedly recognisable as fire, as they have been rendered with a flaming red (which can be called a symbol in itself) like the eruption of a flame.

Whether in Satyug (the epoch of Sita), women draped their *sarees* in this way or not, or if there was a custom of veiling their heads or not, is not something the artist has made an effort to talk about. Here, the artist has used symbols that are resultant of the effects of the epoch that *he* lives in. The presence of the *saree* is only to denote that the painted figure is a woman. The covered head depicts Sita's character—modesty, courteousness, and politeness—which becomes an easy symbol for viewers of today's time to understand. In the original painting, Rama, Lakshmana, and the sages, have all been painted around the fire.

Illustration 16: This line drawing made from the Pattadakal temples found in South India, depicts the incident of Rama and Maarich (the Golden Deer).

Illustration 17: In this Rajasthani style painting from the 17th century, the parrot is warning the heroine ⟨નાયિકા⟩ that if it is not fed good food, it will disclose her secret love-affairs! Since the parrot and the woman are the only two important characters here, other details of objects in the room inside the house have not been depicted and the background is painted red. The outside and the upper part of the same house have been painted with details. The background of the house is painted completely black. The black of the outside and the red of the inside show that this is happening at night. However, the colour of the house is absolutely white and the colours of flowers and leaves—green, red, white, etc.—are depicted as clearly as if seen during the day. Moreover, the tree outside and its black background represent the inner and the outer parts of the image clearly.

Illustration 18: A part of Picasso's painting titled 'Guernica': Here a roaring bull has been used as a symbol of war and its destruction, and to represent the suppressed and suffering humans who are the victims of war, a mother and child have been painted between its legs. These symbols can be easily recognised and understood, and likewise, the comparison of the symbols with the nature and characteristics of the original ⟨situation⟩ (the comparison of war with the strength of the bull to destroy and crush things) is also understandable.

However in Illustrations 19 and 20, there aren't such recognisable symbols. Illustration 19 is a part taken from Picasso's painting titled 'War'. In this, nothing can be recognised. These are 'abstract', non-figurative shapes. However the comparison of war to clutter and confusion, and disgusting pests like scorpions, centipedes, and cockroaches, has been successful in evoking (in the original painting) the impact of war. The colours too play a crucial role.

Whereas Illustration 20 is a detail taken from a painting titled 'Peace', that was made alongside 'War'. Even in this, the shapes are not recognisable (perhaps it is a familiar symbol in Europe, or it bears some relation to their religious scriptures—we are unaware; but for us it remains abstract). Yet, these shapes and their colours, their organised composition, shapes being repeated at regular intervals, etc., all together play a very important role in creating a spirit of peace, order, discipline, and enthusiasm. (Illustration 5 which has appeared earlier ⟨in this article⟩ is also a part of this painting titled 'Peace'.)

18

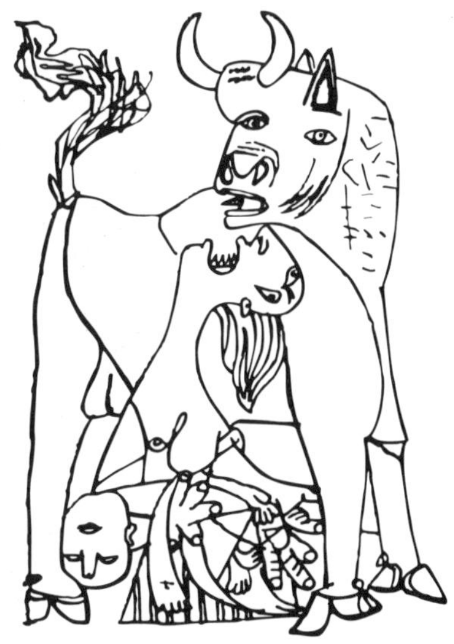

19

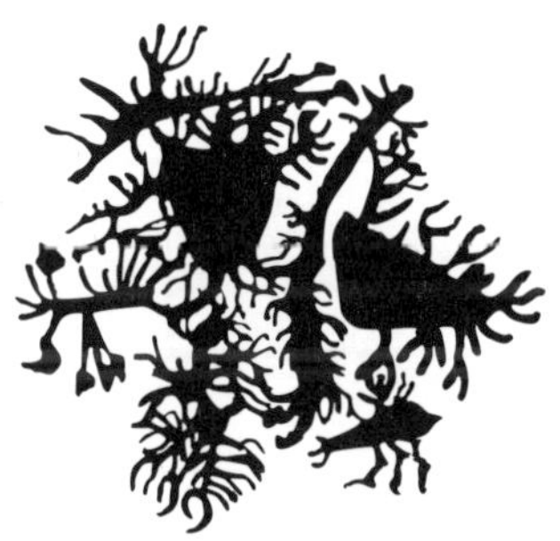

20

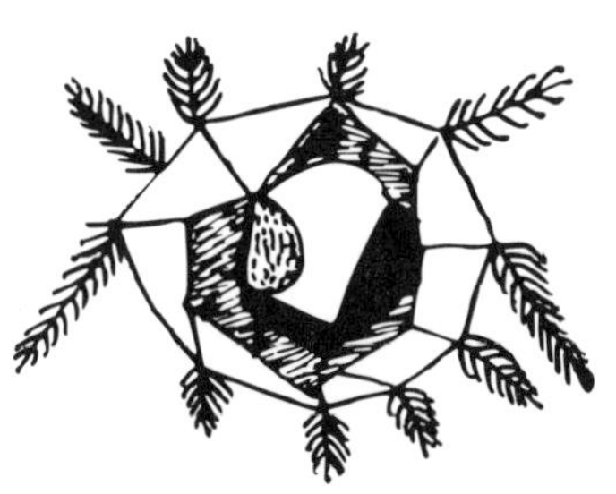

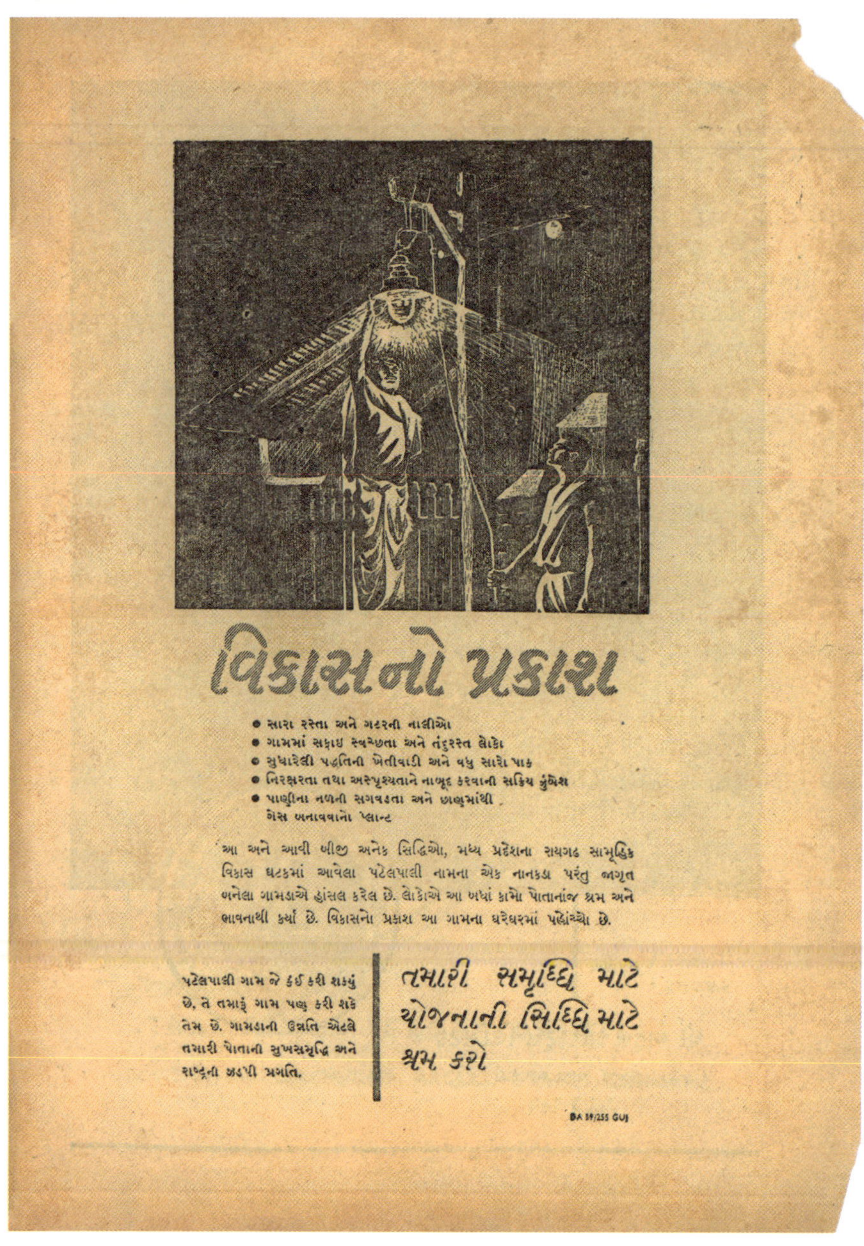

21

⟨A call for development in villages (as initiated and implemented by the villagers) for good roads, proper sewage lines, advanced processes of agriculture, proper tap water systems, and biogas facilities amongst others. The advertisement sets the village of Patelpali in Madhya Pradesh as a benchmark, where the village's progress was a result of people's strength, action, and will. It motivates people to work hard towards such initiatives that will lead to the village's progress and in turn, the nation's speedy development and people's prosperity.⟩

⟨Published in Kumar #432 · December 1959⟩

Figure 21: See the image of an advertisement *'Vikas no Prakash'* (The Light of Development) in the Kumar issue 432 from last December ⟨1959⟩. It shows a burning Petromax and the objects seen in its light. The illuminated area is white, but where there isn't any light, nothing at all is visible.

Illustration 22 is a depiction of a lamp burning on a table and a woman seated on a chair next to it. But unlike Illustration 21 where only the illuminated portions are shown, here all the objects with all their details are drawn clearly. Despite which, to create the effect of the glow of the lamp, 'light and shadow' have been used as symbols. Also, a major portion of the drawing is occupied by black because of which the white areas create the effect of being lit. Had this been rendered only as a line drawing, it wouldn't have the dramatic ambience as is seen here.

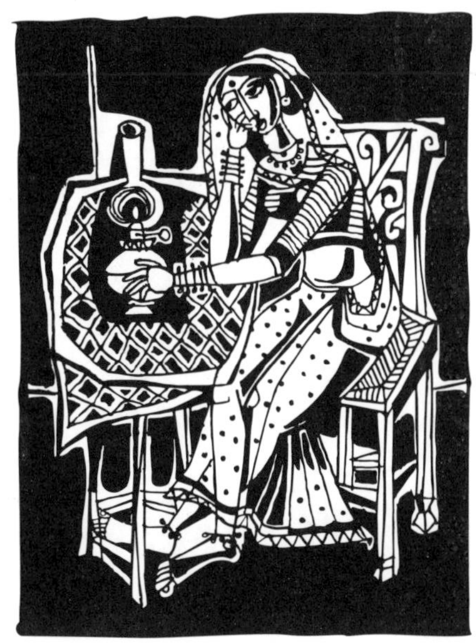

22

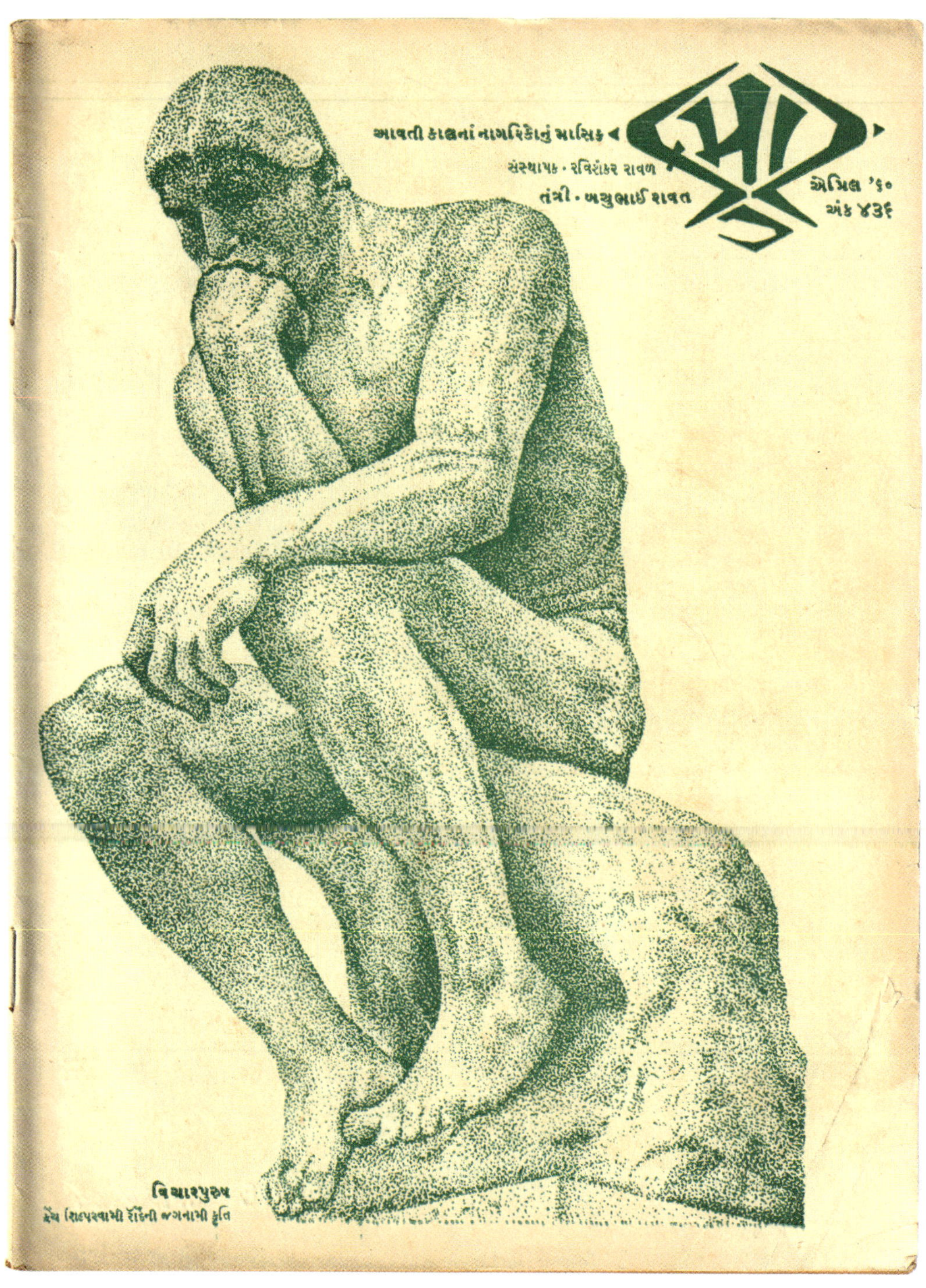

KUMAR #436 · APRIL 1960

Readers Write

A few articles by Shri Jyoti Bhatt in favour of 'Modern Art' have been published in Kumar recently. I am not an artist, but I am interested in art, and I write this inspired by the layperson's sentiments.

Shri Bhatt says ⟨in 'An Article Further Explaining Distortion in Art' (page 80 in this book)⟩ that an image itself is the first step towards distortion. I believe that while making a painting, any artist would be more concerned with how to make it aesthetically pleasing rather than 'distorted'.

The reasons justifying the distortion are baseless. If an artist presents a form stemming only from their own imagination as Shri Bhatt says, then only they themselves can understand it. The artist draws a crow, which in their imagination appeared with a peafowl's feathers, and declares to the world that it is a crow—how could the world accept it? Paintings resulting from the waves of imagination, daydreaming, or the wild steed of the mind cannot be understood by the lay public or an ordinary artist; only that artist alone who has unleashed their mind will be able to understand it.

In the same article, it has been explained in Figure 3 अ and through a part of Figure 3 ब ⟨page 82 in this book⟩, how distortion has taken place. The question arises that is this the only principle that must be borne in mind while attempting distortion? Or should another principle of distortion be applied while making a different painting? As far as I know, the principles of distortion may change from artist to artist. If so much has to be written to explain the distortion in a small section of the painting, how much more will have to be written to describe all the kinds of distortion taking place in the whole painting?

There is only one trend at the moment: 'modern'; 'modern'; but nobody wants to understand that India as a country and such blind mimicry are poles apart. Even if the 'Modern Art' paintings receive top awards at exhibitions, art which fails to move the heart of the viewer is just non-art. In this manner, an artist can create paintings of 'Modern Art' without studying anatomy, perspective, etc; because there are no rules of any kind. A six-year-old child's scribbles can also pass off as 'Modern Art'.

There seems to be no concept on the basis of which 'Modern Art' can be evaluated. Yes... there is only one measure of its evaluation—the artist's imagination, the artist's whim. So what is wrong if we call it 'whimsical art' instead of 'Modern Art'?

—*Kiranchandra Somnath Joshi (Ahmedabad)*

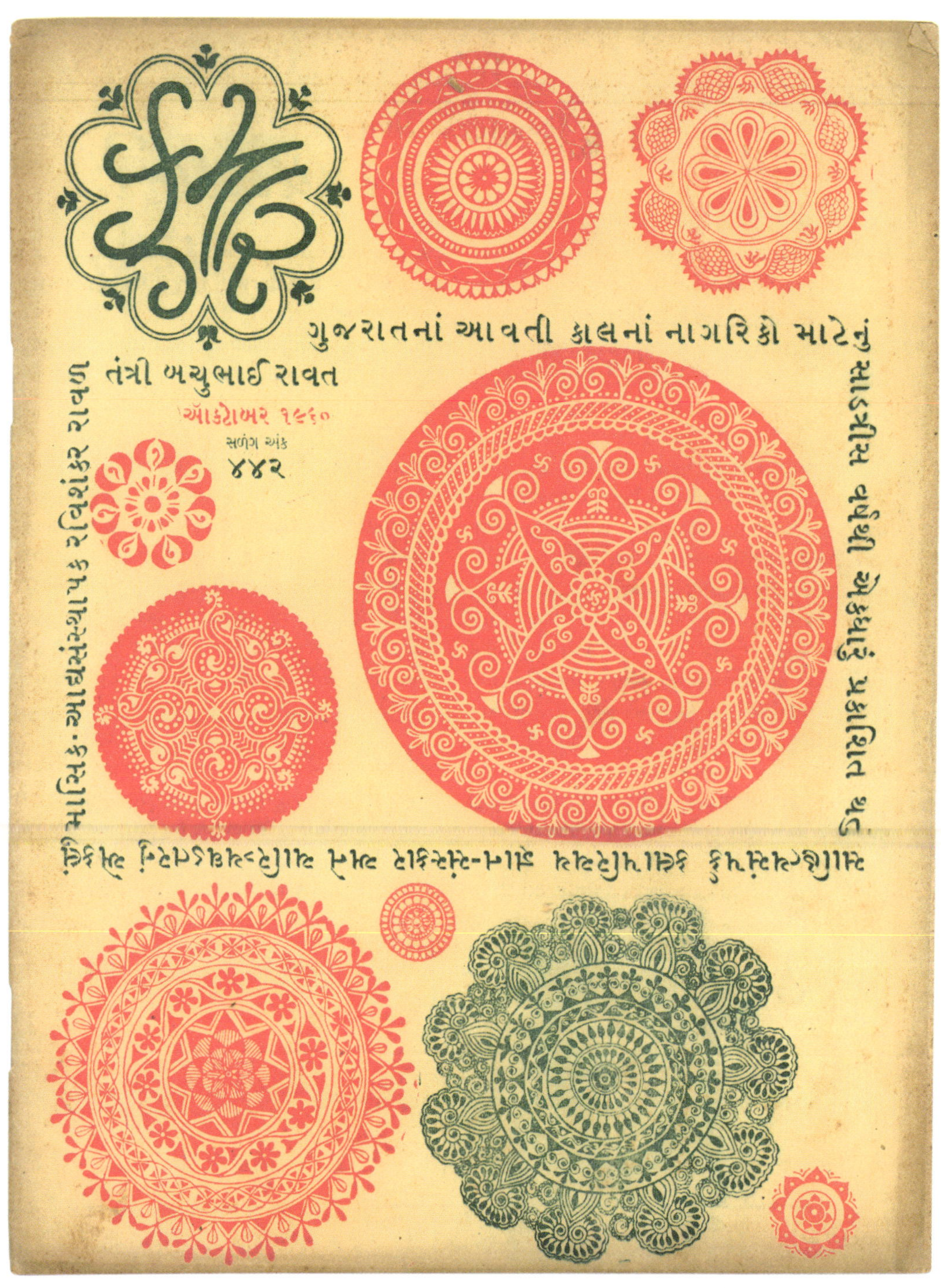

KUMAR #442 · OCTOBER 1960

Readers Write

The quality of the poems published in Kumar is gradually deteriorating and as a justification for this a few statements such as these have been published—"If the poems are inferior in quality, what is the fault of Kumar? When poems from the first half of this century, or from 1875 to 1950, are compared with the modern poems, one will realise that the standard of Gujarati poetry has indeed gone down." I feel that these opinions are half-truths.

I feel that the poems in Kumar are being published according to their 'genre' rather than their 'calibre'. The vision should be to retain perspicuity, along with some novelty of thought and presentation. Moreover, a comparatively simple yet flawless poem by a seasoned poet should also get published. In short, it is the poems that are worth comparing, not the poets.

If seen from this point of view, sometimes one finds many interesting and striking poems by very new poets such as Chandrakant Sheth, Nalin Raval, or Kanu Patel. The fact that poems from the past half or quarter of this century are better than today's is an obviously indigestible opinion.

Along with this, another matter: explaining the types of Modern Art, Jyoti Bhatt's articles were published. In practice, the artist can explain types of art and the vision behind their creations; but that cannot result in the work of art becoming—or seeming—beautiful. If this is the case, then the difference between a garden and a garbage pile, a truth and a lie, beauty and ugliness will collapse, and will result in an unprecedented sentiment of non-duality ⟨અદ્વૈત⟩! There would be a concrete point of view behind the rationale of these divisions, and, if this point of view is not meaningless, then it is essential that these divisions are maintained. Here, there is nothing to be said about the artists' skill or knowledge. Picasso got in a frenzy and decided to start painting like a child—and in turn, his works became the epitome and a unique beauty emerged from it; how can we trust this without any reason?

—*Dinkar Vaidya 'Min Piyasi' (Chuda)*

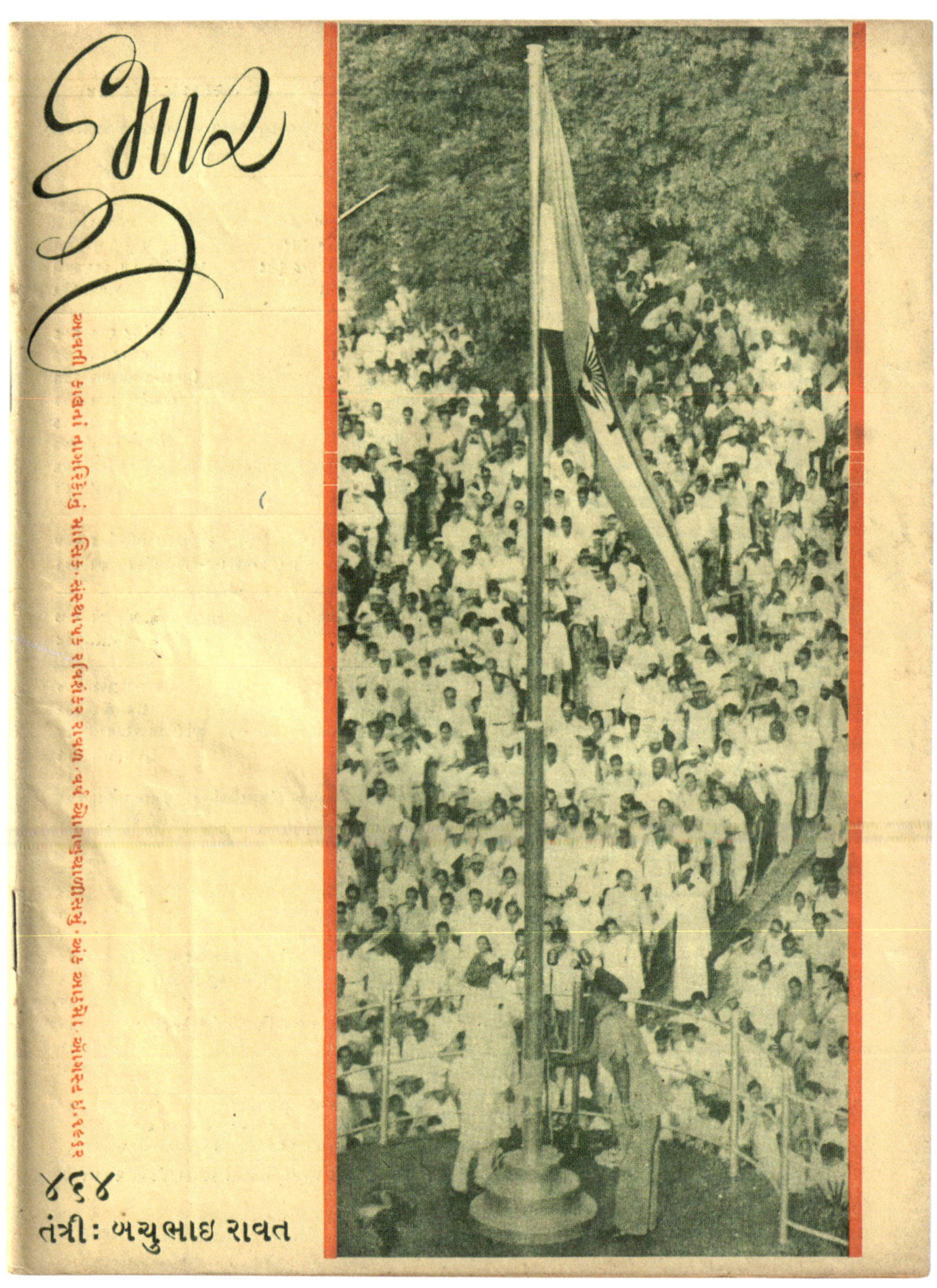

KUMAR #464 · AUGUST 1962

Readers Write

It was a pleasure to see Sheikhbhai's painting in the July ⟨1962⟩ issue of Kumar ⟨page 123 in this book⟩. But it was not so pleasant to read the description of the painting! The artist profile (by Shri Vinay Trivedi) also seemed very wordy. On my way home today, I visited Arun Bose's exhibition. I'm sending the exhibition catalogue along with this; I really liked the cat in it (see image). Why?

It is a very difficult question. Because an intelligent answer will also turn out to be meaningless. Should I say that the pose of the cat seated against the wall is active? Or that the cat's back, that the artist has depicted going beyond the rules of anatomy, is remarkable! Or that the blue cat against the black background creates such a juxtaposition of colour that cats appear to play before our eyes! Or does the artist's power lie in the fact that the cat's leonine face, when observed closely, resembles that of a blood-thirsty demon? Or all of this—and the indivisible sum of it all—creates such a unique atmosphere, that discussing each of its parts separately becomes a hindrance to understanding the picture; it becomes a post-mortem? I had gone to see Arun Bose's exhibition after reading such 'post-mortems' by art critics of 'The Statesman' and 'The Hindustan Standard', and was convinced that in order to appreciate these paintings, I will have to sit in penance for infinite hours in front of such paintings, only then will their

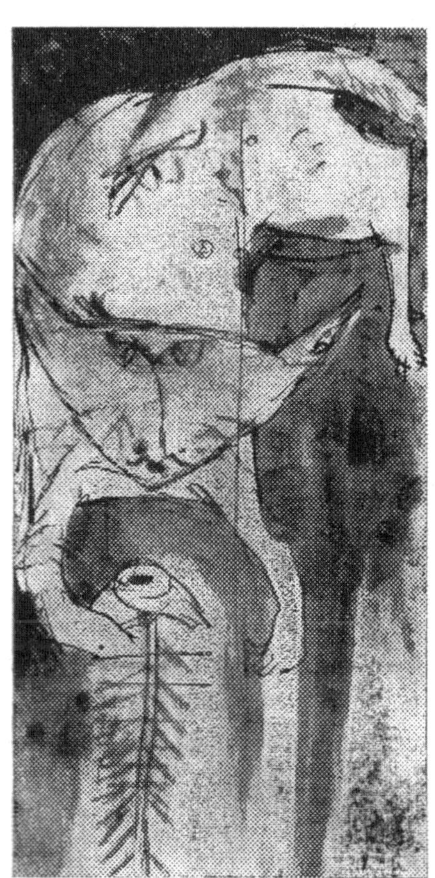

characteristics be understood. The same way that infinite sleepless nights become essential in order to understand the subtle difference between *'hem kalyan'* and *'nat kalyan'*[28]—to truly 'understand' it.

---

28 — *Hem kalyan* and *nat kalyan* are *ragas* within the larger family (or *thaat*) of *raga kalyan*. Individual *ragas* within a larger *thaat* might sound very similar, and it takes a trained ear to perceive the nuances of and differences between the individual *ragas*.

Not everyone can easily attain this, but who says it is necessary for everything to be easily attainable for everyone? How rigorously do *pandits* have to study the Gita to grasp its true essence? Besides, countless people may be reciting it everyday like parrots, and yet we have not disregarded the Gita. This is the fundamental difference between Tulsidas Ji's 'Ramcharitamanas' and 'Gita', and it will remain so. And yet we do not call one 'good' or belittle the other by calling it 'bad' or 'worthless'. If we can cultivate such a scientific vision in the field of art, that will suffice.

—*Jayantilal Mehta (Calcutta)*

[*Wouldn't other readers have different reactions based on this painting of a cat? What kinds?*]

⟨—*Editor*⟩

After seeing the painting 'White Horse' in the July ⟨1962⟩ issue, I write this letter with reference to the debate concerning art that has taken place until now in Kumar. It is said that in Modern Art, the artist attempts to represent impressions from their subconscious in their own styles (which are in most cases gnarly and ambiguous), and despite this clarification being quoted several times, a question still remains, that do only such obscure and gnarly thoughts impress upon the modernist's mind? Why can an object not be represented by conforming to realism and order? And if one cannot make any sense of a painting without having to read its title, why call that a painting at all? (It shouldn't be considered a blunder if one mistakes 'Negro Boxer' for a 'wild plant'!) Although your efforts to clarify the perspectives of Modern Art through the series of texts by Jyoti Bhatt and descriptions underneath the images of artworks are commendable, yet this kind of art still remains hard to swallow.

At times, this art is compared to the uninhibited and expressive art of children. However, in the 400th issue of Kumar ⟨April 1957⟩, the way in which Rasiklal Parikh's painting showed a child's scribbles seems more clear and appealing than the art of these modernists. As long as the characteristics of the subject of the painting are evident, and as long as the contours of the lines and the colour composition indicate artistry, the paintings will surely be appealing; and even if to a large extent they aren't realistic, they will still be delightful. I, and others like me, liked Shri Pradyumna Tanna's incomplete sketches and Shri Shiavax Chavda's quick drawings a lot. I really liked the long-necked and big-turbaned 'Vanjhaaro' in the July ⟨1962⟩ issue. The artist should be congratulated. However it is slightly annoying when one has to see totally obscure and unclear paintings. While it is through studying Kumar that I am nurturing my art appreciation and understanding of art, I am not biased against, nor do I lack faith, in Modern Art; I am only humbly sharing my opinions based on the present. Photographs of two sculptures of Shri Nehru by a Black artist had appeared in Kumar—the slight distortion made by the artist to distil Nehru's versatile personality is one that can be understood. However, what was so magnificent in the 'White Horse' that in order to evoke it ⟨this magnificence⟩, all this ⟨distortion⟩ had to be done? But in conclusion, and in all frankness, I must let you know that I greatly admired 'Saraswati' (Shrimati Prabha Badgelvar) and 'Shaishav-smriti' (Shrimati Mohini Bakshi), both paintings done in the manner of Modern Art.

—*Harikrishna R. Pathak (Songadh)*

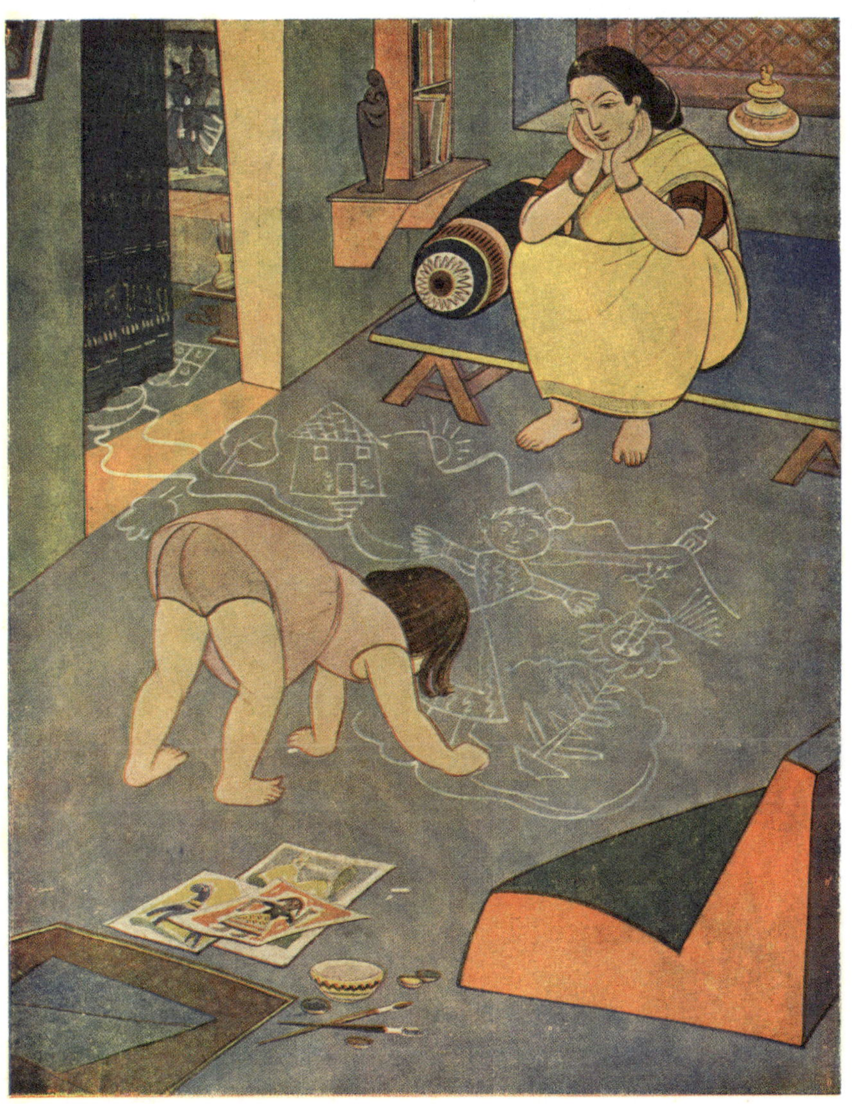

'Bal-Chitrakaar' ⟨Child Artist⟩ · Artist: Rasiklal Parikh
⟨Published in Kumar #400 · April 1957⟩

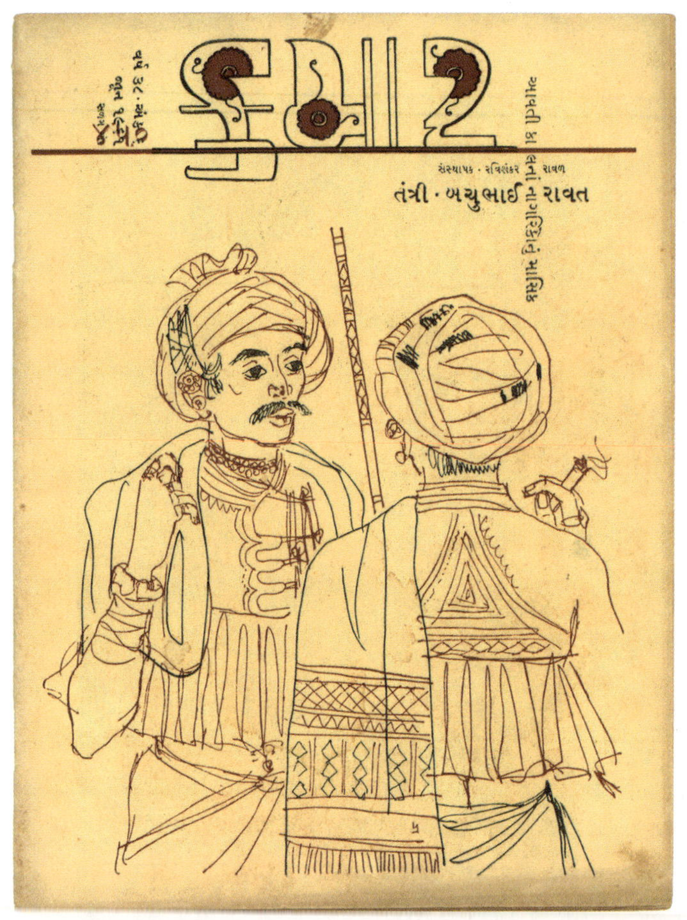

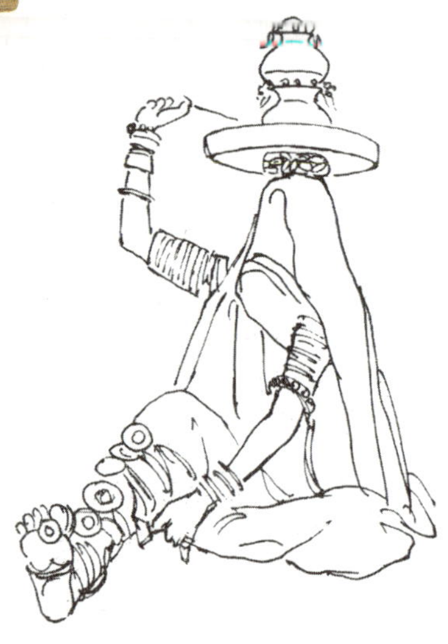

⟨Sketches by Pradyumna Tanna⟩
⟨Published in Kumar #450 · June 1961⟩

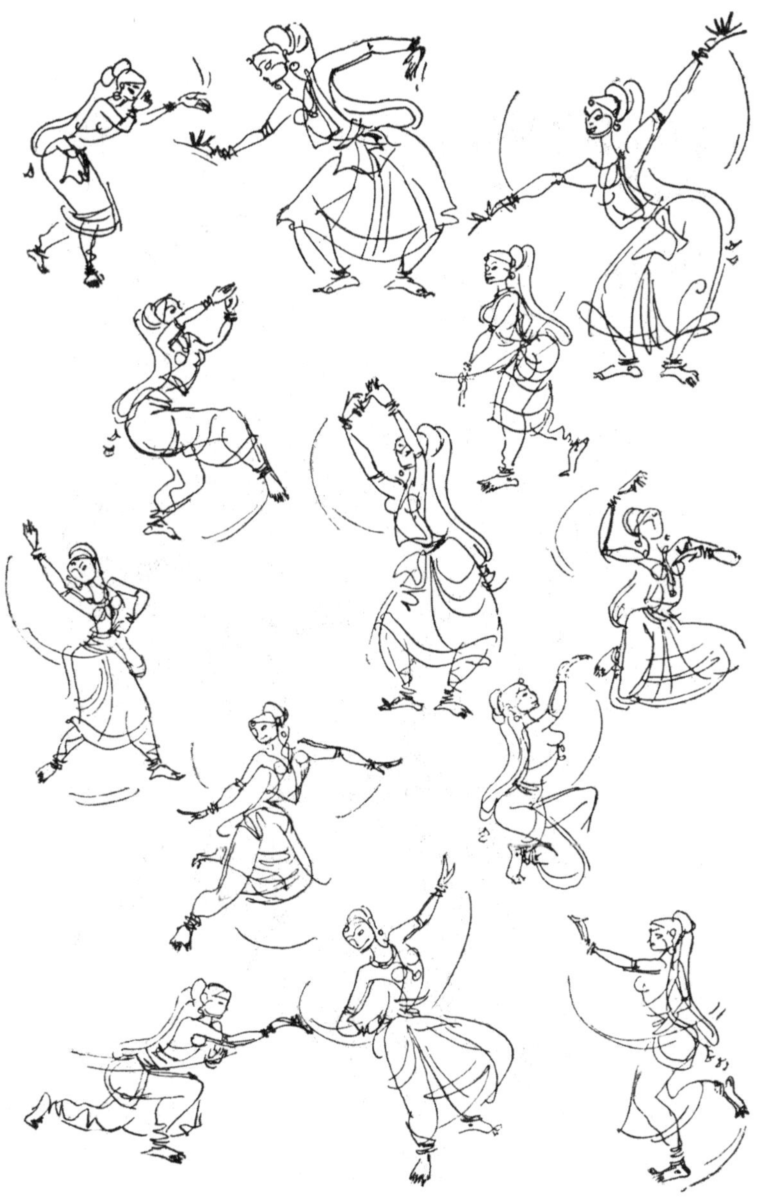

'Dance Movements' · An example of the strength of Shri ⟨Shiavax⟩ Chavda's quick sketches.
⟨Published in Kumar #456 · December 1961⟩

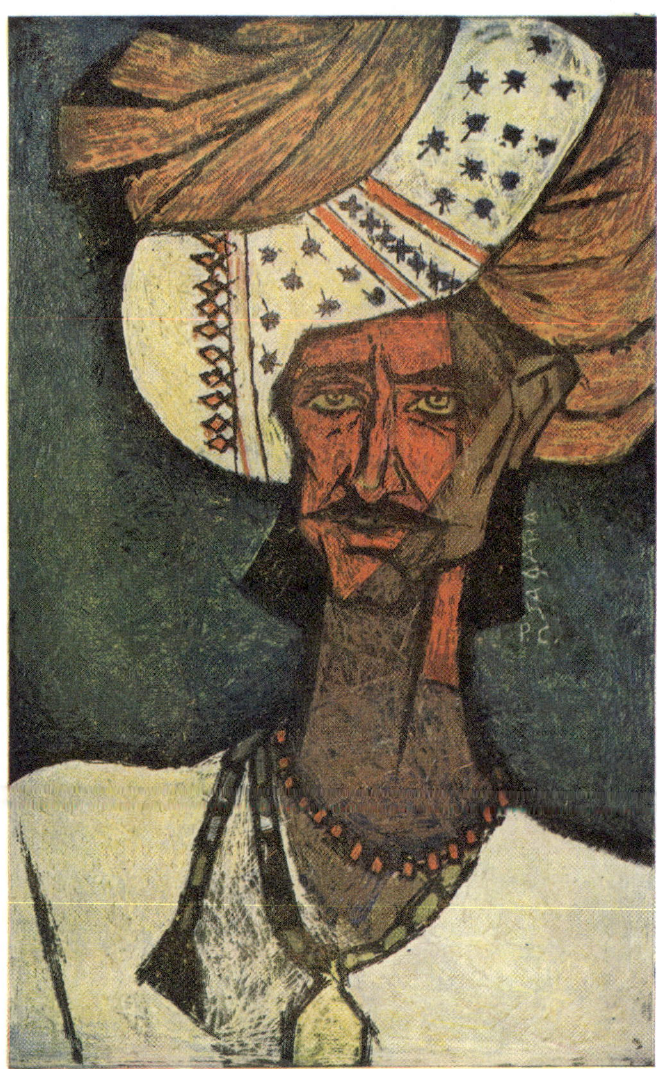

'Vanjhaaro' ⟨Nomad⟩ · Artist: Piraji Sagara
⟨Published in Kumar #463 · July 1962⟩

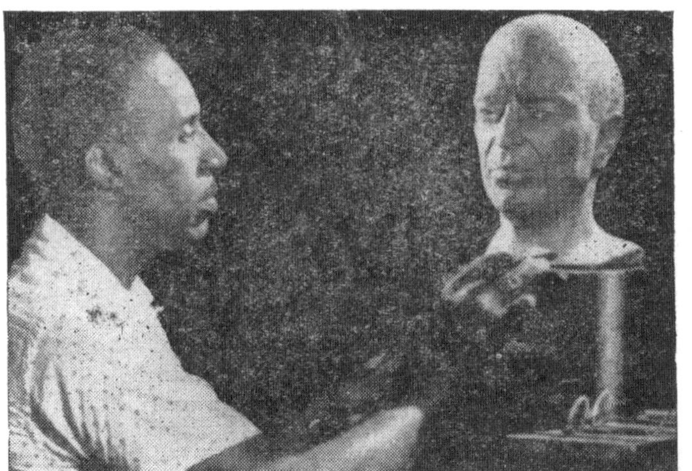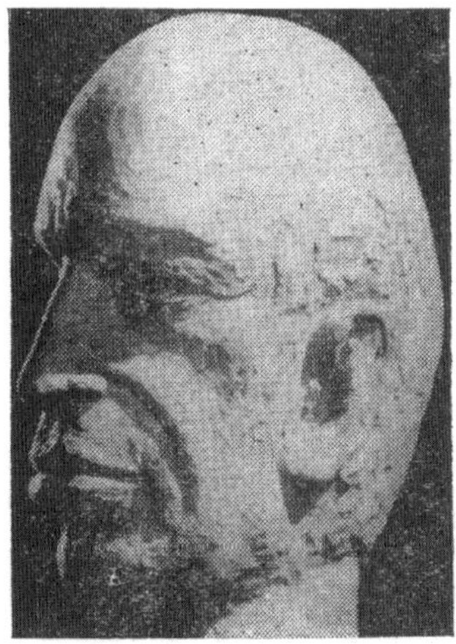

African-American sculptor Mack M. Green and his casted sculpture of ⟨Jawaharlal⟩ Nehru
⟨Published in Kumar #415 · July 1958⟩

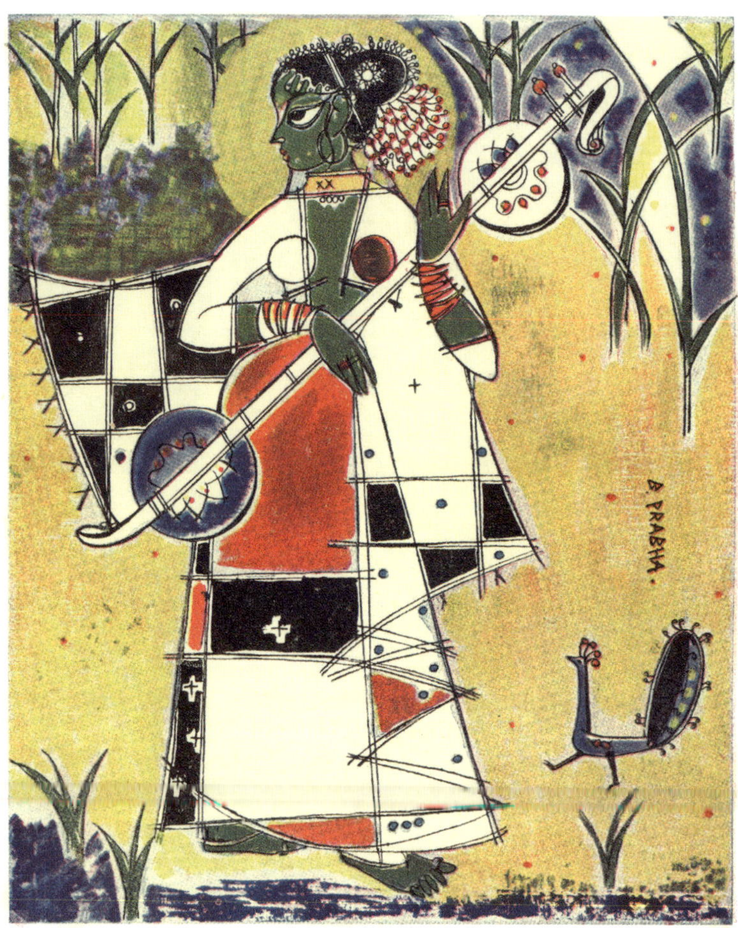

'Saraswati' · Artist: Shrimati Prabha Badgelvar · Image courtesy of the artist
⟨Published in Kumar #435 · March 1960⟩

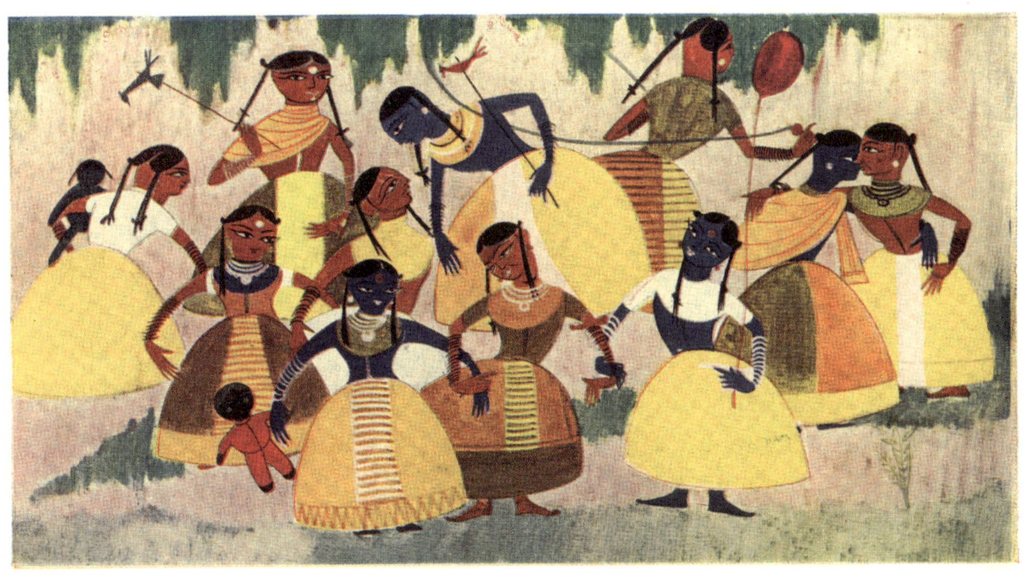

'Shaishav-smriti' ⟨The Memories of Childhood⟩ · Artist: Shrimati Mohini Bakshi · Image courtesy of the artist
⟨Published in Kumar #418 · October 1958⟩

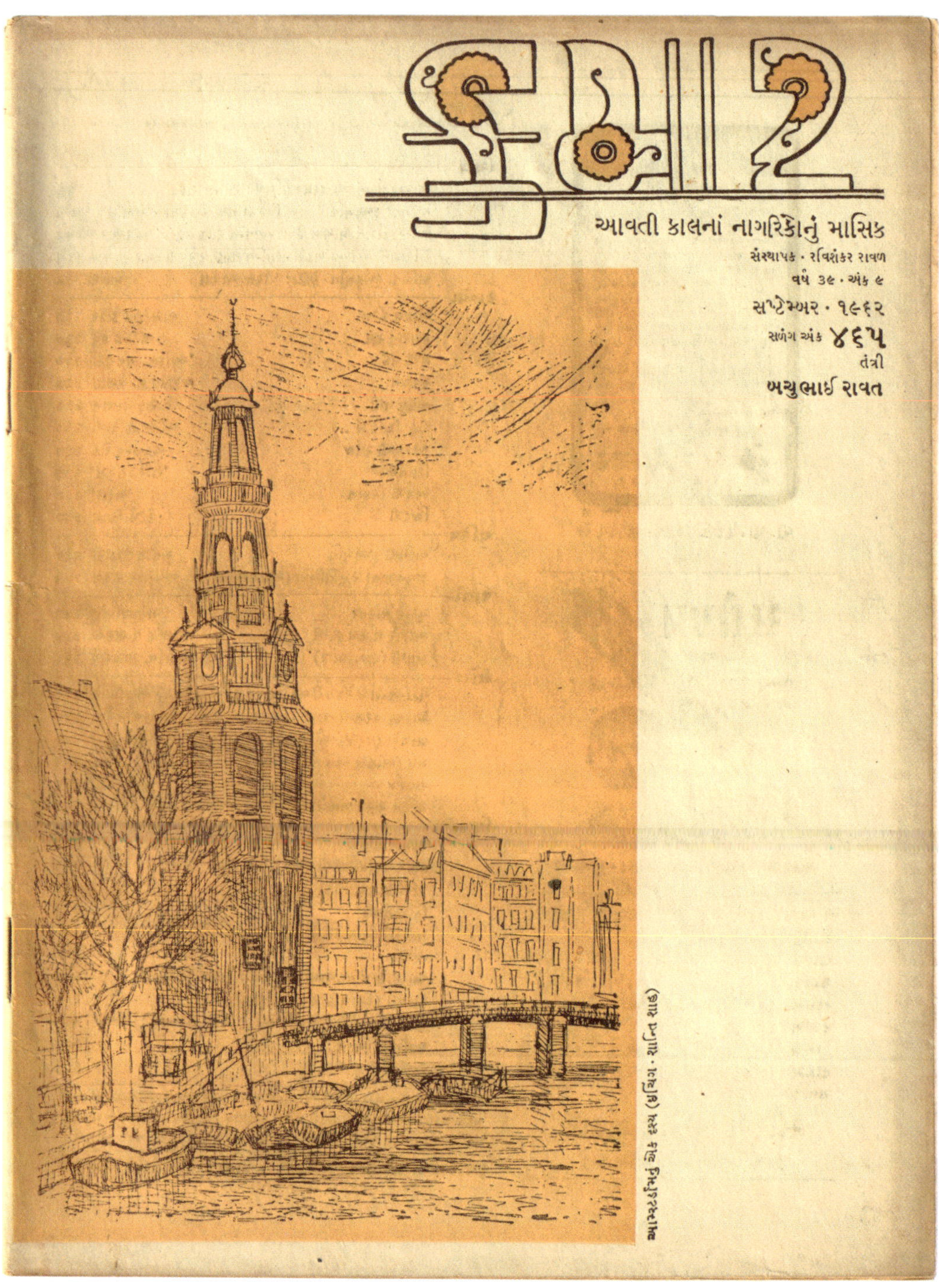

KUMAR #465 · SEPTEMBER 1962

Readers Write

I read Shri Harikrishna Pathak's letter in the August ⟨1962⟩ issue. It is the biggest nuisance of our Gujarati mindset to pass opinions as one pleases without even knowing the ABCDs of art. One must, however, appreciate Pathak for the guts he has shown. He is an art-lover who has read the writings of Jyoti Bhatt, and yet is unable to digest Modern Art.

The fortunate (or unfortunate) reason for this could be that he has misunderstood the definition of art. His effort to understand a painting merely through its title, itself shows his limited knowledge of art. He does not know that a title is not a crucial part of a painting. Parents give different names to their children to identify them, and not because the children show traits that their names indicate! Similar is the case with the title of a painting. In a painting, horses, cows, buffaloes, or men are not things that the art connoisseur needs to understand. The horse in the painting should not be seen as a 'horse', but has to be perceived as a delightful conglomeration of colours. And because the overall shape of that conglomeration of colours somewhat resembles an actual horse, it has been titled 'Horse'. It is but a mistake to believe that the excellence of the painting relies on that 'horse'.

It seems that for my brother Pathak, only that which closely mimics the unbridled art seen in nature is the best kind of art. To sing like a cinema record is not the best music. Similarly, in painting, where is the originality of the artist in merely imitating nature, forsaking the tenets of art? (This can be understood as mimicry.)

Modern Art is 'art for art's sake'. Its representation is based on the artist's personal interests. An artist is not conditioned to represent aspects other than the tenets of art like rhythm, balance, volume, lines and colour, space, or texture. Its excellence lies more in the beauty of the object, than in its meaning.

—*N.G. Bhanwadia (Baroda)*

[*Is it not better to present one's point without being offensive towards the opposition? Amongst artists and art critics themselves, there are different opinions that operate on the subject of the definition of art. To say that only what conforms to one's own notions of beauty is art, and only what one says is true, can be called egotistical.*]

⟨—*Editor*⟩

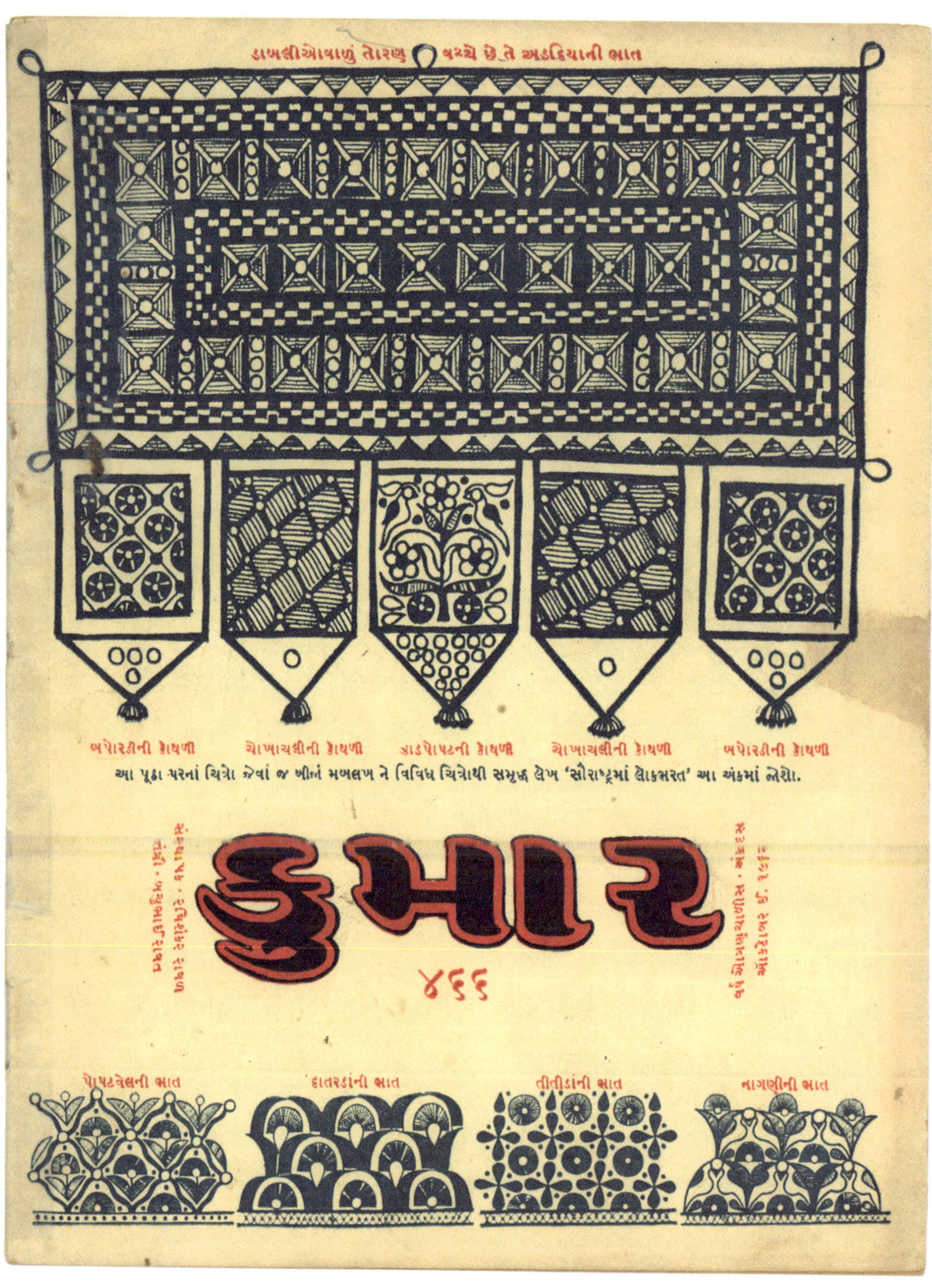

KUMAR #466 · OCTOBER 1962

Readers Write

The deliberations about 'Modern Art' that have been churning for a while now, have been rejuvenated in the Readers ⟨Write⟩ section in the August ⟨1962⟩ issue. When some examples of certain art forms (poetry or paintings) are presented to a person who is interested in them, and when the person understands nothing from seeing these examples; when an attempt to understand it seems like *'adhah shakha mulordhwam'*[29] ⟨with roots above the ground and branches below⟩; or when even after the explanation is provided, one still scratches their head ⟨in confusion⟩—then how is one to make sense of it? However much someone elaborates the meaning of 'Negro Boxer', if its interpretation of possibly being a 'wild plant' does not leave the mind, then what is one to make of it?

Until a new style of art becomes completely popularised, it cannot be fully understood—that is true; but when it cannot be understood at all, or is understood entirely upside-down, then what? Ears habituated to the sounds of music—be it North Hindustani, Carnatic, or Western—can certainly appreciate the rhythm in all; but would we be able to say the same about this new method of painting—Modern Art? In the August ⟨1962⟩ issue, a gentleman has said the practice to merely 'understand' Modern Art, is equivalent to the amount of practice required to understand the Gita. If such is this case, then it is not art. In Kumar, a series of articles explaining Modern Art have been shared by the artist Shri Jyoti Bhatt. From these, this much has been established that Modern Art operates in accordance with certain rules (which is not usually felt while looking at the paintings); but is being bound to rules the only characteristic of art? If artists cannot loosen up and express themselves in their works, then what can possibly come of being bound to rules? Waterworks constructed by a clever engineer can impress the intellect, but not the desire for art.

I have written this ⟨the above⟩ as an ordinary reader, with regards to the appeal in the previous issue, inviting responses to the painting of a cat.

Wouldn't it be good if the length of the section 'Saahitya Sampark' ⟨Literature Review⟩ was increased? If the literary puzzles—that were featured one or two times—were continued, then it will be appreciated by all.

May I (with complete respect) point out a few grammatical errors in Kumar? In the last issue, we saw typographical mistakes in the spellings of the words 'શિર્ષક', 'પ્રશશ્ય', 'વિદ્ધતા', 'ટેલીફોન', etc.*

—*Suresh Desai (Ahmedabad)*

[*We are regretful.]
⟨—Editor⟩

---

29 — An excerpt from a longer verse in the Gita—*"sri-bhagavan uvaca || urdhva-mulam adhah-sakham || asvattham prahur avyayam || chandamsi yasya parnani || yas tam veda sa veda-vit"* which translates to: "The Blessed Lord said: There is a banyan tree which has its roots upward and its branches down and whose leaves are the Vedic hymns. One who knows this tree is the knower of the Vedas."

કુમાર

આવતી કાલનાં નાગરિકોનું માસિક

નવેમ્બર
૪૬૭
૧૯૬૨

સંસ્થાપક · રવિશંકર રાવળ
તંત્રી · બચુભાઈ રાવત

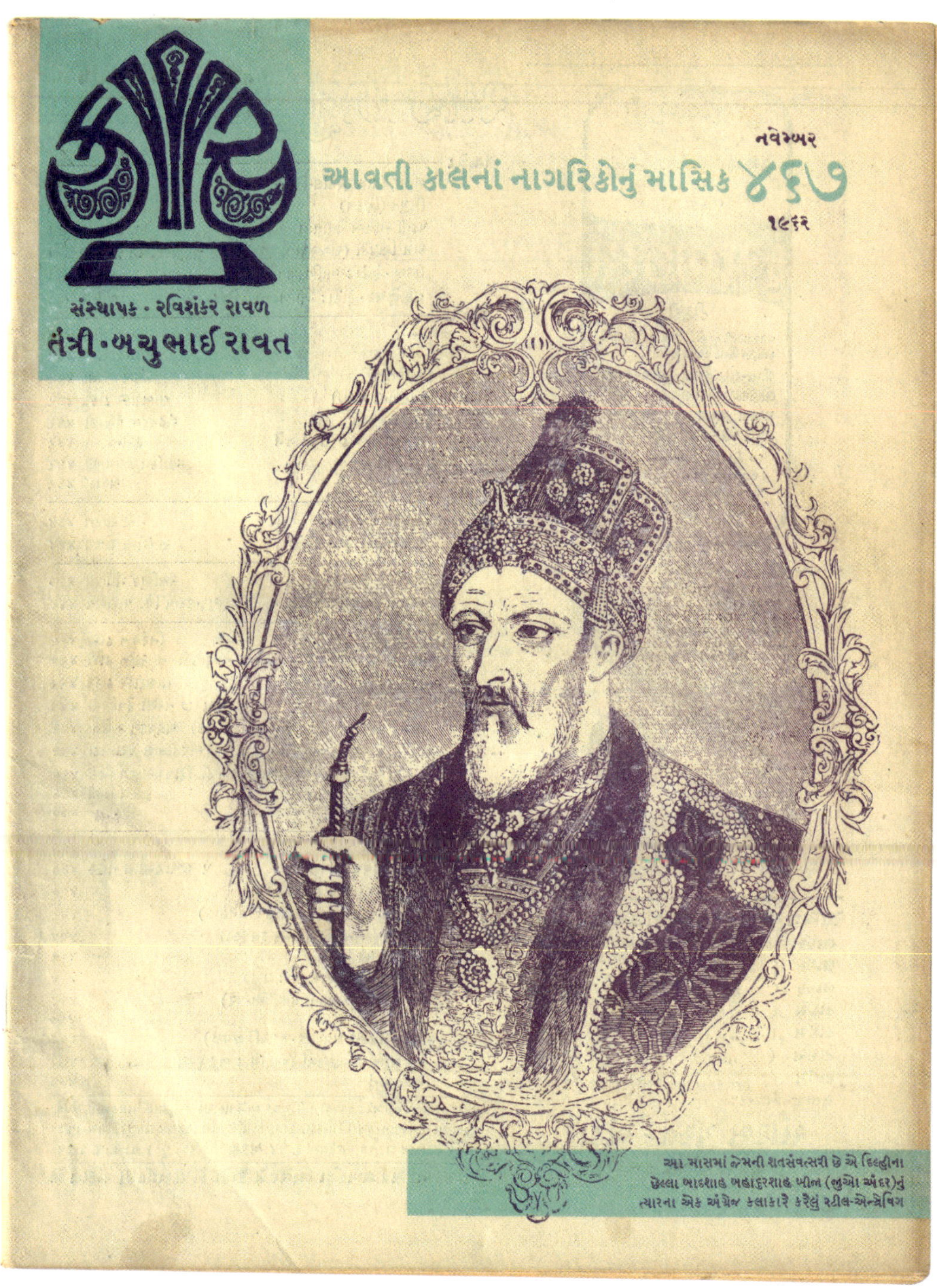

આ માસમાં જેમની શતસંવત્સરી છે એ દિલ્હીના
છેલ્લા બાદશાહ બહાદુરશાહ બીજા (જુઓ અંદર)નું
ત્યારના એક અંગ્રેજ કલાકારે કરેલું સ્ટીલ-એન્ગ્રેવિંગ

Readers Write

After reading my writing ⟨in 'Readers Write'⟩ in the September ⟨1962⟩ issue, I have received cantankerous letters from some readers, and many of them can be summarised as such:

"Music, drama, dance, poetry, prose, film, as well as ancient painting, all these arts can be understood and enjoyed by the masses, so they can satisfy everyone's mind, while Modern Art is the only art which pleases no one except the artists; and also that modern artists create art only for themselves; so, in comparison to other arts, isn't this a drawback of Modern Art?"

However, some people, even artists, believe that, "sometimes art should be created without caring for others, and only for self-satisfaction." Yet, I personally disagree with this opinion. As said by the poet Kalapi, "art which may be consumable and sweet, is not art without a consumer" seems entirely true to me.

Just like a layperson would lighten the burden of one's heart by sharing their feelings of happiness, sorrow, etc. through language, in the same way the artist also pours out the feeling of their heart through painting. Just as there is no satisfaction in unburdening one's emotions in the absence of another to bear the load, there is no meaning to an artist's creation if it has no consumer or person to appreciate it.

Artists always create works for themselves as well as for the consumer, that is a fact. However, to fully understand what emotions the artist wishes to convey through the work, and to derive aesthetic delight, the consumer must be worthy.

Critiquing Abhinavagupta's elaboration on Rasa, Ramanbhai Neelkanth has said, "To take pleasure in and to experience the essence of poetry, the culture of connoisseurship ⟨રસિકતા⟩ is necessary. For those who do not possess this culture in their being, aesthetic compositions are futile. Owing to the numerous experiences of life, all individuals respond to momentary instincts, but without the power of special training, a stable, fixed state of mind ⟨સ્થાયીભાવ⟩ cannot be achieved. Since this power is not related to intellectual pursuits, but to emotions and feelings, scholars with mastery in other subjects are many a time unable to grasp the essence of poetry."

In exactly the same way, due to the lack of appropriate training, when people who are proficient in other subjects fail to derive aesthetic pleasure from Modern Art, then it is their personal fault, and not that of the arts.

Besides, it is impossible to satisfy every individual of the world with a work of art. It is certainly wrong to say that even plays and movies satisfy all viewers. The same play or movie might be appreciated by one and not appreciated by another. The same is true in the case of music, dance, poetry, prose, etc.

While ancient paintings are understandable, modern ones are not—the reason behind this is that people are usually not ready to accept the sudden abolition of prevalent trends to be replaced by some new system. For instance, several years ago, the custom of child marriage was prevalent in some societies. When some leaders attempted to abolish the practice and bring in reform, they were ostracised by society. The same society has today accepted this reform. Much in the same way, today inter-caste marriages are considered sinful in the eyes of some, but after a while these might even become commonplace!

It was the same in the case of the Dutch artist ⟨Vincent⟩ van Gogh. For as long as he was alive, people ridiculed his paintings. But when his works are exhibited today, people come to view them in flocks and herds from far and wide. Similarly, 'Modern' Art is a completely different and novel style compared to the artistic tradition that has been prevalent in India since years—in which subjectivity is of great importance. Thus those who believe that ancient art is at the zenith of the artistic field will neither understand this new art today, nor will they accept it. But as time passes the same populace will gradually understand and even accept it!

—N.G. Bhanwadia (Baroda)

Regarding Shri Pathak's and Shri Bhanwadia's letters about Shri Sheikh's painting, one contains a humble opinion, whereas, the other is a self-authorised erroneous assumption about the superiority of art.

Shri Sheikh's painting, 'White Horse', gives a good understanding of colour, composition, texture, free brushstrokes—but to view these techniques as the 'ideal work of art', to expect everyone to applaud such work without an exception, and to say that those who cannot do so, do not know the ABCDs of art, is not ideal.

Shri Pathak has echoed the discomfort in the minds of a large community of art lovers from around the world towards the strangeness of Modern Art. Even after 60 years of his practice, the number of critics of Picasso, the pioneer of Modern Art, are not a few. To convince oneself that all these people are imbeciles who do not know the ABCDs of art, is blissful self-deception.

Shri Bhanwadia says that in Modern Art the conglomeration of colour has to be admired, but we cannot call the artist who uses this conglomeration to create a greater arrangement or a familiar form as a fraud who is merely into the 'mimicry' of nature. We do not say so for Amrita Sher-Gil, Jamini Roy, Hebbar, or van Gogh, Gauguin, Cézanne, or Degas; likewise, with the nearly 300-year-old, entirely realistic painting by Rubens titled 'Adoration of the Magi' gaining a lot of fame recently and selling for an abnormal price like 37 lakh rupees, we cannot call Rubens, Leonardo, Raphael, Rembrandt, or El Greco as merely imitators mimicking nature. The trend of assuming that those who criticise the obscurity and strangeness of Modern Art are the ones who prefer to look at only attractive and descriptive pictures that resemble technicolour photographs, and then the custom of imposing half-rubbish and immature experiments as ideal art in the public view by proclaiming the slogan 'art for art's sake', has become dated.

If art has some place in the life of the public, and if it must contribute in some way to spark their interest and make them more cognisant of the arts, then there is no need to fear the defamation of either the art or the artist. On the contrary, the fame and relevance of art which can integrate itself into public life will only increase.

To believe that in the past, all the visual arts of the East and the West that were integrated in public life were devoid of the fundamental tenets, and only in this century have the gods of art blessed some modern artists to confer aesthetic consciousness, and moreover the assumption that only in their modern style of painting have the essential elements of art been reborn, is a bit too much.

—Himmatbhai Mehta (Rajkot)

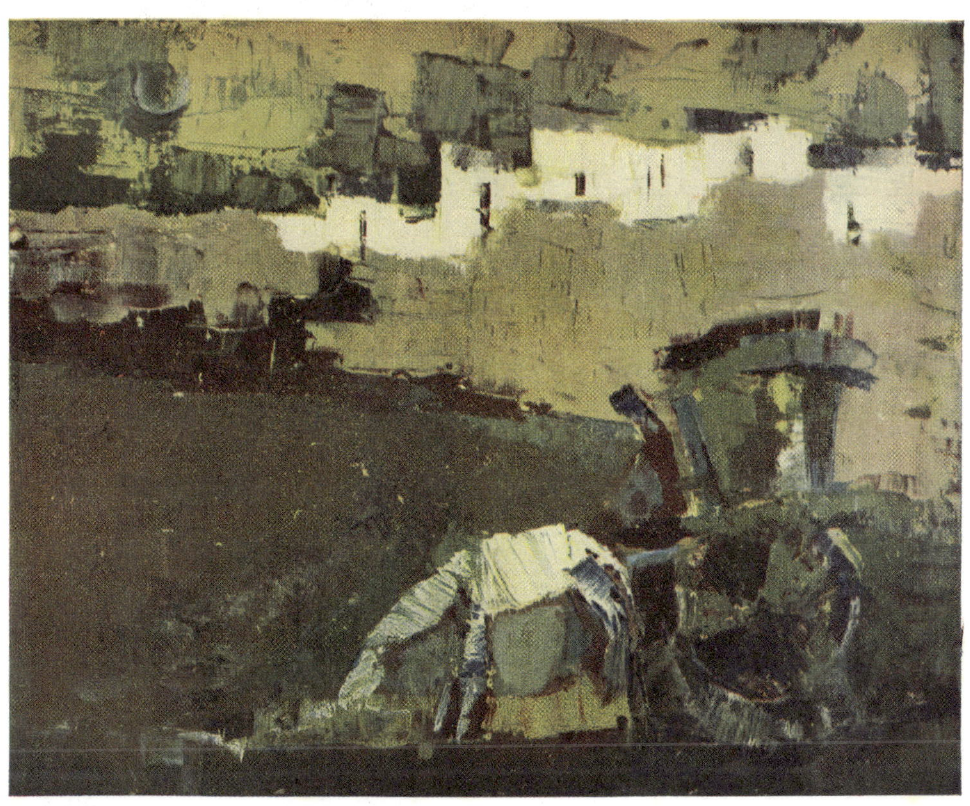

'Safed Ghodi' ⟨White Horse⟩ · Artist: Gulammohammed Sheikh
⟨Published in Kumar #463 · July 1962⟩

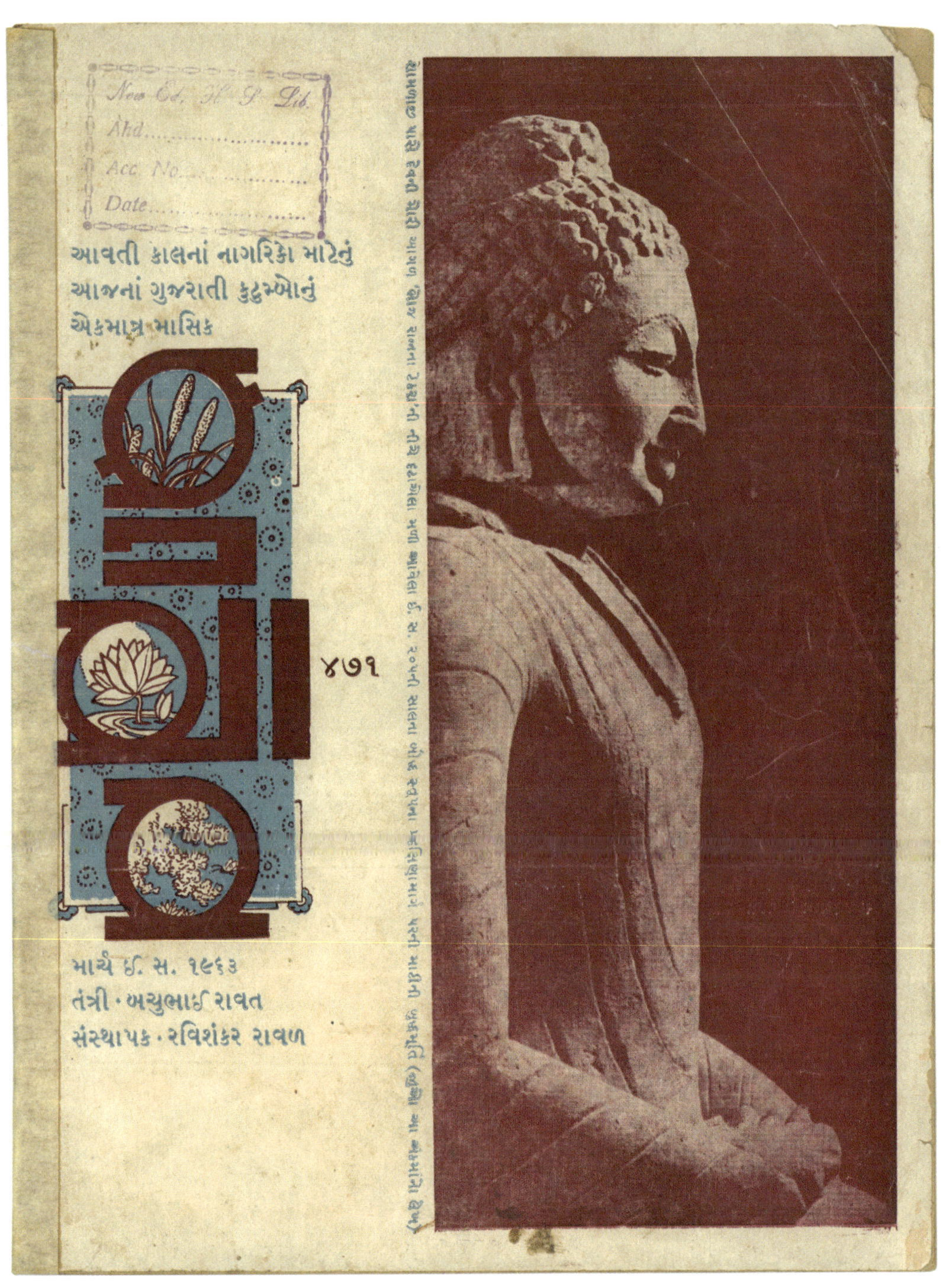

આવતી કાલનાં નાગરિકો માટેનું
આજનાં ગુજરાતી કુટુમ્બોનું
એકમાત્ર માસિક

કુમાર

૪૭૧

માર્ચ ઈ. સ. ૧૯૬૩
તંત્રી · બચુભાઈ રાવત
સંસ્થાપક · રવિશંકર રાવળ

KUMAR #471 · MARCH 1963

Readers Write

I really liked the 'Kalavarta' ⟨Stories of Art⟩ section in the 1963 February issue. It seems as if the articles there were selected in the context of the debate that the readers had with regards to 'Modern Art'. That which did not come into fruition with clarity in the debate, has materialised in the passages given in 'Kalavarta'. The drawing of 'a gathering of people on the verandah overlooking a street' in the last segment of the autobiographical narrative of R.M.R. ⟨Ravishankar Mahashankar Raval⟩, can itself be a theme for a painting. In a village or a city, on every street, such a gathering of young men can be seen often. Two years ago, I had sent a similar drawing of a group of three as a Diwali card to a friend. I am sending a memory-drawing ⟨સ્મૃતિચિત્ર⟩ of this along with this letter. This has been created using the technique written below the image of Shri Khatsuriya, in the February ⟨1963⟩ issue. If you continue providing us with tricks like this that can be easily attempted, then people like us, who are into professions other than art, can also try them out.

—Harikrishna R. Pathak (Sonagadh)

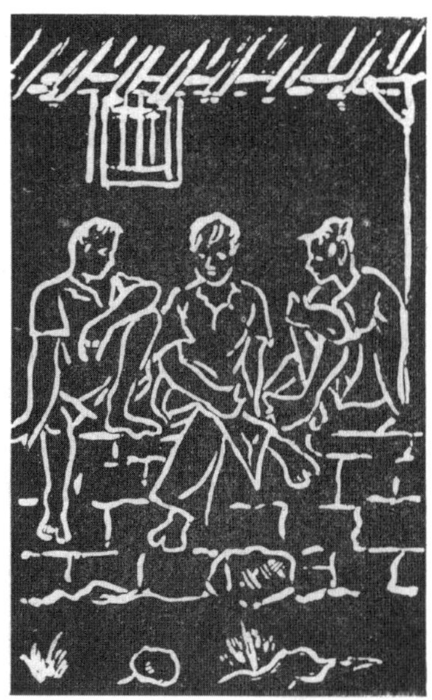

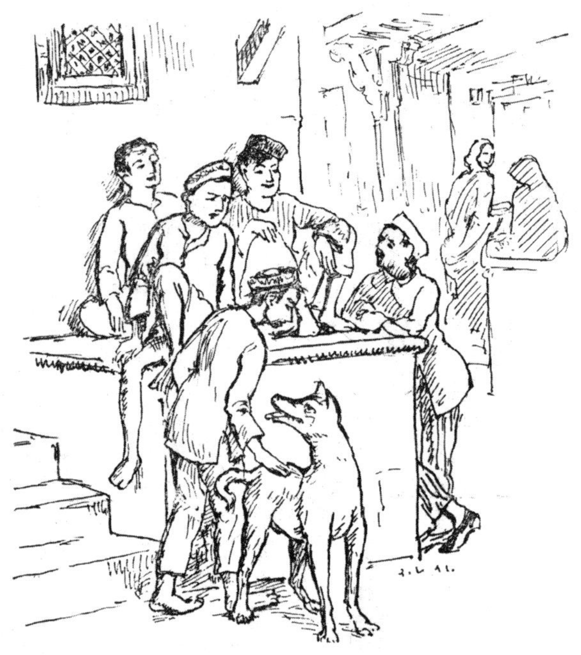

A gathering of people on the verandah overlooking a street · Artist:
Ravishankar Raval

⟨Published in Kumar #470 · February 1963⟩

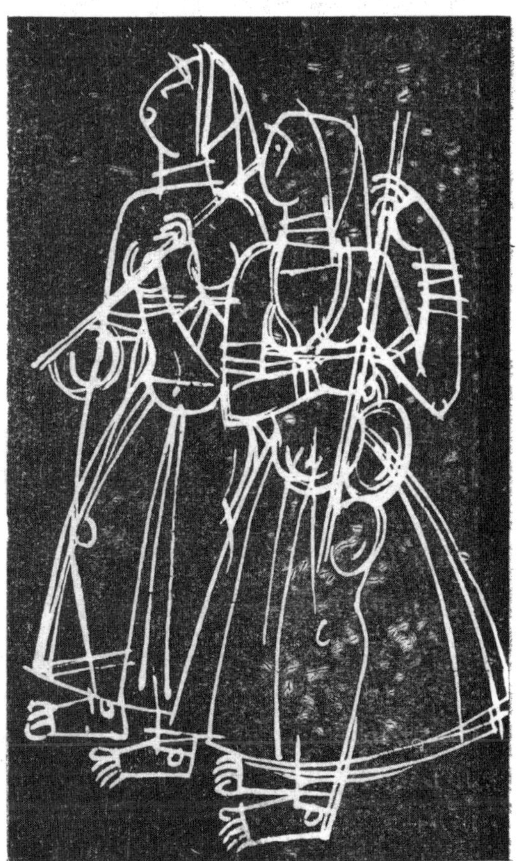

'Bhajnikao' ⟨Hymn-singers⟩ · Artist: Khatsuriya

⟨Published in Kumar #470 · February 1963⟩

⟨The technique as described by Khatsuriya: "Dilute pure
gum arabic, mix a light colour in it, and using the solution so
formed, draw on a sheet of paper. Once it dries, coat the paper
with waterproof ink. Wash the sheet with water once the ink
dries. On washing, you will notice that the gum arabic will
come off the paper, in turn creating a drawing. You can also
use wax crayon and oil crayon instead of gum arabic."⟩

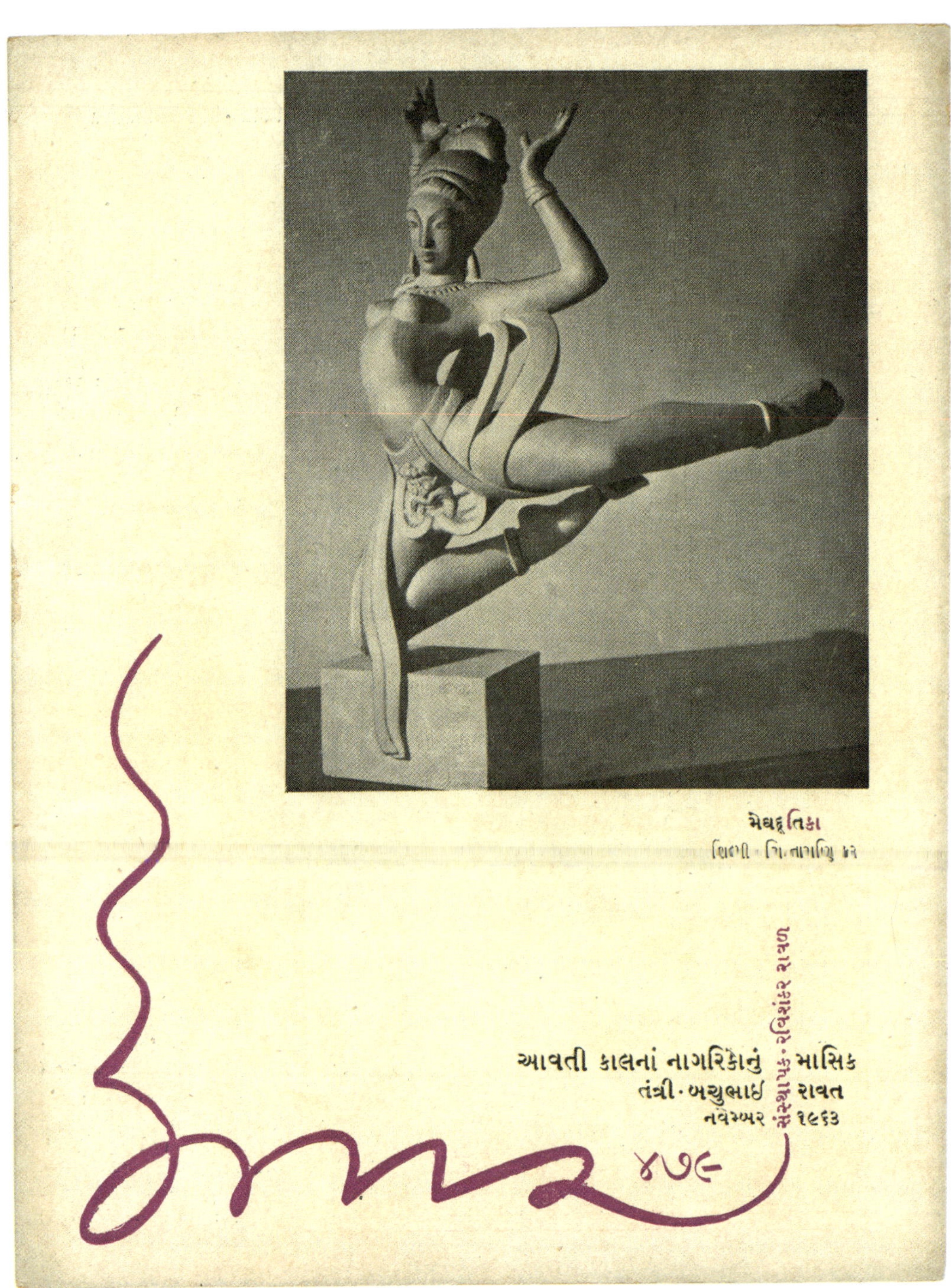

આવતી કાલનાં નાગરિકોનું માસિક
તંત્રી · બચુભાઈ રાવત
સંપાદક · રવિશંકર રાવત
નવેમ્બર ૧૯૬૩
૪૭૯

Readers Write

The poems published in Kumar represent the best poetry in Gujarati literature. Congratulations!

In an issue of Kshitij[30], there is a bibliography of books on the subject of art. In that, Shri Pherozeshah Rustomji Mehta's 'Chitrarasika'[31] is named. But unfortunately, 'not to be read' is written against it. The methods of knowing, understanding, and thinking about art can be of many different kinds. Opinions and reflections can be of many different kinds as well. Thus a stubborn insistence of this kind to say that only one method or thought is the *truth*, should not be appreciated at any cost. Usually, through such periodicals, there is definitely a tolerance-led expectation to know and understand the other's thoughts and opinions. Having a directive of this kind towards those who bear a different ideology than oneself is certainly not appreciated.

—Chandrashekhar (Bhavnagar - 2)

[*Even so, we will need to be tolerant.*]
⟨*—Editor*⟩

30 — A Gujarati literary periodical published in Baroda (Gujarat, India), Kshitij was founded by Prabodh Choksi in 1960, and edited by Suresh Joshi, who is recognised as the father of Gujarati modernist literature. The magazine was known for its articles on art and culture of that time, as well as its cover pages designed and illustrated by artists, including Jyoti Bhatt.

31 — 'Chitrarasika' is a compilation of Pherozeshah Mehta's articles offering his views about appreciating various forms of visual art, published in 1962. Meant to be a primary guide to visual art, Mehta cites many examples of artworks from the Western Classical era, including references of museums and art schools, to talk about their formal, aesthetic, and historical aspects.

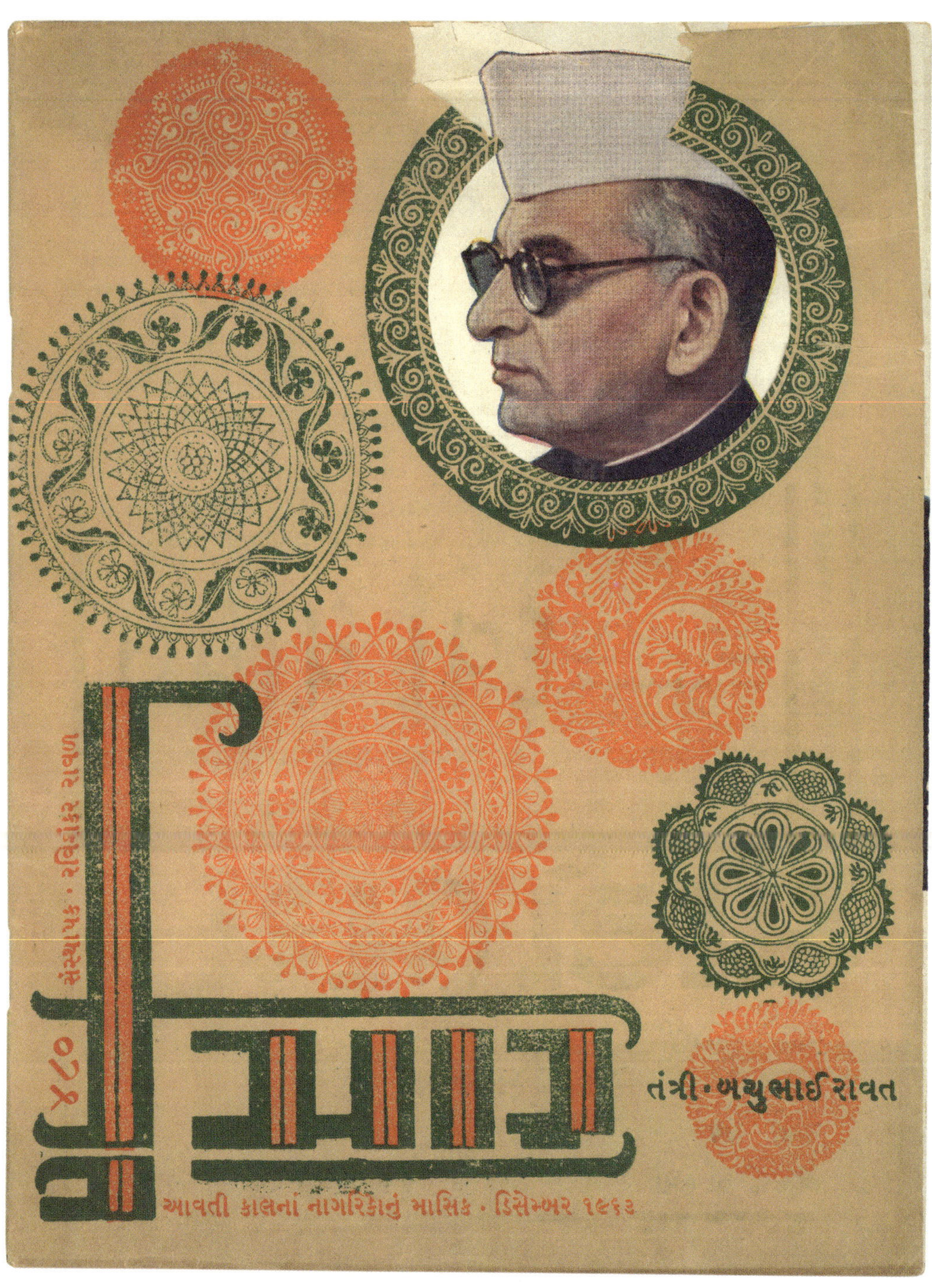

KUMAR #480 · DECEMBER 1963

Readers Write

In the October ⟨1963⟩ issue of Kumar, you have mentioned the weekly 'Gujarati' from Mumbai. In that a column discussing all kinds of politics would be published every week, and I—amongst many other state officials—used to read it regularly. In this, the English column written by Dinshaw Edulji Wacha (later titled Sir), was enthusiastically read by Pherozeshah Merwanjee Mehta. He ⟨Mehta⟩ would greatly praise the political policies of its ⟨the weekly's⟩ editor Shri Ichharam ⟨Desai⟩.[32]

Shouldn't this humble writer receive some kindness, with regards to the opinion of Kshitij ('not to be read')?

With regards to art, uniform criticisms and thoughts are not seen everywhere. 'This side or that'—to decide this, a dice is rolled. When Modern Art crosses even the limit of limits, then one cannot not accept the truth found in the words of this art critic:

"When reason dreams monsters are born," ... "For over forty years now a bewildered public has been faced with the baffling phenomena of Modern Art. It has listened to serious critical discussion not only of the work of bonafide artists but also of the art of children, lunatics, and more recently of chimpanzees. The art, which imposed order on the flux of forms and events at one time, now seems wholly given over to chaos. No wonder that Modern Art is an elaborate joke kept going on by astute publicists." ('Art in Crisis' by Hans Sedlmayr)

—*Pherozeshah Rustomji Mehta (Karachi)*

32 — The weekly 'Gujarati', founded by Ichharam Desai in 1880 in Bombay, published articles on political, social, and literary subjects, and was instrumental in spreading the views of the Indian National Congress (INC). Pherozeshah Merwanjee Mehta and Dinshaw Edulji Wacha were both founding members of the INC.

Here, Pherozeshah Rustomji Mehta's mention of Wacha, Mehta, and Desai seems to refer to the politics of that time. There seems to be some delicate play of politics between the three—in terms of working solely towards an independent nation versus working in toe with the British government. For example, while Desai was arrested for treason by the British for his political writing, Merwanjee Mehta was knighted by the British government for his service as a lawyer, and was in turn instrumental in Desai's release.

Yet, Mehta seems to hint at their interest in (and respect of) each other's opinions even though their stances were not aligned.

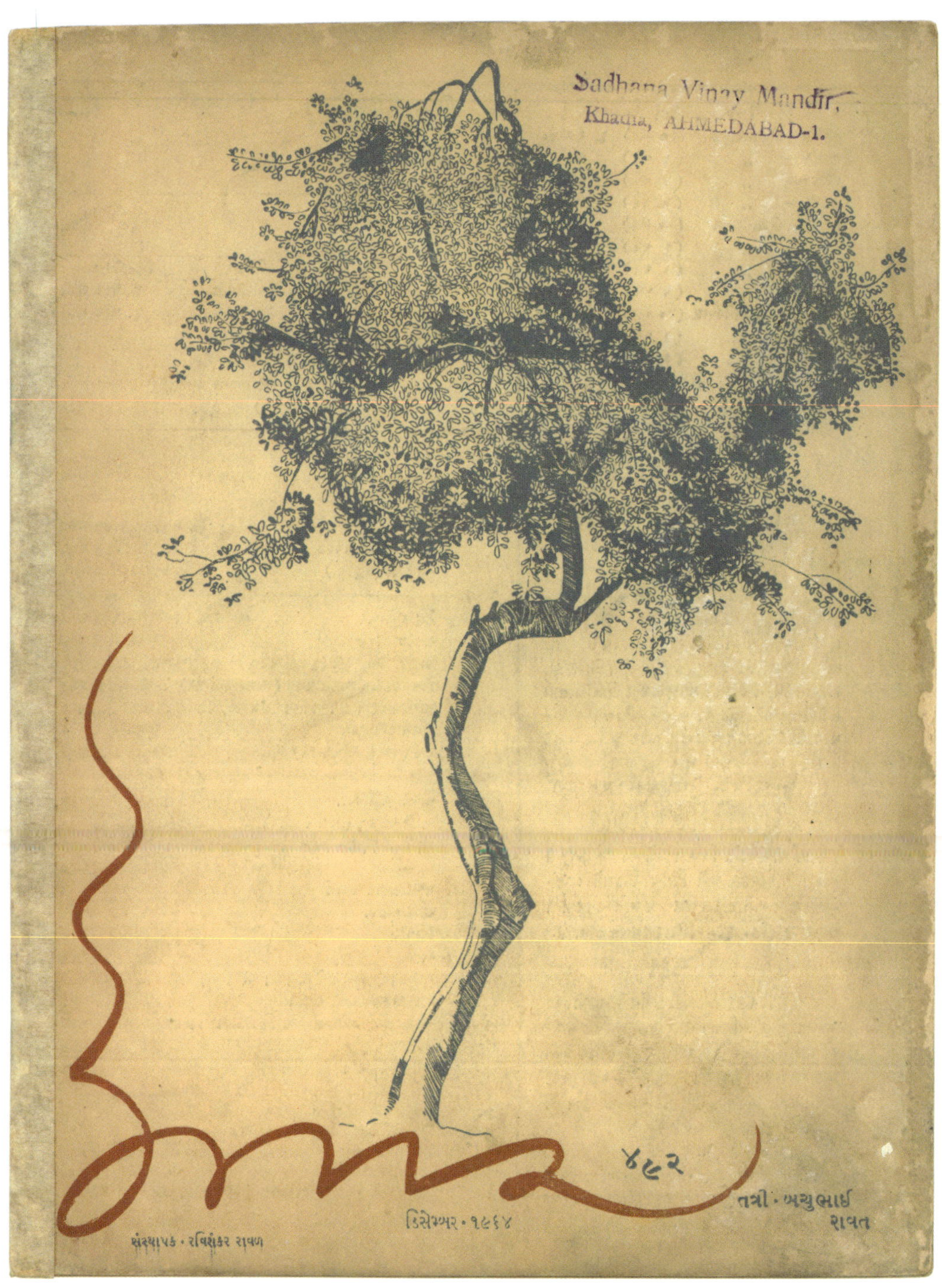

KUMAR #492 · DECEMBER 1964

Readers Write

Recently, I have received a letter from our respected master Shri Vishnuprasad R. Trivedi; in that he has especially mentioned one aspect, which I believe you would get joy in knowing. He writes:

"Your perspective towards the art of painting seems reasonable to me. Today, the upside-down (*shirshasana*) approach that has taken over the arts, is one that I oppose. The philosophy behind it is wrong and it leads a man to destruction. From the arts, the elements of beauty, aesthetics, intent, harmony, arrangement, and restraint, have all been removed by novice artists and their supportive art critics. The reason behind this seems to be to reclaim the original inspirations of art, from prehistoric times. This seems childish. When it comes to culture, one cannot just go back to the past. Through meaningless gestures and antics, you can only create momentary curiosity, but that curiosity will result in foolishness, confusion, and ridicule in a split second. I am hopeful that this epidemic of anti-art that belongs to this era will not continue for long. However, artists and art critics should also make an effort to stop this epidemic." (V.R.T.)

—*Pherozeshah Rustomji Mehta (Karachi)*

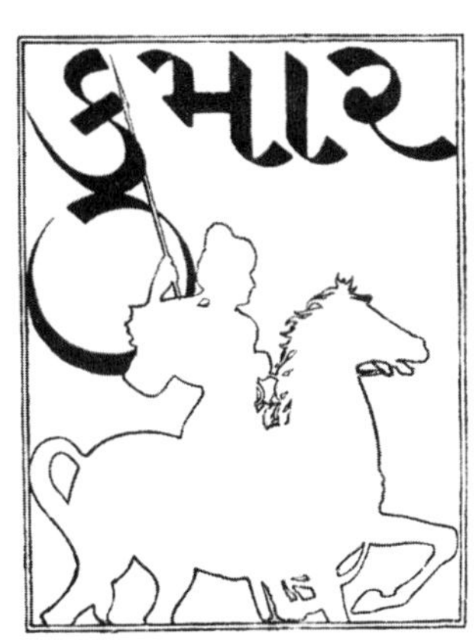

કુમાર

POSTSCRIPT

KUMAR: A PERIODICAL FOR THE CITIZENS OF TOMORROW

Founded in Ahmedabad in 1924 by the artist and educator Ravishankar Raval (1892–1977), and writer and design enthusiast Bachubhai Ravat (1898–1980), *Kumar*—a literary and cultural periodical in Gujarati—can be best described through two of its (many) bylines: 'A Monthly for the Rising Public' (*Ugati Praja nu Masik*) and 'Today's Periodical for Tomorrow's Citizens' (*Aavatikaal na Nagariko Maate nu Aajnu Masik*).

Kumar[1]—which translates to 'a young boy'; one who is at the brink of becoming a man—became a space to "provide material that gives the emerging youth a new vision towards their lives"[2]. In keeping with this spirit and context, the cover image of the very first issue (January 1924) was drawn and designed by Raval, and featured an image of a young man riding a horse. Raval explained this image by stating that the youthful horse stood for the readers' unparalleled enthusiasm, while the gesture of holding the horse's rein symbolised a sense of control over this enthusiasm, through rational thought. The spear in the boy's hand stood for his well-thought-out target, while the young man himself was symbolic of youth—the reader—who was moving towards *tomorrow*.

Born and brought up in Bhavnagar, Ravishankar Raval pursued his studies in painting at Sir JJ School of Art in Bombay in the early 1900s. The roots of *Kumar* can be traced back to this time in Bombay, where theatre and print activities had been flourishing with significant involvement from the Gujarati-Parsi community of the city. It was here that Raval met Haji Mohammad Alarakhiya Shivji, a writer, journalist, collector, and connoisseur of printed matter, who founded the Gujarati periodical *Vismi Sadi* (which translates to '20th Century') in 1916. Inspired by periodicals from the West such as *Nash's Magazine* and *Pearson's Magazine*, Haji's initiative to publish a pictorial periodical was met with enthusiasm

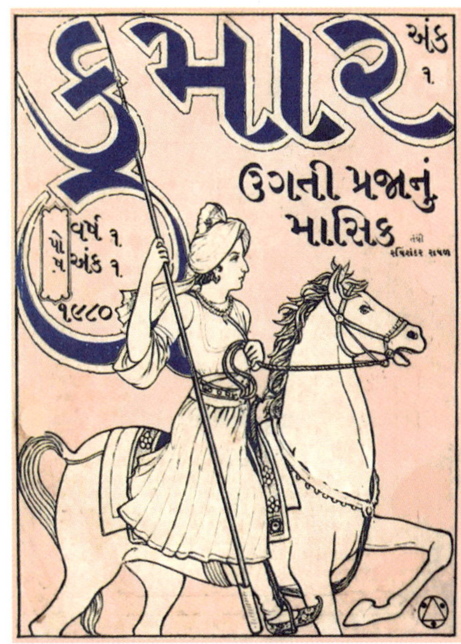

Kumar #1 · January 1924

---

1 — The title was borrowed from a handwritten Gujarati periodical of the same name from the early 1920s run by students of Dakshinamurti Vidyarthi Bhavan (a school in Bhavnagar, Gujarat). However, in the Editor's Note of the first issue of *Kumar* (January 1924), on p. 3, Raval clarified that the periodical was not only meant for young boys (*kumars*), but also for young girls (*kumaris*), and the word *'kumar'* was to be understood as youth in general.

2 — Translated from: 'For the Reader' (*Vaanchnar Ne*), February Issue of *Kumar*, 1924, p. 2.

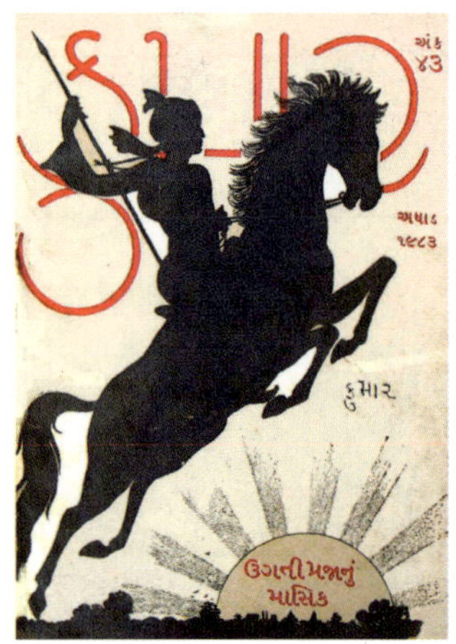

I

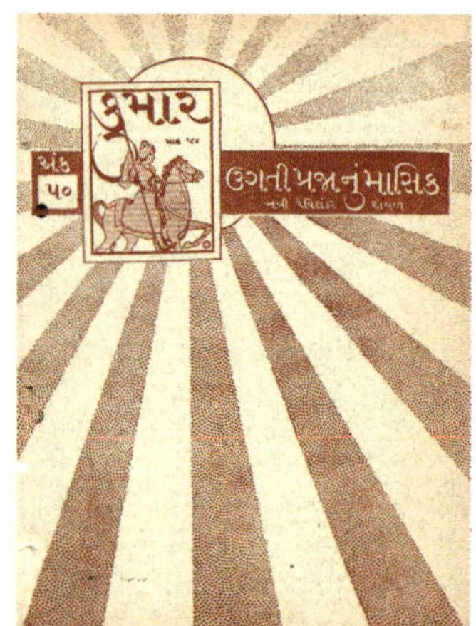

II

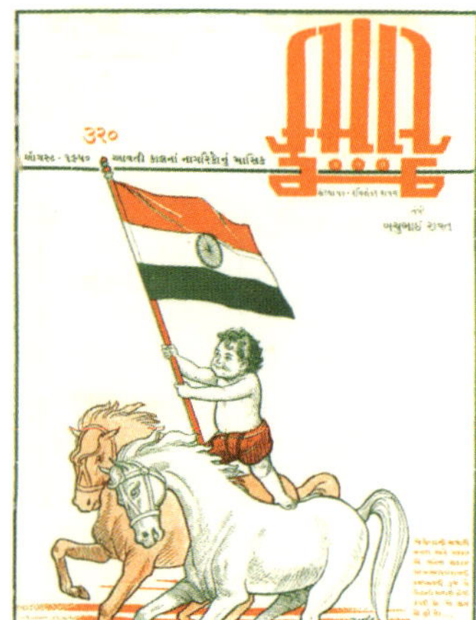

III

Variations of the visual of a young boy riding a horse, as seen on the covers of *Kumar*:

I.   Kumar #43 · July 1927
II. Kumar #50 · February 1928
III. Kumar #320 · August 1950

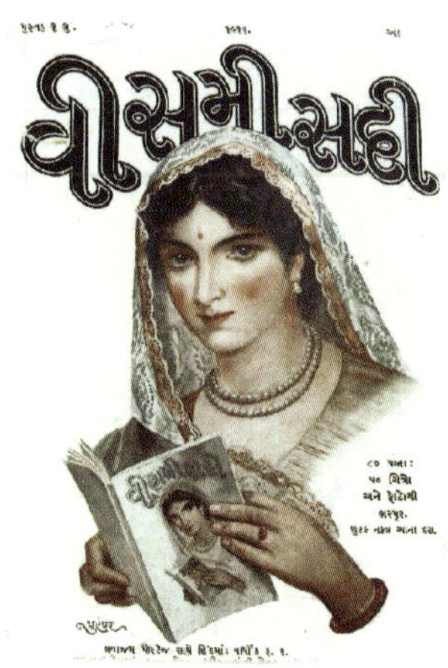

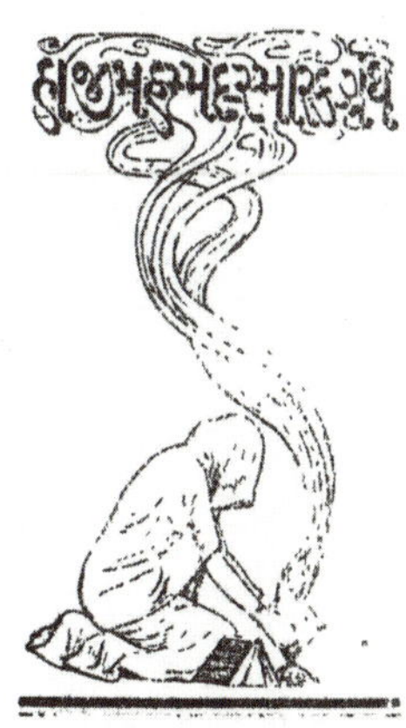

Cover page of the first issue of *Vismi Sadi*, April 1916.

Cover page of *Haji Mohammad Smarak Granth,* published in 1922.

by Raval, a young graduate, who was roped in as a frequent collaborator for illustrations.

During this collaboration with Haji, Raval met Bachubhai Ravat—a writer and journalist born in Ahmedabad and brought up in Gondal, Rajkot. Ravat was then the publisher and editor of *Gyananjali*, a handwritten periodical with pages filled with poems, conversations, decorative drawings, and stories that were reflective of the time.

Both ardent followers of Mahatma Gandhi's ideology, his critique of English-centric education, and encouragement of alternative educational structures, Raval and Ravat began to plot strategies for a periodical that would "offer significant guidance for art, aesthetics or newness, adventure, or social-progress"[3]. In his autobiography, Raval expanded on this further by stating the need for a "periodical that builds a connection between school and home, and in turn offers awareness and discipline in relationships, adventures, and virtues"[4]. This was met by Ravat's vision of *prajashikshan*—education for the masses—through journalism, a profession filled with responsibilities of shaping the social, political, and cultural viewpoints of the public. Thus, in and through *Kumar*, Raval and Ravat's companionship brought together two crucial strands of the evolving public sphere: Print and Pedagogy.

With *Kumar*, Raval and Ravat published a range of content that included poetry, stories, articles, puzzles, jokes, games, how-to's, instructionals, letters from readers, artist profiles, book reviews, announcements, and more, with subjects ranging across history, science, medicine, philosophy, politics, technology, literature, arts, and beyond. The range of subjects covered brought with it a well-honed acceptance of multiple perspectives, facilitated by the accepting yet cautious moderation of the editors (as can be seen in the debate that populates this book

3 — While Raval's hope that Ravat would meet Haji and collaborate with him did not materialise due to Haji's sudden demise, the beginning of their working companionship is marked by *Haji Mohammad Smarak Granth*—a book that Raval and Ravat published as a tribute to Haji.

4 — Quotes translated from: Raval, Ravishankar. *Gujarat ma Kala na Pagaran.* 1967. Kala Ravi Trust and Archer, 2009, p. 333.

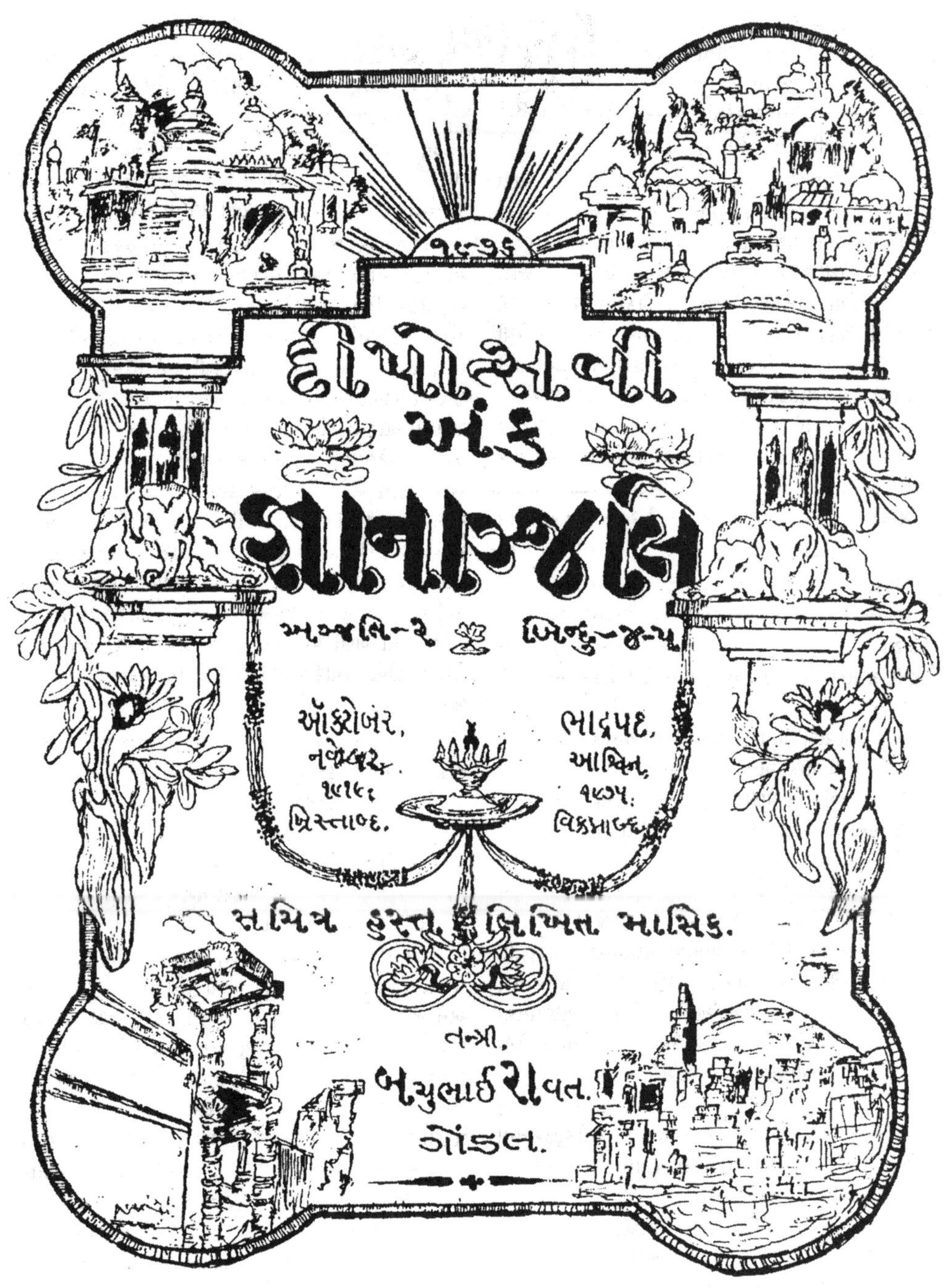

Cover page of *Gyananjali*

Published in the *Bachubhai Ravat Janmashatabdi Visheshaank*
(Kumar #841 · February 1998)

as well). Interjections with clarificatory notes, relevant information, images that add to the dialogue, timely responses to readers, and even calls for other elaborations on subjects were frequent.

With an issue out every month like clockwork for nearly 100 years (and counting), the periodical carried within its pages everything from features on personalities such as President Roosevelt, Samuel Johnson, Marie Curie, and Karl Marx, to columns on beetles and wild boars, in-depth research into design and typography, and articles talking of how one must 'Always Have the Camera on Your Shoulder While Travelling' (*Camera ne Khabhe Bhervine j faro*), to 'The Art of Running Away' (*Bhaagi Jaavani Kala*), and even 'Is the Government Occupying its Seat in Delhi just to Swat Flies?' (*Sarkar Jakh Marva Dilli ni Gaadiye Bethi Chhe?*). Special emphasis was further given to 'new' writings about Gujarat, its history, architecture, literature, artists, and current events, as the editors saw in the periodical an opportunity to inculcate a Gujarati cultural consciousness amongst their readers.

Alongside such textual content, a significant characteristic of *Kumar* was its extensive image-publishing. Photographs, artworks, drawings, sketches, maps, diagrams, and illustrations populated the pages of the periodical with just as much care and attention as the writing, and this was further heightened by Ravat's penchant for design. Ravat's past experience with publishing played a major role in the setting up of *Kumar's* activities. In an interview, Ravat talks of how he not only played the role of publisher, but was also the writer, designer, and illustrator for his handwritten periodicals, which taught him the nuances of design and publishing, and acted as the stepping stones for the founding of the periodical. His work experience at Navajivan Press, amongst other publishing houses, also played a pivotal role in his understanding of vernacular print publishing.

Owing to these past experiences, his handling of the design of *Kumar*—which kept in mind the importance of using space economically without sacrificing on aesthetics—can be seen not only through the layouts of each spread in the periodical, but also through the covers, amongst many other nuanced details.[5]

In spite of the budgetary constraints of image-publishing in the 1920s and 30s[6], *Kumar* published a minimum of three to four full-page colour images in each issue, often representing artworks.[7] Along with these artworks, a range of images of people, places, and events from across the world also found

---

5 — In 1998, *Kumar's* February issue (*Bachubhai Ravat Janmashatabdi Visheshaank*) was published as a special edition to mark Ravat's birth anniversary and focused solely on his contribution to design and typography, within the periodical as well as otherwise. In an essay written in this issue by Ravat titled 'The Art of Image-Publishing in Gujarat' (*Gujarat ni Granthasth Chitrakala*), he talks about the covers, describing how the eye-catching titles, effective compositions of image and text, and the powerful colours ensure that the cover not only hints at what is to come in the pages inside, but also leaves a lasting impression on both the eyes and the mind. This issue also worked as a manual, and introduced various methodologies and processes ranging from page layouts, binding, and fonts, to effective copyediting and printing.

6 — Based in Ahmedabad, Ravat had taken over the responsibilities for printing the initial issues of *Kumar*, and he arranged for this with *Navajivan*, a printing press set up alongside a publishing house of the same name founded by Mahatma Gandhi in 1919. At that time, no other printer was ready to print the periodical, given its complex and diverse design. Unfortunately, *Navajivan* soon refused to continue their production due to financial instability, and *Kumar* took control of their own production and set up the Kumar Karyalaya in 1925.

7 — Most often works of artists from India were featured on these pages, particularly those from Gujarat, including Rasiklal Parikh, Somalal Shah, Chhaganlal Jadav, and Kanu Desai.

space in the periodical. With such ambitious publishing that brought together writings and images from local as well as international contexts, came the question of sourcing them.

To arrive at the visual aesthetics of the periodical, Raval and Ravat undertook extensive research into a number of Western periodicals. Ahmedabad's proximity to Bombay, the centre of trade under the British rule at the time, guaranteed access to a range of periodicals and journals from Europe and America. Amongst these, Raval was greatly influenced by *My Magazine*, a children's magazine published by Arthur Mee from England, as well as Mee's *The Children's Encyclopaedia* and *Children's Newspaper* with regards to content for young readers. He also subscribed to periodicals such as *Boys' Life* and *The American Boy* from the United States, and referred to *Art*, published by Guy H. Lockwood from Kalamazoo (Michigan), to design the title and image of the first cover page of *Kumar*. Recalling how different periodicals were sourced, Raval writes in his autobiography:

"Every Friday, the freshly printed periodicals from England and America would be sold from the [A.H.] Wheeler's stall at the railway station. Before the periodicals that were useful for our work would get sold-out, Bachubhai would reach there. He knew the stall owner—owing to his interest in periodicals—and he would stay there for a few hours, going through all the periodicals of his liking, and purchasing those with stories, writings or collections of images that would pertain to our interests."[8]

Parallelly, Ravat continued pursuing research in printing techniques and technology. He acquired the periodicals *The American Printer* and *The Inland Printer*

to understand the newly updated aspects of printing, ranging from the technical and financial, to the artistic. He also held subscriptions to English periodicals such as *The Strand Magazine*, *The Pall Mall Magazine*, *The Windsor Magazine*, and *The Idler* that influenced his ideas of pictorial journalism.

When seen in the context of the time, these periodicals that made their way to the country approached the need to circulate information, teach, and inspire in very similar manners. Each seemingly influenced by the other, this way of reaching out to the masses became a key marker of modernity as we understand it today—and may have led to why Raval and Ravat found the format of the periodical to work better than others in order to make art and literature accessible to a wider public. It is important to note that in the early 20th century, when neither gallery systems nor today's internet access existed, public access to works of art was primarily facilitated through such print materials. This dependency on print for access to information about art and culture, both local and international, is particularly true for the moment when Modern Art begins to be practised in the subcontinent.

In addition to this collection of periodicals, *Kumar's* resource library also included encyclopaedias, catalogues, dictionaries, storybooks, scientific journals, and manuals, carefully curated to act not only as textual resources, but also as an image bank from where photographs, paintings, and illustrations could be reproduced. Raval and Ravat were also keenly following writings published in other Indian periodicals, weeklies, and newspapers in Hindi, Marathi, and English that reflected social, cultural, and

---

8 — Translated from: Raval, Ravishankar. *Gujarat ma Kala na Pagaran*. 1967. Kala Ravi Trust and Archer, 2009, p. 334.

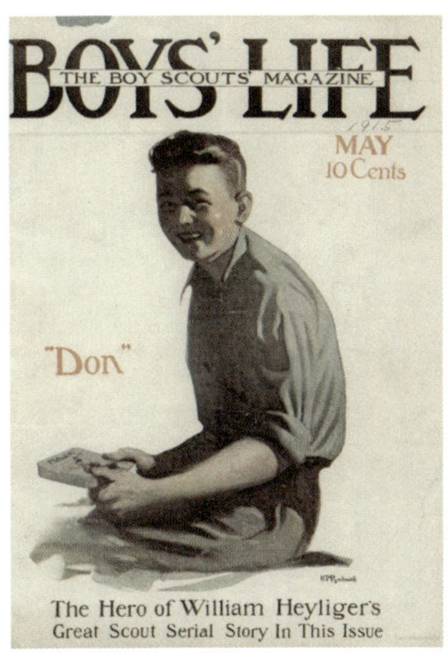

I

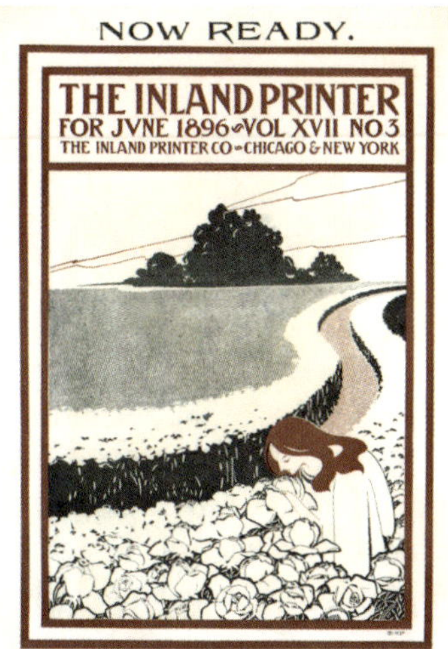

III

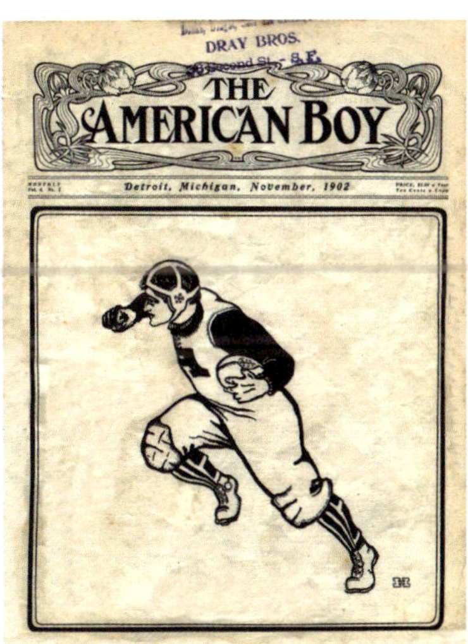

II

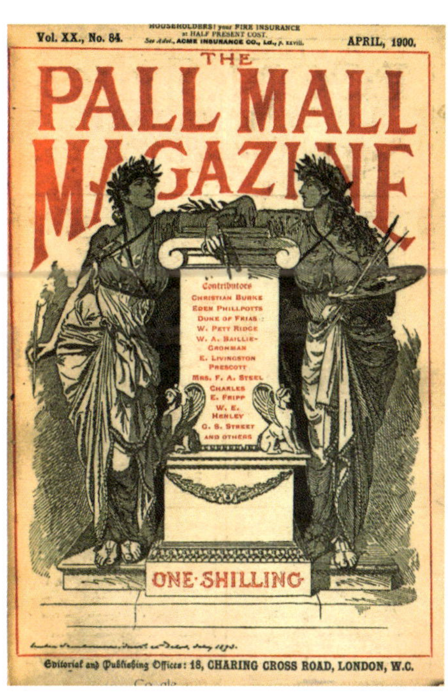

IV

I.   Boys' Life, May 1915
II. The American Boy, November 1902
III. The Inland Printer, June 1896
IV. The Pall Mall Magazine, April 1900

political concerns of that time, and relevant material from these would occasionally get translated into Gujarati.

Kumar's translation practice also played a crucial role in making some important writing on art available to the Gujarati reader. Articles such as 'The Artist's Religion' (a translation of Nandalal Bose's speech from Bengali, *Kalakar no Dharm*), writings by E.B. Havell and Karl Khandalavala, and even a three-part essay by Hermann Goetz titled 'Contribution of Gujarat in the History of Indian Art' (*Hind ni Kala na Itihas ma Gujarat no Faalo*), amongst many others, became a way for local readers to access discourse from across the country and the world.

It is important to note that while the print culture of Bombay had a certain presence, print culture of Bengal too had become quite popular at the time, especially amongst Gujarati artists and educators. In the early 1920s, Raval was invited on a cultural trip to visit Calcutta, Santiniketan, and Banaras. During this trip, Raval met Bengali artists such as Abanindranath Tagore and Gaganendranath Tagore, as well as Ramananda Chatterjee, who was the editor of *Prabasi* and *Modern Review*[9]. He was also introduced to Upendrakishore Ray Chowdhury, a writer and artist who published *Sandesh*, one of the first children's magazines in the subcontinent. Ray Chowdhury would later design the colour blocks for the cover of the first issue of *Kumar*, owing to his mastery of print and block making techniques.

These meetings were formative for Raval, introducing him to practices in the subcontinent that not only resulted in

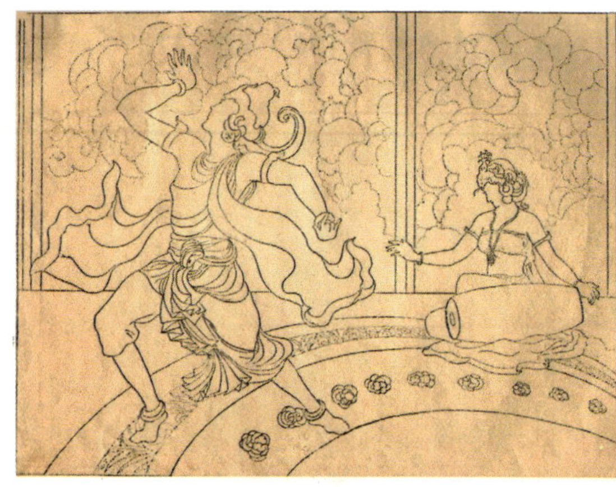

An example of the 'Colour Filling-in Competition' (*Rangpuranini Harifai*), with instructions to fill and send back.

Published in Kumar #96 · December 1931

exchange of ideas, but also of content which could be translated and circulated further. But of course, with circulation also came the need for appropriately moderated discourse, and the desire to effectively bring forth various contesting opinions.

THE PERIODICAL AS A DISCURSIVE SITE

Through its editorial practice, *Kumar* aspired to build a unique discursive space that was engaging and participatory for its readers, one where the usual publisher/subscriber dynamics could be challenged and expanded. With activities such as drawings to be coloured in and sent back (*Rangpuranini Harifai*) and photography competitions where readers could participate by sending in their entries, the objective was to reach the widest possible Gujarati audience, and invite them to be a part of the conversation.[10]

9 — *Modern Review* (founded in 1901) and *Prabasi* (founded in 1907) were two monthly periodicals in English and Bengali respectively. Published out of Calcutta, the periodicals printed parallel content in both languages.

10 — To publicise the newly launched periodical, a two-colour booklet highlighting *Kumar's* purpose and range of writing was printed and circulated within other periodicals and newspapers. This exercise achieved around 500 subscriptions, which was half of what was required for them to run sustainably.

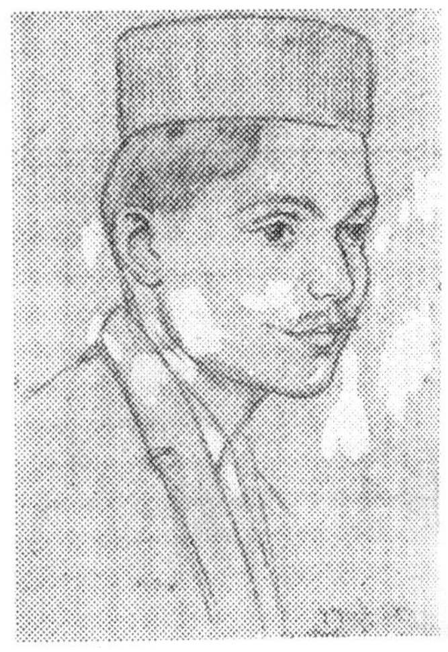

I

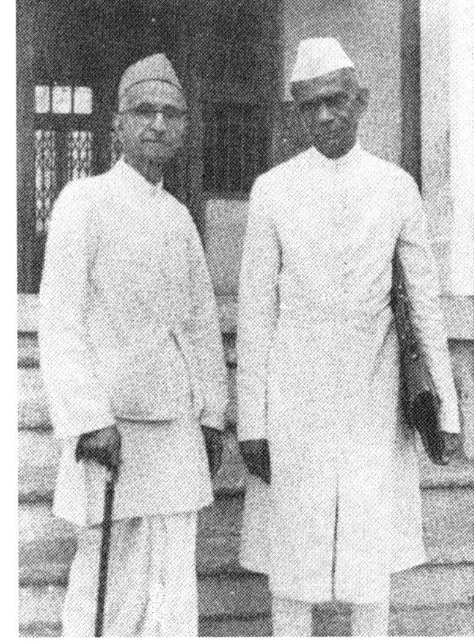

III

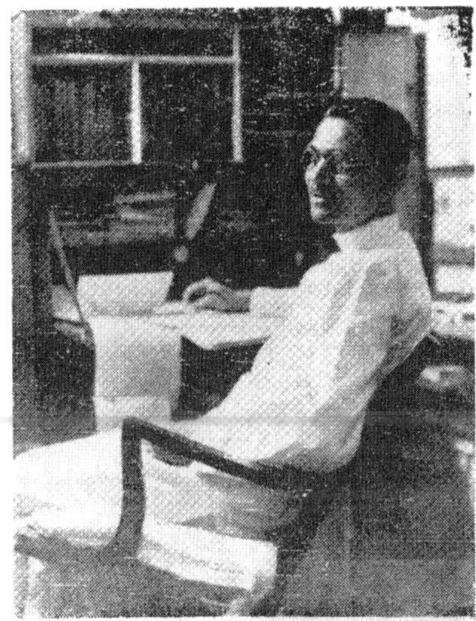

II

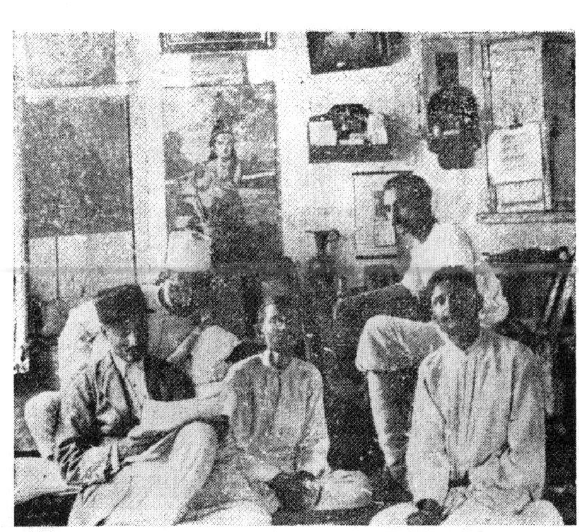

IV

I.   A portrait of Bachubhai Ravat made by Ravishankar Raval.
II. Bachubhai Ravat seated at his desk in the *Kumar* office.
III. The founder-editor of *Kumar* Ravishankar Raval with his
     colleague Bachubhai Ravat.
IV. Five members from the early days of *Kumar*: from the left—
     artist Ravishankar Pandit, Bachubhai Ravat, poet Deshalji
     Parmar, 'Dhumaketu', and Ravishankar Raval (seated on the
     chair behind).

Published in the *Bachubhai Ravat Janmashatabdi Visheshaank*
(Kumar #841 · February 1998)

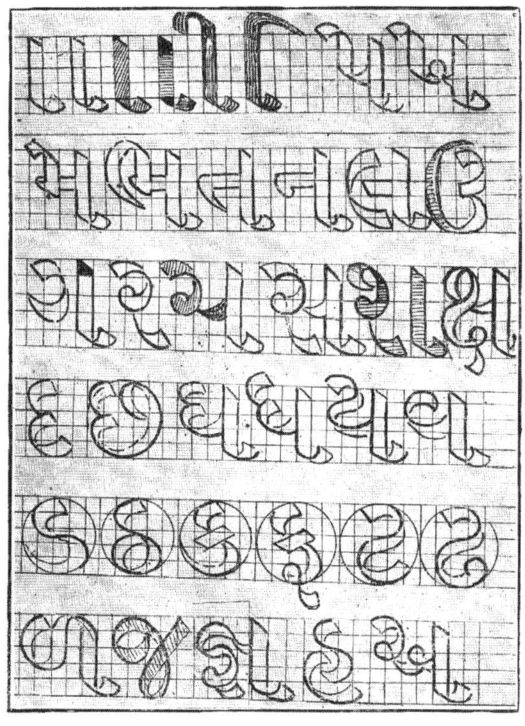

I

II

I. A step-by-step illustration on how to draft alphabets
aesthetically, from the article 'The Art of Writing Beautiful
Alphabets' (*Sundar Aksharon Lakhvani Kala*).

Published in Kumar #10 · October 1924

II. An illustration of Bachubhai Ravat's font Ravat Lipi, from the
article *'Ravat Marod'*.

III. An illustration highlighting the entire process and key steps of
binding a book from the article 'Binding: The Lifeline of Books'
(*Pustak ni Jeevadori: Bandhani*).

IV. An image giving a sense of the process of copyediting from the
article 'Press-Copy and Proof Reading'.
Image caption reads: "Once the signs for each kind of correction
are memorised by the copy editor, the process of proof reading
becomes easy. It's the speed at which the process is carried out
that takes time to master, which gets developed with experience."

II, III, and IV: Published in the *Bachubhai Ravat Janmashatabdi
Visheshaank* (Kumar #841 · February 1998)

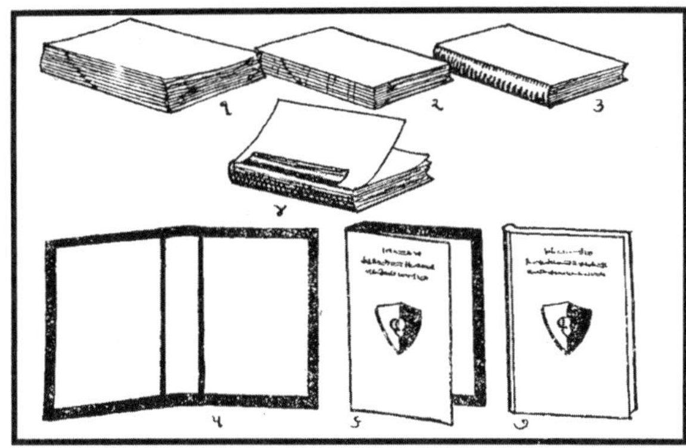

III

ત્યારે 'સાહિત્ય' એટલે શું ?

માણસના આત્મામાં રહેલા ભાવોની ઉત્કટ
વણ્ણવી તે તે બધી સ્થિતિઓ રસાનુભવન હૃદ સંક્ષ
સંતર્પણની સ્થિતિઓ છે. તેવી સ્થિતિ, ભાવ
અને રસના તેવા અનુભવ મનુષ્યમાત્રને સર્વ
સામાન્ય હોવાથી તે સર્વનું પ્રત્યક્ષીકરણ વા
આલેખન જેમાં તેવી રચના-કાવ્ય કે નાટક,
રસભર નિબંધ, નવલિકા કે નવલ-પ્રત્યેક
માણસને માણસ તરીકે આકર્ષે છે અને વળી
કરે છે તેના આત્માને ઐચ્છિક રસમતલ
સ્ફૂર્તિનો અધિકારી ઠરાવે છે.

એવાં આકર્ષણ ને વશીકરણ કરનાર હરેક
રચના તે સાહિત્ય અને તેનો રચનાર તે જ
સાહિત્યકાર અને બીજે નહ. એવા સાહિત્ય-
કારને તો સિસૃક્ષા જે સાચું ને ઉત્કૃષ્ટ
જીવન છે કોઇ સ્થૂળ પદાર્થ કે દૃશ્ય, અથવા
ઊર્ધ અણુધારી અકળ અંતઃપ્રેરણા જ્યારેજ્યારે
એ સિસૃક્ષાને જાગૃત કરે છે ત્યારેત્યારે સા-
હિત્યકારને હાથે એવું ધન્ય ને અમર સર્જન
થઇ જાય છે જે સાહિત્ય સંજ્ઞાને પાત્ર ઠરે છે.

વિજયરાય કલ્યાણરાય

* સિસૃક્ષા એટલે અહનિંશ રચવા કરવાની
માનવ સહજ અનિવાર્ય એષણા.

IV

Kumar's publishing practice also included the production of products such as calendars and artist-portfolios of Gujarati artists, and on occasion prints of artworks within the periodical itself that could be easily removed and displayed on the walls of one's home. There was also a space for 'pen-pals', where readers of *Kumar* would share their addresses looking for correspondents, resulting in many international exchanges and connections.

This participatory encouragement dates as far back as the first ever issue, where Raval introduced the column 'Ask the Editor' (*Puchho Tantri Ne*), along with a template which the reader could use to write back. While this column ran on and off for the next couple of years, under Ravat's editorship it was reintroduced under the name 'Readers Write' (*Vaachako Lakhe Chhe*) in 1952—a column that played an undeniably crucial role in the Modern Art debate.

Responses from readers engaged with not only content published as articles in the periodical, but also served as a space for requests, conversational voices, referential discourse, and expansions on topics that were addressed. Blurring the line between a 'writer' and a 'reader', it is particularly interesting to note that during the course of the debate, Pherozeshah Rustomji Mehta continues to quote references from readers' responses as well as send in responses himself, and Jyoti Bhatt actively sends in responses to articles on other subjects. While the readers themselves were from both within Gujarat (larger cities as well as small towns) as well as from Bombay, Calcutta, and Karachi, it is important to mention here that most often the respondents were well-read, literate Gujarati men, and only on rare occasions would one find a letter from a female reader.

In addition to the active engagement with readers when it came to the generation of content for the periodical, Raval and Ravat's vision also included the desire to make art education more accessible to the public. In the first year of *Kumar*, Raval—an artist himself, and later a mentor to many young artists—published a series of illustrated articles titled 'Drawing is Easy' (*Chitarvu Sahel Chhe*), where he offered tutorial lessons to the readers on how to draw simple images, including faces, bodies, animals, and objects, using lines. This series continued on and off until 1937.

Reflecting on the lack of art education spaces in the country (an opinion that is mirrored in the first reader's response in this book, by Jyotish Jani in 1959), Raval frequently wrote about cultural literacy, art education, and visual culture with an emphasis on Gujarat. He also ran an informal art school (the Gujarat Kalasangh Chitrashala) at his residence, the activities of which were closely followed in the pages of *Kumar*, where from time-to-time drawings and paintings made by his students would be published.[11]

Raval also closely followed the setting up of the Faculty of Fine Arts in 1950 under The Maharaja Sayajirao University of Baroda (MSU)[12], and wrote about its founders—Markand Bhatt and Hansa Mehta—in *Kumar*, elucidating information about the application and admission process for prospective students. This faculty quickly set a benchmark for modern art education and attracted students and teachers from all across

---

11 — Parallel to Raval's pedagogical endeavours, Ravat too ran a club dedicated to photography, and another to poetry, which encouraged continued and focussed discussion and practice on these subjects. These clubs ran long after Ravat's time, and the poetry club runs to this day.

12 — The Maharaja Sayajirao University of Baroda (formerly Baroda College from 1881 to 1949) was the first college founded in post-independence India to offer undergraduate and postgraduate degrees in Visual Arts.

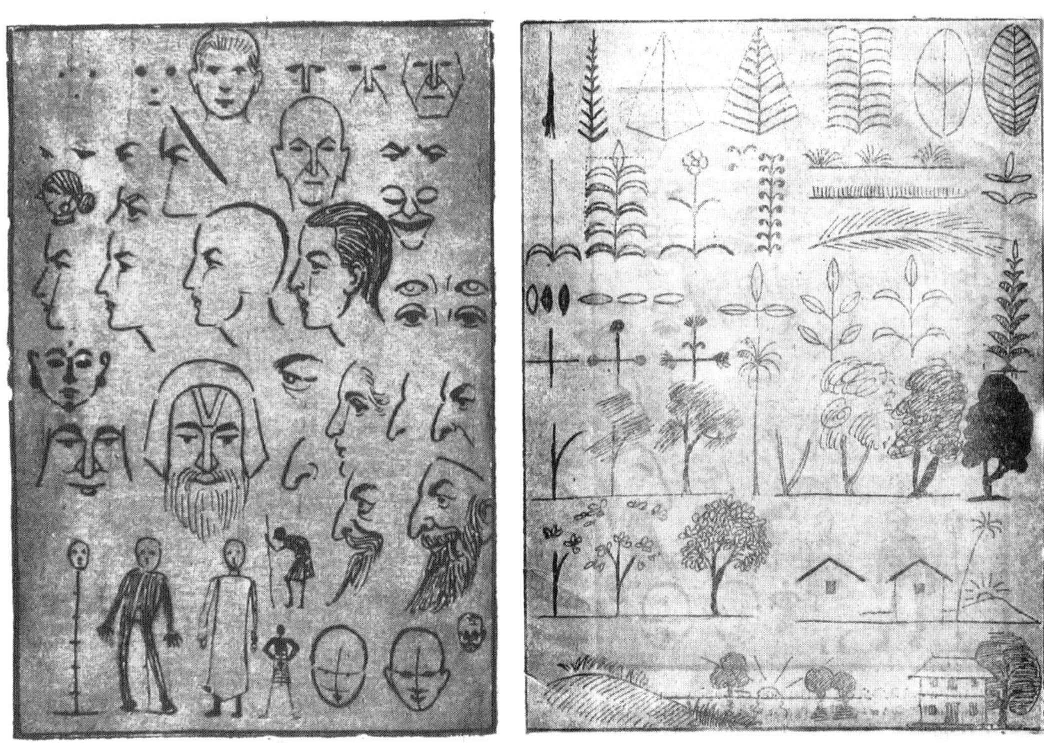

Pages from the article 'Drawing is Easy' (*Chitarvu Sahel Chhe*) by Ravishankar Raval.

Published in Kumar #6 · June 1924

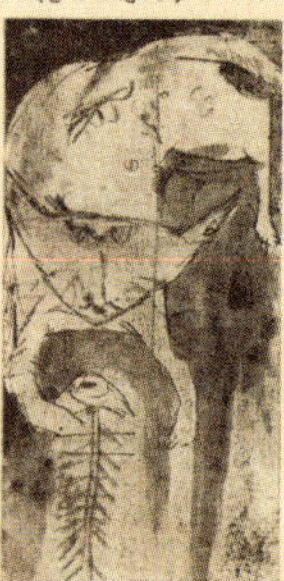

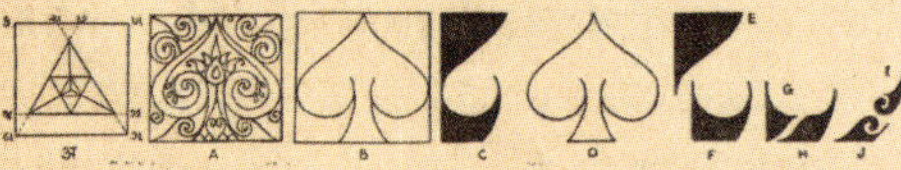

Negro Boxer (હબસી મુક્કાબાજ)
Henri Mattise (હેન્રી માતીસ)
Cut-out (કાગળ કરીને કાઢેલું ચિત્ર)

I

II

I. 'Readers Write' (*Vaachako Lakhe Chhe*)
   Published in Kumar #464 · August 1962

II. The first page of 'Negro Boxer' (*Habsi Mukkabaj*)
    Published in Kumar #428 · August 1959

the country, and it was during this period that Vadodara (and in turn Gujarat) became an important centre for art education.[13]

Following this, the Gujarat State Lalit Kala Academy was established in 1961 in Ahmedabad, separate from the central Lalit Kala Akademi in Delhi, to promote Gujarati artists and their practices. Interestingly, the central Lalit Kala Akademi had meanwhile initiated National Awards for artists, which were given out in three categories: Modern, Academic (realistic), and Oriental (Indian), providing an insight into how art was being framed and studied in that period.[14]

This crucial moment in the history of Gujarat[15] and its position in the world of art, also marks the period when Jyoti Bhatt began his art education at MSU. Having considered Kala Bhavana (Santiniketan) for his higher education, Bhatt heard of the recently established Fine Arts Faculty in Vadodara from a friend, and chose it owing to its proximity to his hometown, and the opportunity to study under N.S. Bendre and K.G. Subramanyan, who were by then well-known in the field. He began his art education in 1950 as part of the first batch enrolled at the Faculty of Fine Arts, going on to study painting and printmaking for six years.

Deeply influenced by the pedagogical practices of Bendre and Subramanyan, as well as his extensive travel and documentation of tribal belts, his practice through the years explored the academic divides between art and craft. His time spent under the guidance of Bendre introduced him to the nuances of Cubism, as well as other modernist styles, which were pushed further through time spent soon after in Italy and then in New York under a scholarship and grant respectively. Soon after completing his education, Bhatt began teaching at the Faculty in Vadodara. From 1959 to 1992, he taught at the painting department, opting for early retirement to focus more on his own practice.

While Bhatt's background is strongly rooted in Gujarat, it is important to note the difference in generation and context between him and Mehta, as an additional entry point into the Modern Art debate.

Pherozeshah Rustomji Mehta, born in Karachi in 1880, was the youngest among eight siblings. Born into a family that came into prominence in the early years when the city of Karachi was being developed by the British as a trading port, his siblings embarked in setting up new businesses. Unlike his brothers, Mehta's interests were in literary activities. He found comfort in working at bookshops, visiting libraries, and feeding his voracious appetite for the spoken and written word.

13 — Alongside its role in modern art education, Vadodara had also become the centre for a modernist periodical movement during the same period, largely under the mentorship of Suresh Joshi, an author, poet, and literary critic. The city became the centre for many important literary periodicals in Gujarati such as *Etad*, *Kshitij*, *Manisha*, *Samput*, *Sayujya*, *Setu*, *Uhapoh*, and others, where modern poets, writers, editors, and artists—including Jyoti Bhatt—frequently collaborated.

14 — Ramnik Bhatt in his reader's response in the April 1959 issue of *Kumar*, refers to Raghav Kaneria's works printed in *Kumar* as part of the announcement when he received the National Award for his sculptures in the Modern Art category, and requests the editors to publish explanatory articles on the subject.

15 — As the Faculty of Fine Arts was coming into being, Gujarat itself was going through many changes. Post the Indian independence, the region of Gujarat that was earlier ruled by the British under the Bombay Presidency became part of the bilingual state of Bombay which merged the princely states of Saurashtra, Baroda, and Kutch. In 1956, the Mahagujarat movement was initiated, claiming for Gujarat the status of an independent state on the basis of linguistic bifurcation. Following this, Gujarat was granted separate statehood on 1st May, 1960. This was also a time when the long-standing claim to a unique cultural identity of Gujarat found footing.

While working as the editor of Karachi's then-daily newspaper *Parsi Sansar ane Lok Sevak*, he published five books in Gujarati on art and culture, in addition to several articles on varying topics. Later, a book titled *Chitrarasika* was published in 1962 which brought together his articles on visual and performing arts, largely from his writings published in *Navchetan* (a Gujarati periodical from Calcutta) and *Kumar*.

As introduced by Ravat within the pages of the periodical, Mehta's eminence as a scholar made him an important resource for others on topics ranging from art and artistic expression, to poetry and styles of elocution. His articles present wit and satire with utmost ease, which can be traced back to the fact that he was one of the few early Gujarati scholars to introduce epigrams into their oration and writing.

Mehta, largely exposed to art through his travels to the art galleries and museums in the West, wrote a number of articles in *Kumar* about Western artworks. His first full length article about Leonardo da Vinci's artwork 'Mona Lisa' called 'The Mystery of That Smile' (*E Smit no Bhed*) was published in *Kumar* as early as 1933. Some of his other articles in *Kumar* were about representations of Venus in artworks, Michelangelo, and the collection in Louvre.

In the late 1950s (as seen in the debate that precedes this), Mehta's scholarly referencing, exposure to art globally, and years of experience in the field of writing, was met serendipitously by Bhatt's youthful determination to explain—and in turn defend—the practices that have been formative to his own artistic work.

While the debate amongst these two authors and the readers of *Kumar* occupied a tiny portion of the periodical's pages—sharing space with a wide variety of other content— its currents continued to resurface in the following two decades, through a number

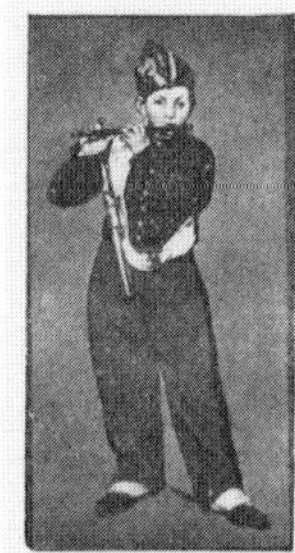
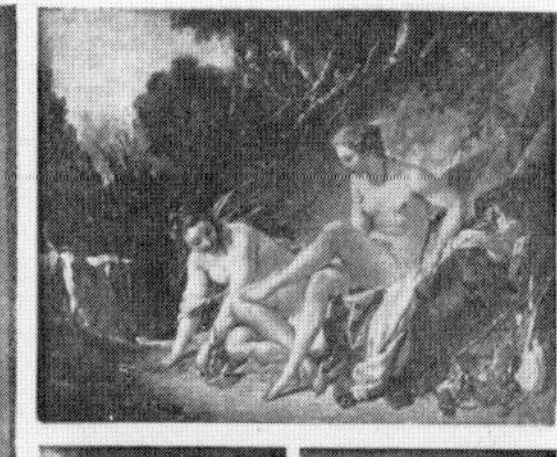
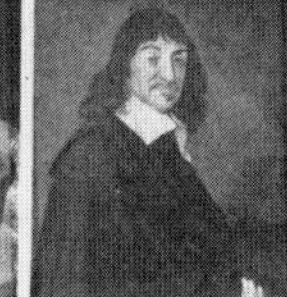

The sixth page of 'Louvre: The World's Largest and Most Prosperous Museum' (*Louvre: Jagatnu Sauthi Jangi ane Samrudh Kaladhaam*) by Pherozeshah Rustomji Mehta.

Published in Kumar #419 · November 1958

of texts and images published under the editorship of Ravat. This could be seen in the regular column 'Story of Art' (*Kalavarta*) and in articles such as 'Are Abstract (Formless) Paintings Meaningless?' (*Shu Abstract (Amurt) Chitro Arthheen Chhe?*). Parallel to this, many modern artists and movements from the West continued to be featured in the periodical, and mentions can be found of auction houses such as Christie's and Sotheby's as well, along with many Indian artists and their works. Marking Raval's 75th birthday, the December 1967 issue was a special 'Art Issue' (*Kala Ank*) where along with 37 images of art works, a number of articles about art in general, and the modern and pre-modern art and architecture of Gujarat in specific, were published.

Bhatt continued writing on a variety of subjects for *Kumar* (with his most recent

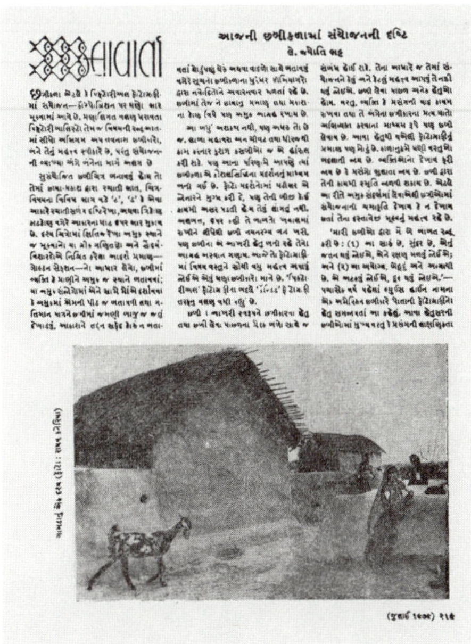

The first page of 'A Perspective on Composition in Today's Photography' (*Aajni Chhabikalama Sanyojanani Drishti*) by Jyoti Bhatt, featuring a photograph by Raghav Kaneria.

Published in Kumar #667 · July 1979

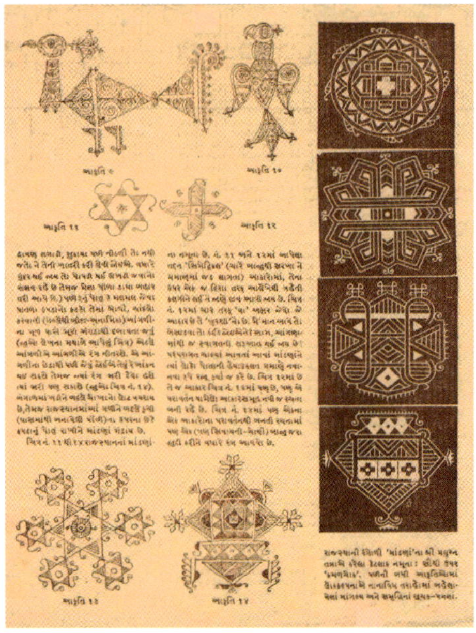

The second page of 'Jyoti Bhatt Teaches: How to Make Rangoli' (*Jyoti Bhatt Shikhve Chhe: Rangoli Kem Paadvi*) by Jyoti Bhatt, featuring illustrations by Pradyumna Tanna.

Published in Kumar #442 · October 1960

text published in 2005) focusing especially on living traditions, and folk and tribal art forms. He also wrote a number of articles on photography, highlighting its practice and history, along with artist profiles of upcoming artists from Gujarat such as Raghav Kaneria, Haku Shah, Khodidas Parmar, and Himmat Shah. Mehta too continued to write for *Kumar* and his last article was on Michelangelo in the 1964 February issue.

In supporting such a wide editorial vision, Ravat had a challenging role to play. In 1942, Raval, burdened by financial hardships, had decided to shut down the periodical. It was then that a few well-wishers of *Kumar* came forward to support it and converted Kumar Karyalaya to a company—Kumar Karyalaya Limited. It was then that Ravat took over the additional responsibility as managing director, parallel to his role as editor. Ravat continued in this position until his death in July 1980.

From August 1980 onwards, Biharilal Taank (who was previously the periodical's sub-editor) took over as the editor until 1987, at which time, owing to financial uncertainties, *Kumar's* publishing was stopped for a period of three years—until 1990. Following this, the board of directors decided to re-launch the periodical, with Dhiru Parikh at the helm. Along with the continued publishing of *Kumar*, Parikh, a writer and poet (and the editor of *Kavilok*, a Gujarati monthly for poetry), also welcomed the idea of archiving and digitising all past issues of the periodical. This herculean task of documentation resulted in a set of CDs which brought together all issues of the periodical from 1924 to 2004 (which served as a valuable resource for the research of this book), made available to the public at a nominal price. Following Parikh's passing in May 2021, Praful Raval, a writer, teacher, and poet took over, and serves as the current editor of *Kumar*. The periodical continues to be published monthly from the very same office in Ahmedabad.

REFERENCES:

— Mehta, Hasit. (Ed.). *Sahityik Samayiko: Parampara ane Prabhav*. Rannade Prakashan, 2012.

— Panchal, S., Tailor, B., and Shukla, J. (Eds.). *Vismi Sadi nu Gujarat*. Samvaad Prakashan, 2002.

— Raval, Ravishankar. *Gujarat ma Kala na Pagaran*. 1967. Kala Ravi Trust and Archer, 2009.

— *Bachubhai Ravat Janmashatabdi Visheshaank*, February Issue of Kumar, 1998.

— "Mijlas", April Issue of Kumar, 1932.

— "Chalo Kumar Karyalaya", April Issue of Kumar, 1932.

— Parikh, Dhiru. "Sampaadan: Ek Sarjanatmak Prakriya", in *Nepathye-thi Prakash-Vartul-Man*, Raman Soni (Ed.). 1996.

— Bhatt, Jyoti. "Roop Naam Jujava", in *Kalagranth: Part 5*, Ramnik Zapadia, Gujarat Kala Pratishthan, 2015.

Images in the postscript are courtesy of *Kumar* archives, the private collection of Anil Relia (Archer Art Gallery, Ahmedabad), and various public domain sources.

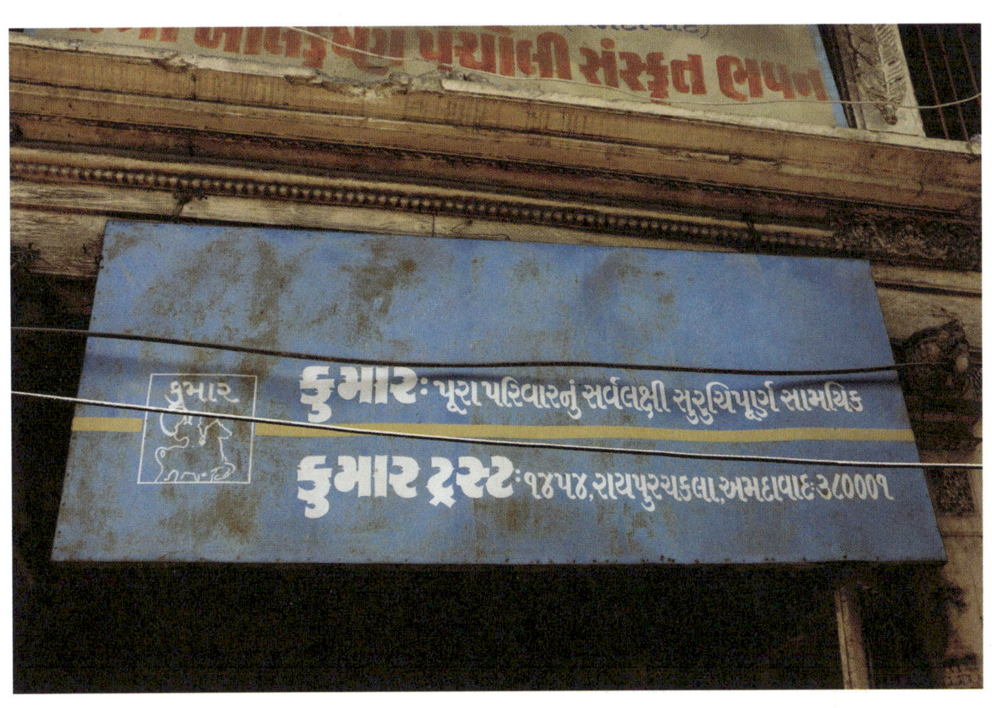
કુમાર: પૂરા પરિવારનું સર્વલક્ષી સુરુચિપૂર્ણ સામયિક
કુમાર ટ્રસ્ટ: ૧૪૫૪, રાયપુરચકલા, અમદાવાદ: ૩૮૦૦૦૧
કુમાર

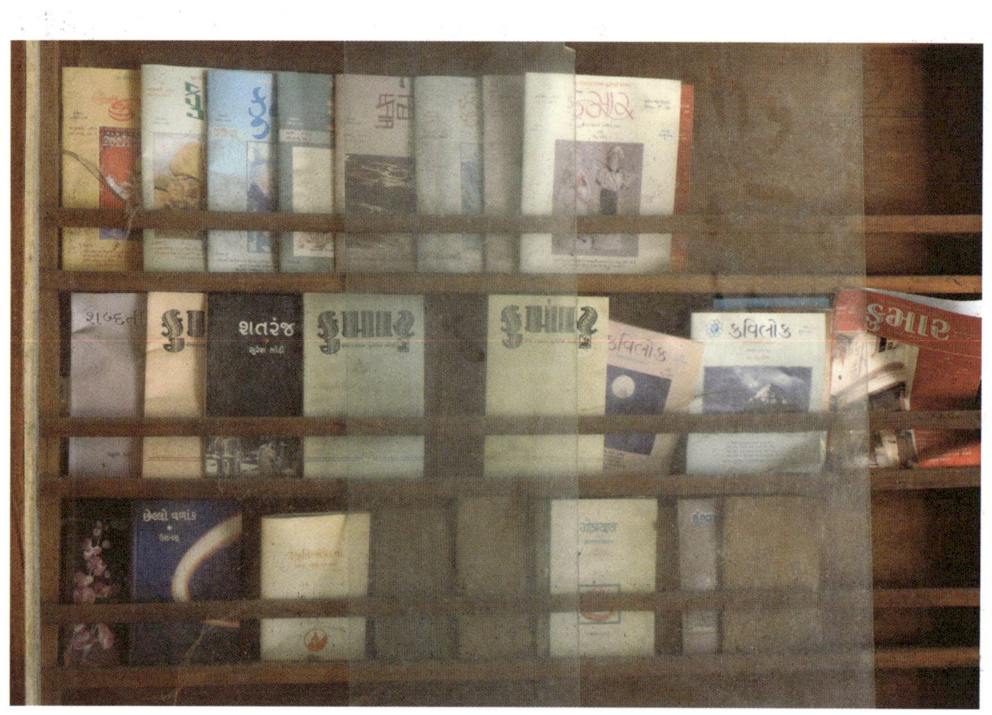

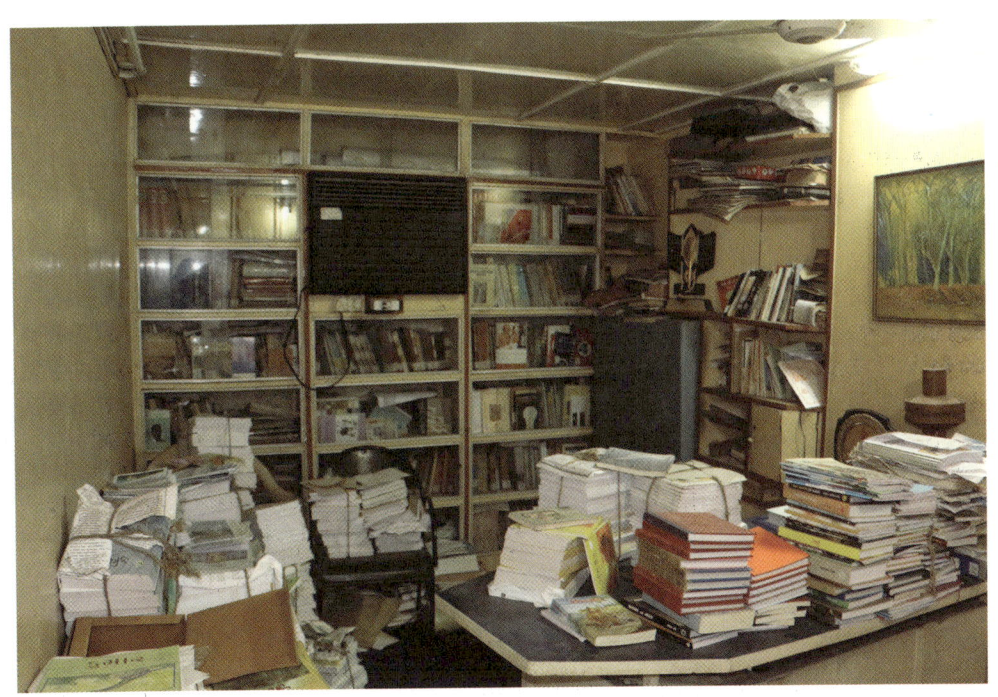

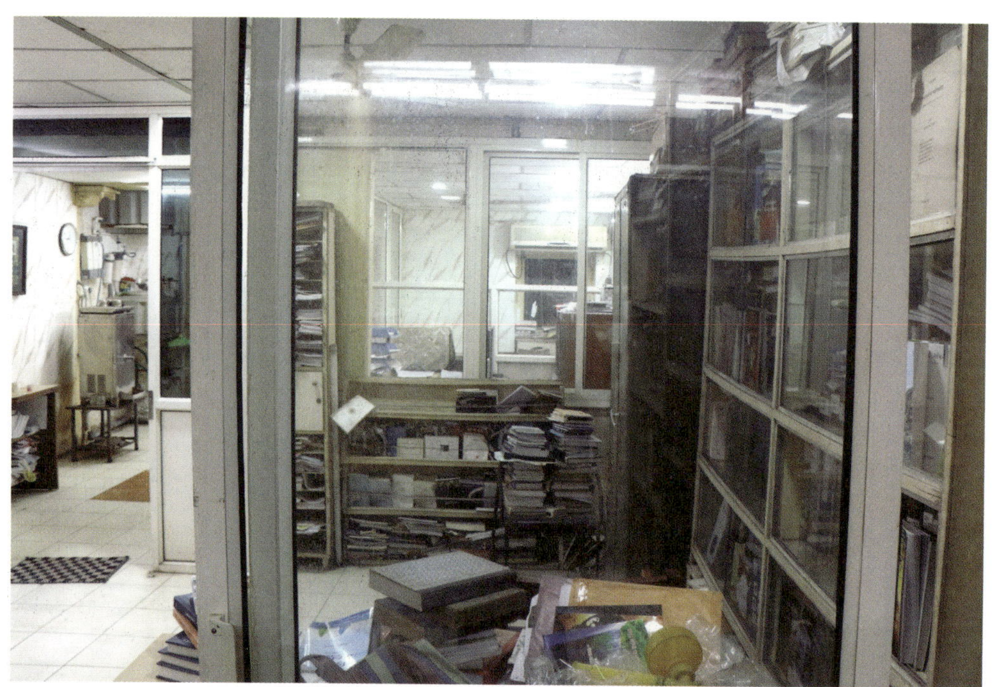

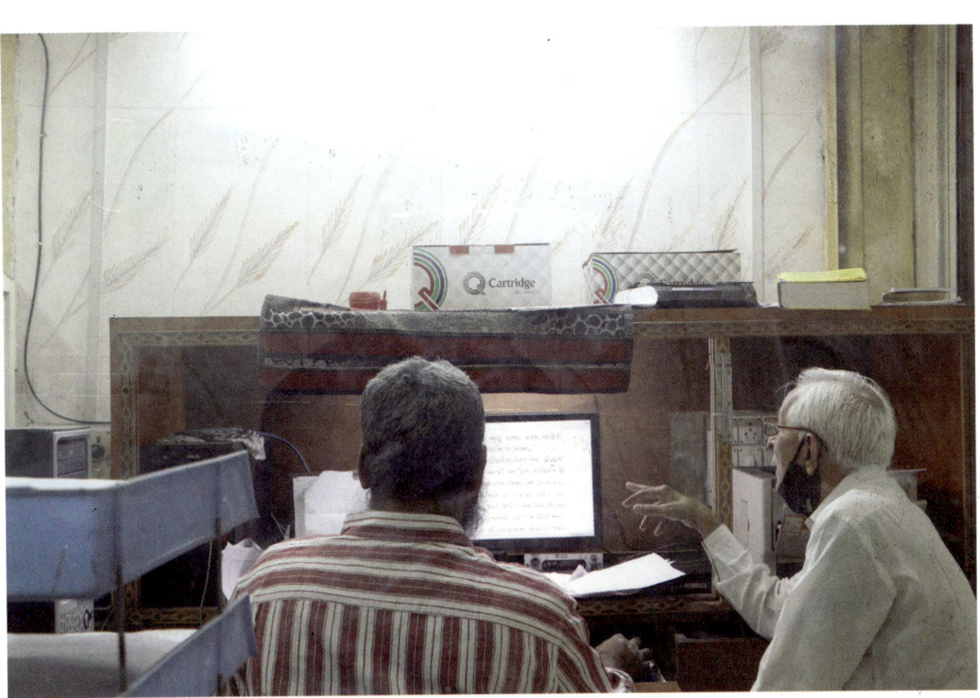

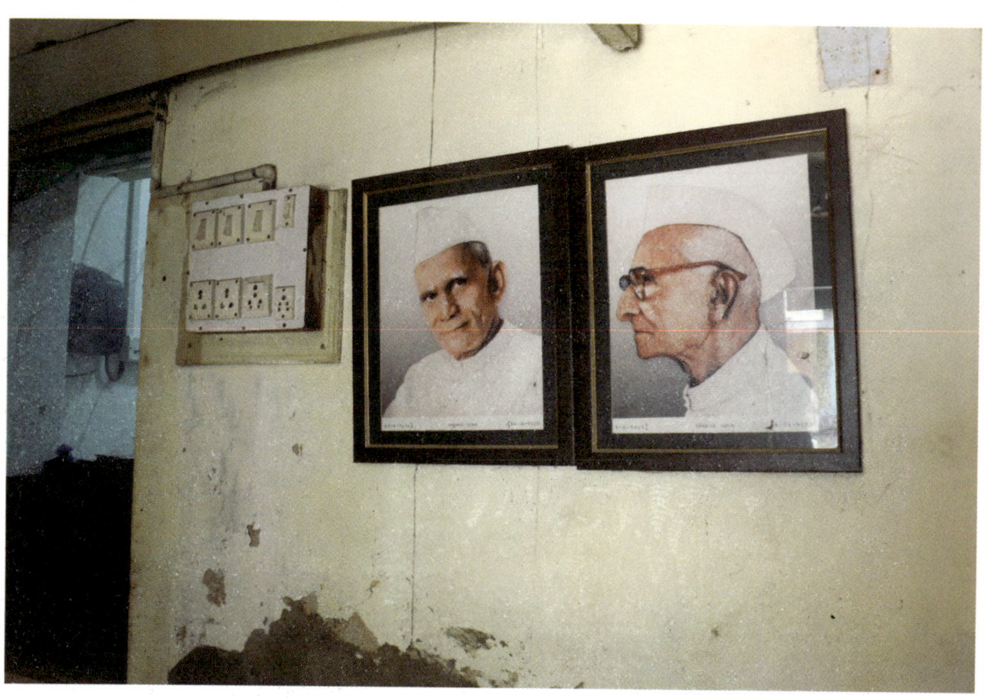

Images taken during a research trip to Kumar's office in Ahmedabad in 2021

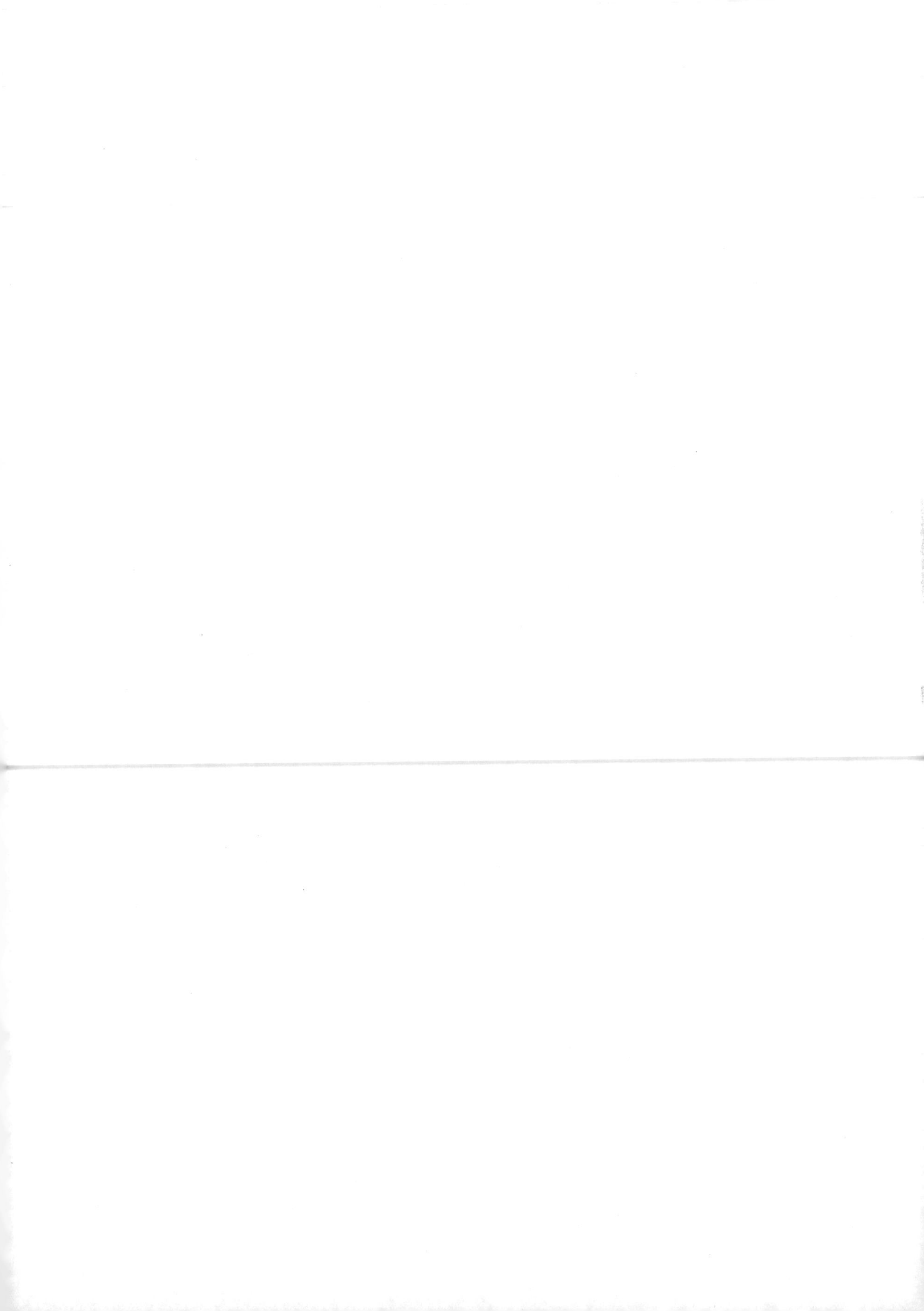

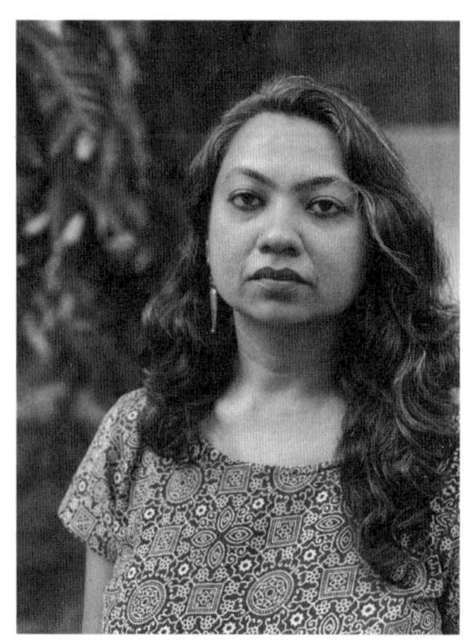

VASVI OZA

Vasvi Oza is an artist, educator, and researcher based in Bangalore. She has previously taught at Azim Premji University and the Karnataka Chitrakala Parishath, and her areas of research include Gujarati print culture, translation, and drawing. She completed her PhD from the English and Foreign Languages University (Hyderabad) in 2016, after having graduated from the Faculty of Fine Arts, The Maharaja Sayajirao University of Baroda (MSU) with a Masters in Painting in 2007.

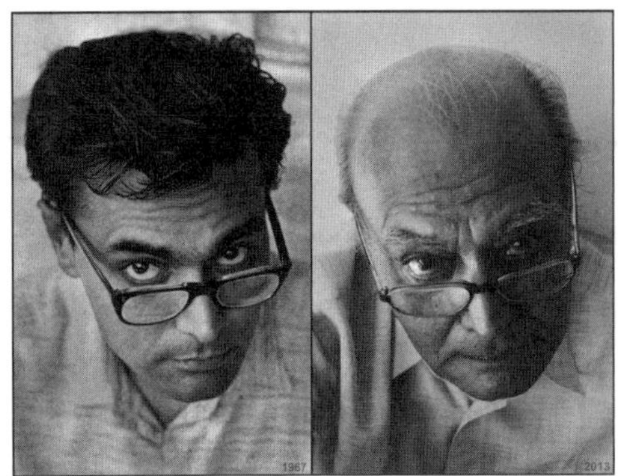

JYOTI BHATT

A renowned painter, printmaker, and photographer, Jyoti Bhatt (b. 1934) lives and works in Vadodara, Gujarat. He was among the first batch of students to graduate from the Faculty of Fine Arts, The Maharaja Sayajirao University of Baroda (MSU) in 1956, where he studied painting and printmaking for six years. Bhatt began teaching at MSU in 1959 and continued to teach there until his retirement in 1992. He studied at the Accademia di Belle Arti in Naples (under a scholarship from the Italian Government) and at the Pratt Graphic Art Center in New York (under the Fulbright & John D. Rockefeller IIIrd Fund Fellowship) between 1961 to 1966. Apart from his art practice, he has also written frequently in Gujarati about art, craft, design, photography, and printmaking, for *Kumar* and other publications.

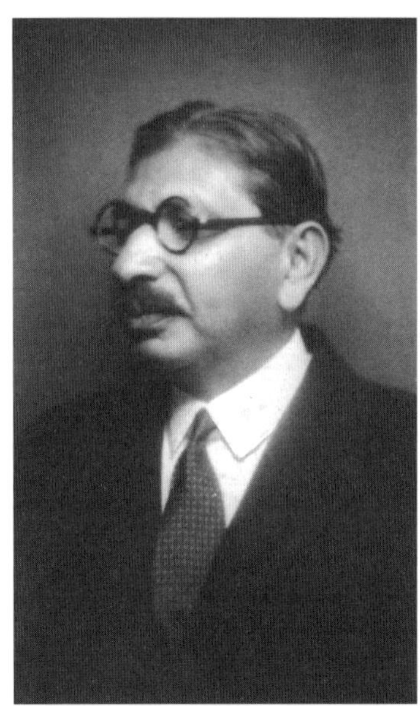

PHEROZESHAH RUSTOMJI MEHTA

Pherozeshah Rustomji Mehta (1880–1971) was a writer and scholar from Karachi. Apart from his writing for periodicals such as *Kumar* and *Navchetan*, he has published five books in Gujarati, including *Chitrarasika* (published by *Kumar* in 1962) which brought together his articles on visual and performing arts. He was also the editor of Karachi's then-daily newspaper *Parsi Sansar ane Lok Sevak* for many years, and was amongst the earliest Gujarati scholars to introduce epigrams in his oration.

Reliable Copy's annual programme is made possible with support from its Publisher's Circle initiative.

Reliable Copy Publisher's Circle 2022–23 has been supported by:

Ark Foundation for the Arts

Bilal Javeed

Chanchalba Amin Charitable Trust

Goethe-Institut / Max Mueller Bhavan Bangalore

Jyoti Bhatt

Mallika Leuzinger

Museum of Art & Photography

Rajjubhai & Sandra Shroff

Rebecca Hanna John

RK Rangan

UPL Limited

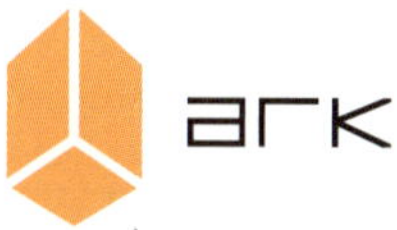

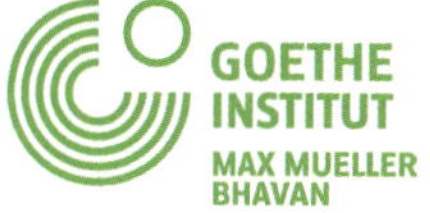

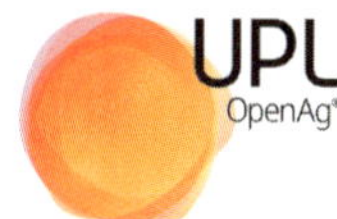

Reliable Copy #7
Modernism/Murderism:
The Modern Art Debate in Kumar
By Jyoti Bhatt, Pherozeshah Rustomji Mehta, and the
readers of Kumar · Translated by Vasvi Oza · 2022

Reliable Copy is a publishing house and curatorial practice
for works, projects, and writing by artists. It is represented
by Nihaal Faizal and Sarasija Subramanian and operates
under Reliable Copy Trust, in association with Press
Works.

Reliable Copy Trust & Press Works,
14/2, Andree Road,
Shanthi Nagar,
Bangalore – 560027,
Karnataka, India

www.reliablecopy.org